Population Policy in Western Europe

Responses to Low Fertility in
France, Sweden, and West Germany

Population
Policy in
Western Europe

C. ALISON McINTOSH

M. E. Sharpe, Inc.
Armonk, New York/London

Copyright © 1983 by M. E. Sharpe, Inc.
80 Business Park Drive, Armonk, New York 10504

Library of Congress Cataloging in Publication Data

McIntosh, C. Alison.
    Population policy in western Europe.

    Bibliography: p.
    Includes index.
    1. Europe—Population policy. 2. Fertility, Human—
Europe. I. Title
HB3581.M37   1982   363.9'1'094   82-5840
ISBN 0-87332-226-6   AACR2

Printed in the United States of America

Contents

ACKNOWLEDGMENTS

This study could not have been started, let alone completed, without the help of many people and organizations. Both intellectually and in practical and personal terms, my greatest debt is to Jason Finkle who kindled my interest in the topic. The ideas that form the core of the study emerged in the course of innumerable discussions between us and are as much his as mine. The completed manuscript profited from the careful reading and critical comments of Barbara Crane, James Chesney, Ronald Inglehart, and Yuzuru Takeshita, of the University of Michigan, and of Thomàs Frejka of the Population Council. I am grateful to them all. Apart from these intellectual contributions, the study could not have been undertaken without the financial support of the Rockefeller Foundation, the Horace H. Rackham School of Graduate Studies, the Center for the Continuing Education of Women, and the Alumni Association, all of the University of Michigan.

It is a pleasure to acknowledge the help of many other persons. The study would not exist but for the willingness of policy-makers and influentials in France, Sweden, and West Germany to give of their time and expertise. I only hope that they see some pale reflection of their countries in my remarks. In particular, I would like to thank Mme. Jacqueline Hecht, Dr. Karl Schwarz, and Dr. Max Wingen who did much to smooth my way in France and Germany. Dr. Wingen has kindly kept me supplied with documents which he thought would be of interest to me. I also benefited from discussions with scholars and officials in universities and government agencies in countries other than those included in the study, and in a number of international agencies. Ann-Sofie Kalvemärk generously sent me successive chapters of her book *More Children or Better Quality?* as they were completed and read an early draft of my third chapter. The final text has been materially improved by her comments. Thomas Anton of the University of Michigan kindly allowed me to read the manuscript of his study *Administered Politics: Elite Political Culture in Sweden* before it went to press. Jean-Claude Chasteland of the United Nations Population Division was good enough to let me examine the replies to the Third and Fourth Population Inquiries Among Governments and provided me with office space while I did so. I would like to thank the authors and editors of a number of books and articles for permission to publish their tables and figures.

On a more personal level, I wish to record my appreciation of the help given by Ruth Merrill. Ruth appointed herself unofficial (and unpaid) research assistant while I was in Paris on and off during the spring and summer of 1978. I don't know what I would have done without her help. Lillian Stafford and Kirsten Alcser performed the essential and difficult task of translating Swedish documents, and Gabrielle Eggers and Martina Myers struggled with the even more difficult German texts. All unofficial translations from these languages are their work; unofficial translations from the French are my own.

I would like to thank Martina Myers, Judy Perry, Beth De-Lap, and Ann Warde for struggling with the computer to transcribe my draft. Judy Perry and Stan Bernstein, of the Center for Population Planning, and David Rodgers and Paul Grosso of the University of Michigan Computing Center, have wrought miracles in getting the manuscript onto tape for printing under the patient and cheerful editorial guidance of Joe Hollander of M. E. Sharpe.

Needless to say, the interpretation and conclusions are mine alone.

Population Policy in Western Europe

DEMOGRAPHIC TRENDS AND POLICIES IN DEVELOPED COUNTRIES

At about the time international attention was turning to the problem of rapid population growth in developing countries, birth rates in the advanced industrialized nations resumed their long-term decline after the brief remission of the "baby boom." In Eastern and Western Europe and in North America the fall in fertility has been precipitous, but the same trend is also visible in Southern Europe and in Australia. By the early 1970s fertility in the West had fallen far below the level required for replacement of the population in the long run,[1] and vigorous pronatalist policies had been introduced in Eastern Europe in an effort to increase the number of births. During the 1970s, first in East and West Germany and later in Austria, Luxembourg, and the northern provinces of Italy, fertility fell so low that the annual number of deaths in these countries now exceeds the number of babies born.[2] Among the industrialized nations, moreover, nearly all the countries that still have a positive balance between births and deaths are in that position only because they have a relatively larger number of women in the reproductive

---

[1]Replacement level fertility is the level of fertility that, in conjunction with existing mortality rates, would result, if continued, in a population growth rate of zero. In other words, it is a level which ensures that each generation exactly replaces itself. Among the various measures of fertility, replacement is indicated by a gross or net reproduction rate (GRR or NRR) of 1.0 and, given mortality rates in developed countries today, by a total fertility rate (TFR) of 2.11 approximately. A more extended discussion of these rates and their interpretation is given in Appendix A.

[2]For an up-to-date discussion of the fertility decline, see Jean Bourgeois-Pichat, "Recent Demographic Change in Europe: an Assessment," *Population and Development Review* 7, 1 (March 1981), pp. 19–42.

years, and not because their fertility per woman is high enough to ensure demographic replacement.

There has been a remarkable similarity in the timing and patterning of the fertility decline in countries that vary widely in geographical location, religious composition, political system, and economic structure. The downturn in the curve appeared simultaneously in 1964 in all the major nations of Western and Northern Europe, and just a few years earlier in Canada, the United States, and Eastern Europe.[3] Even minor fluctuations in the rate of decline since 1964 have appeared at the same time in a number of Western European nations. Scholars are at a loss to understand this similarity of behavior among peoples of such diverse ethnic, social, political, and economic backgrounds. Many fall back on the "explanation" proffered by Jean Bourgeois-Pichat:

> Progress in contraception would lead one to think that the decision to procreate would, henceforth, be taken in the intimacy of the awareness of couples, whereas formerly it was determined by the cultural heritage of societies. In fact, couples seem to be strongly obedient, unconsciously no doubt, to great currents of opinion; how else can one explain the reversal in the movement of fertility at the same time in most of the countries of Europe.[4]

If reproductive decisions are motivated not only by the conscious desires of individual couples but also by changes in fashion, there is as much reason to anticipate a reversal of the present trend in the future as to expect a continuation of the decline. Very recently, indeed, there have been indications that in Northern and Western Europe and the United States, birth rates may have reached their lowest ebb. As Figure 1 shows, in some countries there has even been a slight upturn in fertility. Nevertheless, because of changes in the norms governing marriage and the family, and the availability of near-perfect means of preventing unwanted children, many demographers believe

[3]Institut National d'Etudes Démographiques (INED), *Natalité et politique démographique*, Travaux et Documents, Cahier no. 76 (Paris: Presses Universitaires de France, 1976), pp. 14–15 and figures on pp. 45–46.

[4]Jean Bourgeois-Pichat, "Baisse de la fécondité et decendence finale," *Population* 31, 6 (November-December 1976), p. 1077. For an elaboration of this proposition, see idem, "Recent Demographic Change in Europe."

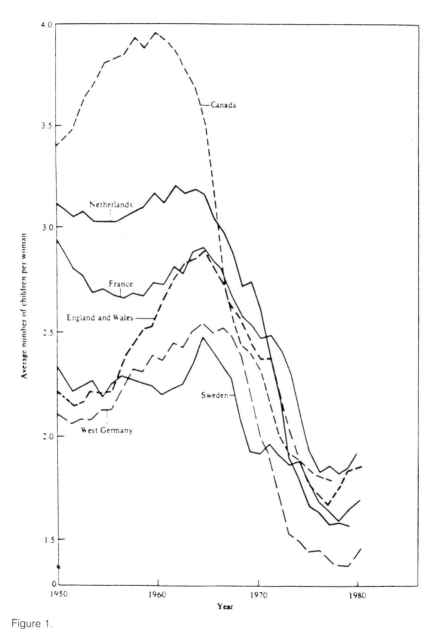

Figure 1.

Trends in the total fertility rate in selected countries of Western Europe and in Canada, 1950–80.

Source: Reprinted with the permission of the Population Council from Jean Bourgeois-Pichat, "Recent Demographic Change in Western Europe: An Assessment," *Population and Development Review* 7, no. 1 (March 1981): p. 28.

that a spontaneous increase in the birth rate sufficient to ensure replacement of the population is unlikely.[5] Furthermore, the longer an upturn is delayed, the less the likelihood that it will suffice to bring deaths and births into balance, since low fertility erodes the "buffer" provided by large cohorts of women in the childbearing years.

Low fertility and declining rates of population growth pose difficult problems for government and society: changes in age-structure and a growing number of elderly dependents, especially the very old, severely strain the financial bases of social security systems; aging work forces introduce unwanted rigidities into the operation of labor markets; exacerbated depopulation of rural areas calls into question the design and implementation of regional development policies. While many economists nowadays appear to believe that economic growth is possible under conditions of population stagnation, albeit at a lower level than in the recent past, the demand generated by a growing population is helpful in cushioning the worst consequences of errors in investment.[6] Moreover, extremely rapid changes in fertility, such as we have just experienced, bring with them problems of accommodation as cohorts of markedly different size work their way through the age-structure, causing waves of expansion and contraction in the need for child care, schools, jobs, social and medical services, and pensions for the elderly.[7] Above all, even if satisfactory adjustments can be made to zero population growth, and to the problems of transition to that level, no one can speak with certainty about the social and economic consequences of an absolute decrease in population numbers.

[5]See, for example, Karl Schwarz, "La baisse de la natalité en Allemagne fédérale," *Population* 33, 4–5 (July-October 1978), pp. 1015–16; Charles F. Westoff, "Marriage and Fertility in the Developed Countries," *Scientific American* 239, 6 (December 1978), pp. 51–57.

[6]This point was made by economists during the birth decline of the 1920s and 1930s. See, for example, John Maynard Keynes, "Some Economic Consequences of a Declining Population," *Eugenics Review* 29 (April 1937), p. 14; Gunnar Myrdal, *Population: A Problem for Democracy* (Cambridge, Mass.: Harvard University Press, 1940), pp. 151–60 (reprinted in 1962).

[7]For a good discussion of some of the social policy implications of population stabilization or decline, see David E. C. Eversley, "Welfare," in *Population Decline in Europe*, ed. Council of Europe (London: Edward Arnold, 1978), pp. 115–42.

As difficult as are these and similar problems for a society to deal with, for many people the prospect of declining population growth brings with it anxieties of a more fundamental nature. There are signs that many European political elites fear that an aging society will lose its dynamism and sense of adventure, that it will lack young men to guard its frontiers, and that its empty spaces will fill with peoples of more vigorous but alien extraction. In a world in which the developed countries yearly provide a smaller proportion of the global population,[8] some social analysts fear that the reluctance of the young to bear children portends the demise of Western civilization and culture.[9] It is not surprising, therefore, that there is a discernible pronatalist sentiment among European governments.

Notwithstanding their anxieties, governments in the liberal democracies face serious moral and political constraints on their capacity to induce even the modest rate of population growth that would serve, they believe, to prevent the most obviously troublesome consequences of population stagnation or decline. Demographic inertia—the fact that changes in birth

[8]According to the United Nations' "most likely" projection, the population of the "more developed regions," which comprised 27.1 percent of total world population in 1975, will constitute only 20.5 percent in the year 2000. See United Nations, Department of International Economic and Social Affairs, *World Population Trends and Prospects, By Country, 1950–2000* (New York: United Nations, 1979, ST/ESA/SER.R/33), p. 6, table 3. For this projection "more developed regions" includes: Northern America, Japan, Europe, Australia, New Zealand, Eastern Europe-USSR.

[9]These points were frequently made during the 1930s and 1940s and still appear, though less commonly, in the literature today. See, for example, Alva Myrdal, *Nation and Family* (New York: Harper and Brothers, 1941), pp. 104–5 (reprinted by the M.I.T. Press in 1968); Gunnar Myrdal, pp. 160–61; United Kingdom, Royal Commission on Population, *Report* (London: HMSO, 1949), p. 126; Ansley J. Coale, "Should the United States Start a Campaign for Fewer Births?" *Population Index* 34, 4 (October-December 1968), pp. 467–74. The most persistent campaigner on these themes over a long period has been the eminent French demographer, Alfred Sauvy. For example, see, *L'Europe et sa population* (Paris: Les Editions Internationales, 1953); *La montée des jeunes* (Paris: Calman-Levy, 1959); *Zero Growth*, trans. A. McGuire (Oxford: Basil Blackwell and Sons, 1975); *Le Plan Sauvy* (Paris: Calman-Levy, 1960; "Les conséquences du vieillissement de la population," in Gérard-François Dumont et al., *La France Ridée* (Paris: Le Livre de Poche, 1979), pp. 61–118. The same points were made by respondents in interviews undertaken for this study in France and West Germany in 1978.

rate take twenty years to manifest themselves in the active population—tends to exert a dampening effect on the sense of urgency experienced by politicians at the same time as it calls for action *now* if the supply of labor is to be assured at the turn of the century. It is also difficult to mobilize political support for expensive pronatalist measures in a period of financial stringency and high unemployment such as is being experienced today.

A more enduring impediment to action may be the commitment of Western governments to the causes of women's equality with men and their right to control their own fertility. As women's access to education and to work without fear of discrimination on account of marriage, pregnancy, and motherhood has been increasingly guaranteed by the state, inducements to devote their lives to childrearing seem to have lost their attraction for most women. Even more significantly, all but a few Western states now guarantee relatively free access to modern contraceptives and legal abortion, even if social practice in some areas is still resistant to the full realization of legislative intentions. Throughout the 1970s most expert observers believed that the net antinatalist effect of these measures far outweighed the pronatalist effect of the social and family benefits provided by the same governments.[10] Furthermore, as one student of these measures has observed, "the tendency is to extend these individual rights and to protect them more efficiently; in the liberal democratic countries of Western Europe this tendency would seem irreversible."[11]

Low population growth has reached the political agenda in virtually all the industrialized nations. Throughout Europe, in particular, a majority of governments has established or revitalized population commissions to monitor population trends and advise on policy;[12] national and international conferences and

[10]For example, see Massimo Livi-Bacci, "Population Policies in Western Europe," *Population Studies* 28, 1 (July 1974), p. 200; Paolo de Sandre, "Critical Study of Population Policies in Europe," *Population Decline in Europe*, ed. Council of Europe (New York: St. Martin's Press, 1978), pp. 145–70.

[11]Livi-Bacci, p. 192.

[12]See Bernard Berelson, ed., *Population Policy in Developed Countries* (New York: McGraw Hill, 1974).

seminars are proliferating;[13] public discussion has been thorough—and at times intense. In their responses to the Fourth UN Inquiry Among Governments on Population and Development in July 1978, thirteen of forty-one "developed" countries indicated that they considered their rate of natural increase "too low" and that they felt "full" or "some" support of fertility would be appropriate.[14] In addition to these thirteen, several Eastern European countries that have managed to raise fertility by means of vigorous pronatalist policies now profess to be satisfied with their rates of natural increase.[15] Finally, a number of developed countries have adopted what the United Nations terms an attitude of "watchful waiting" and have indicated that they may intervene in the future should this become necessary to maintain a stationary or slightly growing population.[16]

[13]For example, fertility decline was one of the most important topics at the Second European Population Conference organized by the Parliamentary Assembly of the Council of Europe in 1971. As a result of this conference, the Council of Europe established a Committee for Population Studies (CAHED) whose members are senior demographers from each of the member states. CAHED meets regularly to discuss the social (and policy) implications of demographic trends. In September 1976 the Council of Europe organized a Seminar on the Implications of a Stationary or Declining Population in Europe. The papers presented at the conference have been published under the title *Population Decline in Europe*, ed. Council of Europe, 1978. In 1977 the Center for Population Research, National Institutes of Health, organized two conferences on low fertility. Papers from the first conference have been published under the title, *Social, Economic and Health Aspects of Low Fertility*, ed. Arthur A. Campbell (Washington, D.C.: U.S. Government Printing Office, 1979). Papers presented at the second conference have been published as *The Economic Consequence of Slowing Population Growth*, eds. Thomas J. Espenshade and William J. Serow (New York: Academic Press, 1978). At the end of 1980 a colloquium on population trends and policies in Europe, organized by INED, brought together demographers and legal experts from France and six Eastern European countries. See Michel L. Levy, "Préoccupations natalistes en Europe de l'Est," *Population et Sociétés*, no. 143, January 1981.

[14]United Nations, Department of International Social and Economic Affairs, *World Population Trends and Policies: 1979 Monitoring Report*, vol. 2 (New York: United Nations, 1980), pp. 16–17 and table 33.

[15]Ibid., p. 17.

[16]Ibid.

Governmental Responses to Low Population Growth

Notwithstanding the similarity of demographic trends and the evidence of concern about them, the actual policy responses of governments vary markedly. In Eastern Europe, soon after fertility reached replacement level, five of the seven low fertility countries[17] started to implement comprehensive and coordinated policies intended to encourage childbearing. Among Western nations only France is attempting seriously to raise the birth rate. As Table 1 shows, moreover, many countries in the west and north of Europe have rates of fertility and natural increase at least as low as those in Eastern Europe when pronatalist policies were first introduced there, and in some cases considerably lower. In order to provide a background for a more detailed study of France, Sweden, and West Germany, therefore, it will be of interest to briefly explore the range of pronatalist measures introduced in recent years by governments in some other Eastern and Western countries.

Policy responses in Eastern Europe

Birth rates fell dramatically in Eastern Europe in the late 1950s when most of the socialist countries followed the example of the Soviet Union and legalized abortion on demand. In these countries, where reliable contraceptives were almost unknown, legal abortion was seized on by women as an important means of preventing unwanted fertility. By the early 1960s, in several countries the number of abortions performed came to equal if not exceed the number of live births, and gross reproduction

[17]Two of the nine Eastern European socialist states do not suffer from low population growth. Albania's population is still growing at about 2 percent per annum. In Yugoslavia, despite wide regional disparities, overall fertility is approaching replacement level. The rate of population growth is still relatively high (approx. 0.8 percent) because of earlier high fertility. See United Nations, Department of International Social and Economic Affairs, *Selected Demographic Indicators By Country, 1950–2000* (New York: United Nations, 1980), pp. 171, 177. For a discussion of possible impediments to the formulation of either national or regional pronatalist policies in Yugoslavia, see John F. Besemeres, *Socialist Population Politics* (White Plains, N.Y.: M.E. Sharpe, Inc., 1980) pp. 227–46.

rates fell alarmingly.[18] The demand for abortions was particularly heavy in Romania, where they soon came to outnumber live births by four to one, and where the crude birth rate fell from 25.6 to 14.6 per thousand between 1955 and 1965.[19] The Romanian government's response to what was seen as a demographic disaster was very different from the responses of other Eastern European governments. At the end of 1966, without warning, the government imposed restrictions which made legal abortions virtually impossible to obtain and, simultaneously, banned the importation and local manufacture of contraceptives.[20] At much the same time, the Family Code was modified by a decree which stated that marriage could be dissolved only in exceptional cases.[21] The effect of these policies was almost instantaneous, the birth rate more than doubling in the following year. Despite the impressive immediate impact of the policies, the effect was short-lived, as couples soon found other ways to avoid conception or resorted to illegal abortion. Nevertheless, although the birth rate has declined again, it has remained at a level which ensures replacement of the population.[22]

The responses of Bulgaria, Czechoslovakia, and Hungary are much more characteristic of Eastern European reactions to low fertility. Concerned about future labor force growth as well as the health effects on women of repeated abortion, these countries started early in the 1960s to develop coordinated approaches to eliminating obstacles to childbearing. With some differences in detail and timing, Bulgaria, Czechoslovakia, and

[18]Robert J. McIntyre, "The Effects of Legalized Abortion Laws in Eastern Europe," in *Research in the Politics of Population*, ed. Richard L. Clinton and R. Kenneth Godwin (Lexington, Mass.: D. C. Heath, 1972), pp. 185–86.

[19]Ibid.

[20]Michael S. Teitelbaum, "Fertility Effects of the Abolition of Legal Abortion in Romania," *Population Studies* 26, 3 (November 1972), pp. 405–17; William Moskoff, "Pronatalist Policies in Romania," *Economic Development and Cultural Change* 28, 3 (April 1980), pp. 602–3.

[21]Vladimir Trebici, "Law and Fertility in Romania," in *Law and Fertility in Europe*, eds. Maurice Kirk, Massimo Livi-Bacci, and Egon Szabady (Dolhain, Belgium: Ordina Editions, 1976), pp. 523–24, 527–28; Moskoff, p. 604.

[22]Bernard Berelson, "Romania's 1966 Anti-Abortion Decree: The Demographic Experience of the First Decade," *Population Studies* 33, 2 (July 1979), pp. 209–22; Levy, "Préoccupations natalistes en Europe de l'Est."

Table 1

Population Policy and Selected Demographic Indicators in Developed Countries
(latest available year)

	NRR Latest available year		NRR Lowest year		Infant mortality 0/00%	Natural increase 0/00%	Population growth 0/0%
A. Countries with measures to raise fertility*							
Bulgaria	1.05	('76)	1.00	('65–69)	21.8	5.0	0.51
Finland	0.79	('78)	0.71	('63)	12/0	4.3	0.36
France	0.88	('78)	0.88	('76)	11.4	3.9	0.30
Germany (East)	0.90	('78)	0.73	('75)	13.2	0.0	0.02
Greece	1.03	('77)	1.03	('75)	20.3	6.5	0.59
Luxembourg	0.70	('78)	0.69	('77)	10.6	-0.4	-0.01
B. Countries with measures to maintain fertility*							
Albania	1.61	('80)§	n.a.		86.8†	25.2	2.21
Czechoslovakia	1.16	('75)	0.95	('68)	18.7	6.9	0.59
Hungary	0.97	('78)	0.81	('64)	24.3	2.6	0.29
Ireland	1.66	('75)	1.66	('75)	15.7	10.9	1.04
Poland	1.05	('77)	1.04	('68)	22.4	9.7	0.96
Romania	1.15	('79)	1.13	('75)	31.2	10.0	0.78
Yugoslavia	1.00	('77)	1.00	('77)	33.6	8.7	0.82
USSR	1.07	('78–79)	1.07	('78–79)	27.7‡	8.5	0.94

C. Countries without fertility incentives*

Austria	0.77 ('79)	0.77 ('78)	14.9	-1.2	-0.05
Belgium	0.80 ('78)	0.80 ('78)	11.9	0.7	0.31
Canada	0.84 ('78)	0.84 ('78)	12.4	8.3	1.14
Denmark	0.77 ('79)	0.77 ('79)	8.9	1.8	0.13
Germany (West)	0.65 ('78)	0.65 ('78)	15.5	-2.5	-0.29
Iceland	1.27 ('74)	1.27 ('74)	10.8	12.1	-1.02
Italy	0.91 ('77)	0.91 ('77)	17.6	3.6	0.37
Netherlands	0.76 ('78)	0.76 ('78)	9.5	4.4	0.51
Norway	0.84 ('79)	0.84 ('77)	9.2	2.8	0.34
Portugal	1.16 ('75)	1.16 ('75)	38.9	8.8	0.85
Spain	1.32 ('74)	1.32 ('74)	15.6	10.3	0.85
Sweden	0.80 ('79)	0.77 ('78)	7.7	0.4	0.08
Switzerland	0.73 ('77)	0.73 ('77)	9.8	2.3	-0.08
United Kingdom	—	—	11.7	0.1	-0.05
England Wales	0.83 ('78)	0.81 ('77)	—	—	
Scotland	0.82 ('78)	0.80 ('77)	—	—	
United States	0.86 ('78)	0.85 ('75)	14.0	6.5	0.94

Sources: *Population Index* 42, 2 (Summer 1981), pp. 402–14; *U.N. Demographic Yearbook*, 1978, table 4.
Notes:
*Policy classification from UN World Population Trends and Policies: 1977 Monitoring Report, vol. II, table 67, p. 127.
†1971.
‡1974.
§Estimate. *UN Selected Demographic Indicators, 1950–2000.*

Hungary introduced vigorous measures in three broad areas.[23] First, all three countries have placed some restrictions on access to legal abortion, especially in the case of a first or second child. Though the measures currently in force are far from draconian, all women seeking an abortion are at least required to appear before a special commission to get permission for the operation. It is felt by some, both patients and commissioners, that this procedure is itself a potent deterrent to legal abortion.[24] While attempting to limit the number of abortions, these countries have tried to make modern contraceptives more widely available; nevertheless, it is likely that women in Eastern Europe do not yet have such easy access to contraceptive services and advice as do their sisters in the West.

The second series of measures introduced in Eastern Europe is intended to reduce the difficulties experienced by women who have to care for young children while holding a full-time job. In addition to trying to increase the number of places in nurseries and kindergartens, Bulgaria, Czechoslovakia, and Hungary have made it possible for women to stay home with a new baby for periods varying from one to three years after the birth. Generally speaking, women receive full pay, or nearly full pay, for five or six months and then become eligible for an allowance which approximates the minimum wage. Young mothers who take the extended post-maternity leave have their jobs held for them or are given equivalent jobs on their return to work. Moreover, their promotion rights are safeguarded, and the time counts as work in the calculation of a retirement pension.

Third, building on the system of maternity and family allowances already in effect before the specifically pronatalist measures were introduced, the three countries have all implemented a series of measures designed to reduce the financial

[23]For discussions of Eastern European policies, see Robert J. McIntyre "Pronatalist Programs in Eastern Europe," *Soviet Studies* 27, 3 (July 1975), pp. 366–80; Alena Heitlinger, "Pronatalist Population Policy in Czechoslovakia," *Population Studies* 30, 1 (March 1976), pp. 123–35; Jerzy Berent "Fertility Trends and Policies in Eastern Europe in the 1970s," in Campbell, pp. 31–46.

[24]See, for example, the sources cited by Hilda Scott, *Does Socialism Liberate Women?* (Boston: Beacon Press, 1974), pp. 144–45.

burden of children. Again with variations in the details, these countries have introduced or increased lump-sum birth grants, family and children's allowances, and low-interest loans for building or buying a house. The various allowances increase in amount for successive children, with the emphasis usually falling on the third child. Because these governments do not want high rates of population growth and appreciate that few couples in advanced societies want large families, the financial benefits usually decrease for the fourth and subsequent children.

The three remaining low fertility countries of Eastern Europe have adopted divergent approaches to low population growth. East Germany, whose fertility decline has paralleled that of the Federal Republic, did not fully liberalize abortion until 1972 and has not imposed any new restrictions since that date. Throughout the 1970s, however, the government introduced a program of incentives similar to those of Bulgaria, Czechoslovakia, and Hungary, which has had some success in raising fertility.[25] In Poland exceptionally rapid population growth in the postwar years prompted the Gomulka regime to introduce antinatalist measures during the early 1960s. Since then fertility has fallen almost to replacement level, and before its collapse in 1980, the Giereck government was becoming increasingly convinced of the need to stimulate the birth rate. Nevertheless, the population will continue to grow for some time as a consequence of the earlier baby boom, and competent observers consider that the government's efforts so far fall short of constituting a pronatalist policy.[26] Assistance to the family includes small family allowances and birth grants, paid and unpaid maternity leave, and loans to assist student marriages. Poland also has an extensive network of family planning

[25]United Nations, Department of International Economic and Social Affairs, *Population Policy Briefs: Current Situation in Developed Countries, 1980* (New York: United Nations, January 1981, Serial No. ESA/P/WP.72), pp. 13–14. See also Dr. Akkermann and Karl-Heinz Mehlan, "Law and Fertility in the German Democratic Republic," in Kirk et al., pp. 179–89.

[26]For an excellent discussion of population trends and policies between 1945 and 1970, approximately, see Janusz A. Ziolkowski, "Poland," in Berelson, *Population Policy in Developed Countries*, pp. 445–48. For an analysis of more recent developments, see Besemeres, esp. pp. 119–25 and 137–54.

clinics, and abortion is permitted for a wide range of medical and social reasons, though it is not available on demand.[27] The Soviet Union, finally, is faced with a situation in which subreplacement fertility in the European republics is offset by high fertility in the Central Asian regions. For some time the government has to want to increase the birth rate in the low fertility regions but has experienced ideological difficulties in adopting a regionally differentiated policy.[28] At the Twenty-sixth Party Congress in February 1981, a way was found that appears to lead out of the impasse. A decision was made to introduce two new measures "step by step, in different regions of the country."[29] The two measures, a lump-sum birth grant and partly paid maternity leave, are unlikely to be sufficient, by themselves, to make a significant difference in the birth rate. Nevertheless, the decision to take a regionally differentiated approach paves the way for the evolution of a more comprehensive policy at a future date.

It is still too early to make a final judgment about the effectiveness of Eastern Europe's pronatalist policies. As Figure 2 shows, there have been fluctuations in fertility rates in all the low-fertility countries during the period under discussion. Nevertheless, with the exception of East Germany, all the countries with pronatalist policies have been able to keep the birth rate at or above replacement level. Careful analysis of the fertility effect of individual measures in a number of these countries suggests, however, that the measures may simply have encouraged couples to advance the date of their planned births without increasing the total number of children desired or expected.[30]

---

[27]UN, *Population Policy Briefs*, pp. 27–28. See also Ewa Kozlowska and Jan Wojtyla, "Law and Fertility in Poland," in Kirk et al., pp. 505–15.

[28]See, for example, David M. Heer, "Three Issues in Soviet Population Policy," *Population and Development Review* 3, 3 (September 1977), pp. 229–52; Alfred J. Di Maio, "The Soviet Union and Population," *Comparative Political Studies* 13, 1 (April 1980), pp. 97–136.

[29]Cynthia Weber and Ann Goodman, "The Demographic Policy Debate in the U.S.S.R.," *Population and Development Review* 7,2 (June 1981), pp. 279–95.

[30]Roland Pressat, "Mesures natalistes et relèvement de la fécondité en Europe de l'Est," *Population* 34, 3 (May-June 1979), pp. 533–48.

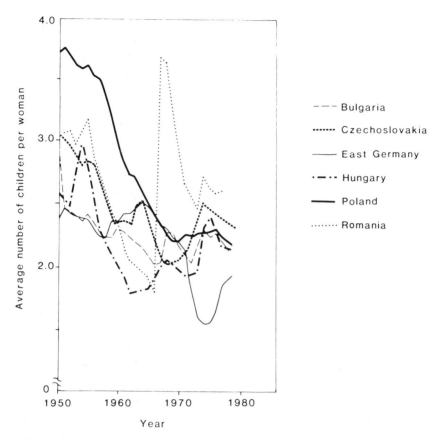

Figure 2.

Total fertility rates in selected Eastern European countries.

Source: Adapted from Levy, "Préoccupations natalistes."

Western policy responses

More than a decade after fertility fell below replacement level in most Western European countries and in North America, these nations are still hesitant to tackle directly the question of low population growth. Many Western governments have demonstrated their concern by establishing agencies and procedures for monitoring demographic trends, but few have stated their intention of trying to modify the birth rate. In most Western nations the period of fertility decline has also been one of liberal abortion reform and increasing availability of free or low-cost family planning services and supplies. Except, possibly, in the United States, there are no indications that these liberal policies might be reconsidered in the near future.

The most common response, especially in those continental European nations that already had well-established family policies prior to the birth decline, has been to upgrade the level of assistance given the family. The new measures may include an increase in child or family allowances, modest extensions of paid maternity leave, and help in obtaining suitable housing.[31] While the increases in allowances may be substantial, governments deny a demographic objective and claim that the purpose of the transfers is to offset the degradation in living standards experienced by families with children. In most cases, moreover, the measures are too narrow in scope to constitute a serious demographic policy. A partial exception to these remarks is Luxembourg, where deaths have exceeded births in the indigenous population since 1966 and in the total population, including immigrants, since 1972.[32] Alarmed by the decline of its tiny population, which numbered only 358,000 in 1980, the government has announced its intention of extensively revising its program of family assistance. The new measures include substantial increases in family allowances and birth grants, and sixteen weeks of maternity leave on full pay. The government is also discussing the possibility of indexing family allowances to wages and introducing a new allowance to encourage parents to stay at home to care for young children.[33] There seems little doubt that there is a

---

[31]Brief, up-to-date statements of the positions and policies of all "developed countries" can be found in UN, *Population Policy Briefs*. For more extensive discussions of policies which may affect fertility in European nations see the relevant chapters in Kirk et al. For recent statement about the attitudes and policies of France, West Germany, the United Kingdom, and the Netherlands, see Henk J. Heeren, "Pronatalist Population Policies in Some West-European Countries," paper presented at the Population Association of America, Annual Meetings, Washington, D.C., March 26–28, 1981.

[32]Grand-Duchy of Luxembourg, Ministry of National Economy, *La démographie du Luxembourg: passé, présent, et avenir*, report prepared by Gérard Calot (Luxembourg: Service Central de la Statistique et des Etudes Economiques [STATEC], 1978), pp. 25–28, including table 1.15 and figure 1.4.

[33]UN, *Population Policy Briefs*, p. 22.

pronatalist intent behind the program, although it has not been formally stated.

Three countries, France, Greece, and Finland, have adopted numerical targets for population growth. Except in France, however, the policies actually enacted fall far short of what would be required to influence the birth rate. At the time they adopted demographic goals, Greece and Finland were worried about the combined effects of low fertility and heavy out-migration. In 1971 Greece announced its intention of aiming for a population growth rate of approximately one percent per annum. The tax structure was modified in favor of large families, and small family allowances were introduced. After 1974, however, the return of large numbers of former emigrants enabled Greece to attain its demographic goal without further resort to pronatalist population policy.[34] In 1975 and 1976 Finland identified numerical population targets for each individual county and indicated that it would strengthen family and social policy should the population in any county fall below the target. Since that time population growth has been considered satisfactory, and no new measures have been introduced for demographic reasons.[35]

Before leaving the topic of Western responses to low population growth, it will be of interest to look briefly at a group of nations that have long been exceptionally tolerant of a low rate of natural increase. Neither during the birth decline of the 1930s nor today have the United States, the United Kingdom, nor any of the English-speaking dominions overseas evinced real concern over low fertility—though Canada and Australia, both countries with large masses and small populations, wish to increase the size of their populations through immigration.[36]

Contemporary attitudes to low population growth in this group of countries are clearly shown in governmental reactions to the recommendations of commissions of inquiry into population trends in both the United Kingdom and the United States. Both President Nixon's Commission on Population Growth and

[34]Ibid., pp. 15–16. See also N. Louros, J. Danezis, and D. Trichopoulos, "Greece," in Berelson, *Population Policy in Developed Countries*, pp. 151–92; and George Siampos, "Law and Fertility in Greece," in Kirk et al., pp. 337–61.

[35]UN, *Population Policy Briefs*, pp. 15–16.

[36]Ibid., pp. 2–3, 8–9.

the American Future and Great Britain's Population Panel were created around 1970 for very similar reasons. In the context of international alarm over global population growth, both commissions were requested to study national demographic trends and their likely consequences for the two countries, and to advise on the need for special policies to modify population trends. The commissions, which reported in 1972 and 1973, came to much the same conclusions.[37] Both groups found that their countries had little to fear from population stabilization. Both argued that demographic change would do little to lessen the major social and economic problems likely to confront the two nations, although they thought that a slower rather than a more rapid rate of population growth would present fewer obstacles to achieving national goals. Both commissions noted that fertility would fluctuate spontaneously around replacement level, and both concluded that there were no demographic reasons for restricting access to contraceptive services and legal abortion.

Although the two commissions found no reason to recommend the introduction of policies intended to modify the birth rate, they noted that the work of many government departments is influenced by demographic trends. Observing that policymakers were ill-informed about the consequences of population change, both commissions advised that more demographic research and analysis be undertaken. Most importantly, in both the United States and the United Kingdom the commissions recommended that offices be established at the highest level to oversee and coordinate the population-related work of government. The British government endorsed the report of the Population Panel, creating a cabinet-level office to coordinate population activities and initiating an intensive program of population research and analysis.[38] The report of the United States' Com-

---

[37]United States, Commission on Population Growth and the American Future, *Population and the American Future* (Washington, D.C.: Government Printing Office, 1972), esp. ch. 16. (This report has also been published by Signet Books, New York, 1972.) United Kingdom, Central Policy Review Staff, *Report of the Population Panel* (London: HMSO, 1973), esp. pp. 1–12.

[38]The report of the first study appeared in 1978. See United Kingdom, Office of Population Censuses and Surveys, *Demographic Review: A Report on Population in Great Britain* (London: HMSO, series DR, no. 1, 1978).

mission was less cordially received, and no action was taken with regard to the proposed Office of Population Growth and Distribution. Moreover, no action was taken on the very similar recommendations of the House Select Committee on Population, which reported in 1978.[39]

The Definition of Population Policy

The preceding pages have indicated that European nations, including some in the West, have introduced a variety of measures intended to stimulate fertility. Not all of these efforts amount to population policy as defined in this study. The words "in this study" are stressed because population policy has been defined innumerable times without the emergence of a consensus on its meaning.[40] Many of the differences that have appeared can be traced to a general failure by authors to specify the purposes for which their definitions have been developed. There are obvious conceptual and methodological differences between an analysis that seeks to understand the population objectives of governments and the means by which they are to be achieved, for example, and one that seeks to assess the impact of governmental behavior on demographic structure and events. The latter objective clearly involves a much wider range of measures. It is desirable therefore to clarify the sense in which the term is used here.

The definition employed here has been designed to facilitate the identification of public policies that have been adopted for the purpose of influencing a demographic variable—either fertility or population growth. For this purpose a population policy may be regarded as "a specific set of government objectives relative to the population magnitude and/or composition with the instruments by which it may be possible to achieve these

[39]United States, House of Representatives, 95th. Congress, 2nd Session, *Final Report of the Select Committee on Population*, Domestic Consequences of Population Change, pp. 43–57 (1978).

[40]For discussions of the many definitions of population policy, see United Nations, *Determinants and Consequences*, pp. 631–61; Edwin Driver, *Essays on Population Policy* (Lexington, Mass.: Lexington Books, D. C. Heath, 1972); R. Kenneth Godwin, ed., *Comparative Policy Analysis* (Lexington, Mass.: Lexington Books, D. C. Heath, 1975).

objectives."[41] Implicitly, this definition contains four elements which should be present: (1) a statement on the part of government of its demographic goals; (2) a course of action to achieve these goals; (3) the designation or creation of an agency to be responsible for implementing the course of action; and (4) an allocation of resources to the agency to carry out its mandate.[42]

Although this definition gives an impression of precision and, in principle, facilitates the differentiation by an observer of a "real" from a "symbolic" policy or the "mere expression of sentiment," it cannot be applied mechanically, as governmental behavior is seldom as neat and coordinated as the definition implies. There are occasions, for example, when governments clearly formulate and announce their demographic goals; there are many other times, however, when policy objectives remain unstated. Not infrequently the latter situation may obtain when there is a lack of consensus on goals and to state them would engender political controversy. National objectives may also be obscure when demographic policies are developed within several ministries without overall coordination. Public policies, moreover, frequently evolve over a period of years, and statements of objectives, courses of action, and allocations of resources may be out of phase with one another at any given time. The identification of a population policy, therefore, calls for more than a formal checking for the presence of the four components of the definition; most commonly it requires careful search in the files of government officials, discussions with policy-makers, and subjective weighing of a variety of facts and opinions.

The study of pronatalist population policy is additionally complicated by the need to distinguish pronatalist measures from other social policy instruments. Frequently the distinction lies only in the intentions of government which, as has just been indicated, may be obscure. Governments desirous of raising the

[41]The definition is given here in the form attributed to Joseph J. Spengler and Otis Dudley Duncan by the United Nations in *Determinants and Consequences*, p. 632. In fact it is a composite of the definition given by Spengler and Duncan in an editorial passage on p. 441 of *Population Theory and Policy* (Glencoe: The Free Press, 1956) and that given by Spengler on p. 456 of the same volume.

[42]This discussion is based on Finkle and McIntosh, "Policy Responses to Population Stagnation in Developed Societies," in Campbell, pp. 277–78.

birth rate rely to a considerable degree on such measures as generous family allowances, maternity grants, assistance with housing, and income tax relief for couples with dependent children, all measures that may also form part of a family policy devoid of any intent to influence fertility. Although there may be times when the intentions of government can be inferred from certain characteristics of the measures, such indicators may be badly misleading. Among population policy analysts, for example, it is almost a convention to regard as pronatalist family allowances that are "progressive," in which, that is, the payments are larger for third and later children than for the first one or two. Until recently, however, the most progressive system of family allowances in Europe was found in the Netherlands where, according to two scholars who have made a study of the scheme, "Family allowances were never considered as part of the demographic policy. On the contrary, they played a role in wage policy."[43] Family allowances in Great Britain have also been progressive since their inception in the 1940s; but here again there has never been a pronatalist intent, and the size of the allowances has always been too small to exert an unintended pronatalist effect. My research has suggested, moreover, that in the climate of opinion that prevails in Western Europe today, governments may look with favor on a blurring of the distinction between family and pronatalist policy. The critical distinction between pronatalist and family policy is, of course, that the former must be intended to influence fertility; the problem of identification turns, once again, on the issue of governmental intentions.

Scope and Purpose of the Study

This study is an attempt to provide an explanation for the differential response of European—and especially Western European[44]—governments to low fertility and low population

---

[43]Philip van Praag and Louis Lohlé-Tart, "The Netherlands," in Berelson, *Population Policy in Developed Countries*, pp. 309–10.

[44]Fertility decline and pronatalist policies in Eastern Europe have already attracted considerable scholarly attention in the West. In addition to the sources already cited, see Jerzy Berent, "Fertility Decline in Eastern Europe and the Soviet Union," parts 2 and 3, *Population Studies* 24, 2 (July 1970), esp. pp. 286–92; Henry David, *Family Planning and Abortion in the Socialist*

growth. Although low population growth is a matter of interest and concern, and increasingly of legislation, little systematic investigation has been carried out on governmental attitudes toward population stagnation in Western Europe or on the factors that lead policy-makers to consider the adoption of public policy to stimulate population growth. In much of the literature there is an implicit, even explicit, assumption that population policy can be explained in terms of demographic conditions and trends. If population growth reaches above a certain level, the government will introduce antinatalist measures; if fertility falls more than is comfortable, efforts will be made to stimulate fertility.

There is a certain cogency in this argument insofar as governments are unlikely to introduce population policies in the absence of some signal from the environment that demographic trends are suboptimal. As the previous discussion indicates, however, demographic trends and conditions are not sufficient to explain why one country will introduce a population policy while another, in similar demographic circumstances, will not. By itself the demographic explanation cannot shed light on how governments define their levels of tolerance of population trends. More importantly, as one eminent demographer observed some years ago, while population policy is strictly speaking an effort by government to influence a demographic trend, the demographic goal of the policy is always seen as instrumental to some other objective—a cleaner environment, the quality of life, the strength of the state. "Never, apparently," he concluded, "is a demographic goal sufficient by itself to justify a population policy."[45] This study

---

Countries of Central and Eastern Europe (International Research Institute, American Institute for Research, Washington, D.C., 1970); Egon Szabady, "Interdependence Between Fertility Changes and Socio-Economic Developments in East European Countries," *Population Review* (New Delhi), 16, 1–2 (January to December 1972), pp. 9–17; David M. Heer, "Recent Developments in Soviet Population Policy," *Studies in Family Planning* 3, 11 (November 1972), pp. 257–64; Milos Macura, "Population Policies in the Socialist Countries of Europe," *Population Studies* 28, 3 (September 1974), pp. 369–79.

[45]Kingsley Davis, "The Nature and Purpose of Population Policy," in *California's Twenty Million*, ed. K. Davis and Frederick Styles (Berkeley, Cal.: University of California Press, 1971) p. 6.

is an attempt, therefore, to identify the factors that influence the population-related decisions of political leaders in Western Europe.

Why France, Sweden, and West Germany?

The selection of a small number of countries to represent the diversity of Western nations with low fertility poses a delicate problem of balance between what is theoretically and methodologically desirable and the limited resources available. Ideally, if universal generalizations are to be made, the study should be based on a random sample of Western nations; however, since three countries was the most that could be handled, it seemed preferable to select them with care. France, Sweden, and West Germany were chosen largely because all three countries have a history of governmental concern for population growth, and all three were among the small group of Western European nations that adopted pronatalist policies in the 1930s and 1940s. The experiences of the three countries show similarities as well as differences, but each country presents a characteristically different type of policy response. More than any other group of Western nations, France, Sweden, and West Germany have all, in one way or another, left their marks on Western conceptions of population policy. Because of their histories, furthermore, the choice of these three nations also permits a relatively long time perspective, adding depth to the analysis and giving some assurance that it will not be confounded by factors of ephemeral significance.

France, Sweden, and West Germany also represent much of the diversity of Western Europe. Although they share many things in common—all may be classified as liberal democracies, for example, and all have highly developed market economies—they nevertheless vary in many significant ways. Each country represents one of the three major ethnic and linguistic groupings of Western Europe: Latins, Germanic peoples, and Scandinavians. Two of them, France and Sweden, embody the two great divisions of western Christendom: Roman Catholicism and Protestantism. West Germany is geographically divided on this variable and provides an interesting point of comparison within her own borders. Politically, while Sweden has now broken a forty-four year stretch of Social Democratic government, France and West Germany have tended more to the political right and both have rather centrist governments at the present time.[46] On the dimension of governmental organization and structure, the three countries provide a range of variation, from a relatively high level of centralization in France and Sweden to the extreme decentralization of West Germany. It may be hoped, therefore, that empirical generalizations drawn from this small but relatively diverse sample may inspire more confidence than might have been the case had the sample been more homogenous.

Plan of the book

The following chapter outlines an alternative to the demographic explanation for the adoption of pronatalist policies and presents the three hypotheses that mark the starting point of the investigation. In Chapter 3 there is a discussion of the emergence of pronatalist sentiment in the three countries of the study and of the factors that led up to the adoption of pronatalist policies during the 1930s and 1940s. The next three chapters deal with the policy responses of France, Sweden, and West Germany today. Chapter 7 addresses the reasons behind the differential responses of the three Western European nations and advances some hypotheses for the differences between Eastern and Western attitudes to low fertility and pronatalist policy. Finally, for readers who have an interest in policy formulation *per se*, Appendix B contains a discussion of the analytical framework adopted for the study.

[46]Since this paragraph was written, France has also broken a long stretch of government by the right by electing the socialist François Mitterrand to the presidency.

II

THE DETERMINANTS OF POPULATION POLICY: AN ALTERNATIVE EXPLANATION

From earliest times the size of the population has occupied a leading place in the thinking of philosophers and theorists of the state and in the practical policies of rulers. In public policy, however, it is seldom that empirical realities independently determine a government's course of action; more commonly it is perceptions of these realities that shape a government's decision.[1] Although the link between demographic variables and fertility policy is weak and indirect, the way in which a country's demographic situation is defined by its leaders and what are seen as the likely consequences of demographic trends are critical elements in the formulation of policy. An overview of population theories and policies, both historically and today, suggests that the attitudes of governments toward population growth are principally determined by what are perceived to be: (a) the relationship between population and national power, and (b) the relationship between population and the economic well-being of the society. In practice, however, it is hypothesized that what a government will actually decide to do about its demographic situation will depend not only on these two variables but also on the role of the state in the society. That is, the actions of governments will be determined in large measure by the degree to which they possess the power, authority, and inclination to shape the structure of the society and the lives of its citizens.[2] As these relationships seem so fundamental in determining governmental responses to demographic trends, they deserve some explanation and elaboration.

[1]For an elaboration of this assumption, see Appendix B.
[2]Jason L. Finkle and Alison McIntosh, "Policy Responses," pp. 278–81.

Population and National Power

The belief that population numbers are directly related to national power is one of the most persistent themes in the history of population theory and policy. The larger the nation, the more soldiers it could mobilize for its armies; the more densely populated the land, the better it could resist the incursions of its neighbors; the more rapid the growth of population, the more easily could men be spared to found colonies, engage in international trade, and carry abroad the national language and culture. In societies and cultures as diverse as the Hebrew tribes of the Old Testament, the great civilizations of Greece and Rome, and the emerging nation-states of modern Europe, governments have encouraged marriage and fertility, protected the public health, and safeguarded the cultural integrity of the people in order to promote the power and strength of the nation and further its international influence.[3]

In Greece the regulation of marriage and procreation was regarded as of great importance for repairing the depredations of war. Sparta, the most martial of the city states, was singled out by classical writers as also the most pronatalist. Under the laws of Lycurgus, marriage was compulsory in Sparta, and celibacy was punished by the imposition of special taxes, serious civil indignities, and political disadvantages,[4] while fathers of three and four sons were accorded special privileges.[5] Procre-

[3]Charles Emil Strangeland, *Pre-Malthusian Doctrines of Population: A Study in the History of Economic Theory*, Studies in History, Economics and Public Law, vol. 21, no. 3 (New York: Columbia University Press, 1904); David E. C. Eversley, *Social Theories of Fertility and the Malthusian Debate* (Oxford: The Clarendon Press, 1959); David V. Glass, *Population: Policies and Movements in Europe* (Oxford: The Clarendon Press, 1940); Johannes Overbeek, *History of Population Theories* (Rotterdam: Rotterdam University Press, 1974); Hugh Last, "The Social Policy of Augustus," Cambridge Ancient History, vol. 10, *The Augustan Empire, 44 B.C. - A.D. 70* (Cambridge: The University Press, 1934), pp. 425–64; L. P. Wilkinson, "Classical Approaches to Population and Family Planning," *Population and Development Review* 4, 3 (September 1978), pp. 439–55.

[4]Edward P. Hutchinson, *The Population Debate* (Boston: Houghton Mifflin Company, 1967).

[5]Aristotle, *Politics*, bk. 2, ch. 9, para. 18; Lycurgus, cited in Strangeland, p. 28; Wilkinson, pp. 444–45.

ation was also encouraged in Rome when that city was still a city-state bent on conquest.[6]

In more modern times the reactions of European governments to the military exploits of Napoleon Bonaparte at the start of the nineteenth century provide the supreme illustration of the perceived link between population and national power. Napoleon's ability to recruit a mass army and to sustain enormous losses was generally attributed to the size of France's population, which far exceeded the population of any other European nation except Russia.[7] But Russia, because of her underdevelopment, was not seen to possess military power commensurate with the size of her population. As the century wore on and Germany's population came to equal and then surpass that of France, European attention turned with some alarm to the military threat posed by Germany. Simultaneously, in Germany anxiety rose over Russia's impending "population explosion."[8] *Relative* population growth thus came to be a factor in international relations. In the words of Quincy Wright:

> Under conditions of international rivalry a country falling behind in the population race perceives that time is against it and consequently initiates preventive war. Germany's aggressiveness in 1914 and 1939 has been attributed to the fact that it was faced by an increasing population disadvantage compared with Eastern Europe.[9]

A different conception of national power and its relation to population evolved during the time of the Roman Empire and

[6]Strangeland, p. 44.

[7]Napoleon is reputed to have boasted to Metternich, "I can afford to expend thirty thousand men a month." It should be noted, however, that Napoleon's army, like those of other nations at the time, was made up of about 50 percent foreign mercenaries. See Samual E. Finer, "State- and Nation-Building in Europe: The Role of the Military," in *The Formation of National States in Western Europe*, ed. Charles Tilly (Princeton: Princeton University Press), p. 146.

[8]Quincy Wright, *A Study of War* (Chicago: Chicago University Press, 1942), p. 1135; Ivan Stanislavovich de Bliokh, "Population Pressures as a Cause of War," trans. Michael Boylsov, *Population and Development Review* 3, 1–2 (March-June 1977), pp. 129–36, excerpted from *The Future War from the Point of View of Technology, Economy and Politics* (St. Petersburg, 1898).

[9]Quincy Wright, *The Study of International Relations* (New York: Appleton-Century-Crofts, 1955), p. 362; Hans J. Morgenthau, *Politics Among Nations*, 5th ed. (New York: Alfred A. Knopf, 1973), p. 126.

was expressed in the famous population laws of Augustus. Augustus's conception of national power and the legislation that followed from it are of interest to us today as they anticipated by 2,000 years many of the concerns that underlie contemporary population legislation in Europe. Faced with the need to rule an empire, Augustus realized that military strength alone would not suffice to control potentially rebellious subjects in far-flung regions of the world. Only a "Romanization" of the indigenous leadership in each of the distant colonies could ensure their allegiance to Rome. To inculcate a sense of admiration for Rome among local leaders, it was essential, in Augustus's opinion, to promote a sense of pride in Roman culture and a sense of cultural identity in administrators and officials sent to govern the colonies. Augustus's population laws were thus designed to strengthen the senatorial class by repairing the dissolute morals that undermined their authority and, among other things, encouraged patrician families to restrict their fertility. A second objective was to protect the cultural integrity of Rome by regulating the rate of absorption of aliens into Roman society and citizenship. Thus Augustus imposed strict controls to reduce the rapid rate of manumission of slaves.[10] Although European nations differ from Rome in that they no longer rule vast empires, their leaders appear to view a sense of cultural identity as an essential ingredient of national power as they define it today. A desire to protect the cultural integrity of the society lies behind many of the restrictions on immigration that have recently been imposed in Europe.

Population and the Economy

The relationship of population size and growth to economic prosperity, as distinct from national power, has been a matter of concern and of difference among scholars and statesmen at least since the time of the Renaissance in Europe.[11] There is an immense literature dealing with population aspects of economic

[10]Last, "Social policy of Augustus."

[11]The fourteenth-century Arabic statesman and philosopher Ibn Khaldun presented an analysis of population in which he displayed a sophisticated understanding of "business cycles" and their relation to population growth. Ibn Khaldun linked these cycles to the rise and fall of states. See *An Arab Philosophy of History, Selections from the Prolegomena of Ibn Khaldun of Tunis*

theory, and it is impossible here to do more than briefly outline the three main positions that have appeared and reappeared over the years. From the first perspective, chronologically speaking, a large and growing population is seen as beneficial to a society, providing a basis for increasing division of labor and technological progress and generating economic growth.[12] A contrary view of population-economic relations, associated primarily with Malthus, emphasizes the pressure of population against subsistence, which it regards as impeding the rise of living standards and as setting an upper limit on population growth. From a Marxian perspective, finally, the growth of population is regarded as dependent on the form of social and economic relations and is viewed positively in a socialist society.

The congeries of theories associated with mercantilism was the first to assign a positive economic effect to a large and growing population.[13] While there were differences among mercantilists about both the proper ends of the state and the sources of wealth—that is, whether power or wealth should be the ultimate objective and whether wealth resided in goods, bullion, or the people who labored to produce them—mercantilists agreed that labor was by far the most important factor of production. It followed that all possible means should be employed to increase the size and productivity of the labor force. Mercantilists observed that high population densities were conducive to industry and commerce and that they supplied the necessary population base for the establishment of colonies, which were desired for the opportunities they provided for trade. Although some mer-

---

(1332–1406), trans. and arr. by Charles Issawi (London: John Murray, 1950). E. P. Hutchinson has commented that the writings of Ibn Khaldun show that a tradition of scholarship existed in this field that has been lost to the West. See, Hutchinson, p. 15.

[12]One economist, Colin Clark, has recently argued that population growth may be a stimulus to development in the Third World. See *Population Growth and Land Use* (London: Macmillan and Co., 1967); also Colin Clark and Margaret Haswell, *The Economics of Subsistence Agriculture*, 3rd ed. (London: St. Martin's Press, 1967).

[13]The following passage is greatly dependent on the discussions in Strangeland, pp. 118–94; Joseph J. Spengler, "Mercantilist and Physiocratic Growth Theory," in *Theories of Economic Growth*, ed. Bert F. Hoselitz (New York: The Free Press, 1960), pp. 3–64, 299–344; Hutchinson, pp. 28–109; and United Nations, *Determinants and Consequences*, pp. 35–37.

cantilists believed that continued population growth would ultimately outstrip the ability of the land to support the population,
probably the most common assumption was that the product of
the soil would increase with the amount of labor expended on it.
If not, food, like any other commodity, could be imported from
the colonies or other foreign nations.

In the latter part of the eighteenth century there arose a new
school of economic theorists for whom land was the most important factor of production and agriculture the most strategic sector
of the economy.[14] In the belief that agricultural prosperity required a regime of free competition, the physiocrats pushed for a
reduction in state intervention. They believed, further, that the
nonagricultural sectors of an agrarian society would also function
at an optimal level when agriculture flourished.[15] Most physiocrats, as well as the Utilitarian philosophers with whom they were
associated, believed that agricultural production could be greatly
expanded by technological progress; they also thought that population growth could be kept voluntarily within acceptable limits
through the perfectability of mankind and society.[16] Thus physiocrats, like mercantilists, tended to favor population growth.

The economic ideas of statesmen and the policies of governments in regard to population growth changed markedly as the
population theory associated principally with Malthus became
known and accepted in Europe and America.[17] Malthus wrote
his famous *Essay on the Principle of Population* partly in reaction to what he thought to be the naïveté of Godwin's assumption that agricultural production might be increased almost
infinitely.[18] Malthus was also reacting against what he con-

[14]Spengler, "Mercantilist and Physiocratic Growth Theory," pp. 54–55;
United Nations, *Determinants and Consequences*, pp. 36–37.

[15]Spengler, "Mercantilist and Physiocratic Growth Theory," p. 55.

[16]The English philosopher William Godwin and the French Marquis de
Condorcet are among the Utilitarians best known to population scholars.
Robert Malthus wrote his famous essay on population largely in response to
the social and economic theories of Godwin and Condorcet.

[17]Karl Polanyi provides an extended discussion of this change in thinking
and the economic conditions that motivated it. See *The Great Transformation*
(New York: Rinehart and Co., Inc., 1944), pp. 77–102.

[18]Thomas Robert Malthus, *An Essay on the Principle of Population*, 1st
ed., 1789. The edition used in the present study is that of Philip Appleman
(New York: W. W. Norton and Co., Inc., 1976), ch. 10, pp. 65–75.

sidered to be Godwin's baseless conjectures about the "future extinction of passion between the sexes" and "the indefinite prolongation of human life."[19] In the first edition of the *Essay*, Malthus set out the core of his theory asserting that:

> The power of population is indefinitely greater than the power in the earth to produce subsistence for man. Population, when unchecked, increases in geometrical ratio. Subsistence increases only in an arithmetical ratio. A slight acquaintance with numbers will show the immensity of the first power in comparison of the second. By that law of our nature which makes food necessary to the life of man, the effects of these two unequal powers must be kept equal. This implies a strong and constantly operating check on population from the difficulty of subsistence. The difficulty must fall somewhere and must necessarily be severely felt by a large portion of mankind.[20]

Convinced of the "absolute impossibility from the fixed laws of our nature, that the pressure of want can ever be completely removed from the lower classes of society,"[21] Malthus contended that little was to be gained by the provision of relief to the poor. Since the principal and most permanent cause of poverty was set by natural law and had little to do with forms of government or the unequal distribution of property, poverty could not be relieved by means of public poor relief; knowledge that financial assistance was available would only encourage profligacy and procreation. Malthus contended that the only effective, and indeed the kindest, way to reduce the misery of the poor was to encourage prudence and restraint in marriage and reproduction.

Malthus's principle of population gained wide currency during the first half of the nineteenth century and was incorporated by economists of the classical school into their theory of economic growth. In essence, classical economic theory viewed the supply of labor as dependent on the demand for it. So long as additional investments were expected to return a profit, capital accumulation would continue and with it a demand for labor; wages would remain above the subsistence level, and population would

[19]Ibid., Ch. 11, pp. 76–78.
[20]Ibid., ch. 1, p. 20.
[21]Ibid., p. 36.

increase. Eventually, however, owing to the fixed quantity of land, diminishing returns would set in, and profits and wages would decline. At the point where profits were no longer possible, wages would be at subsistence level, capital accumulation would cease, and there would be a stabilization of income.[22]

During the latter part of the nineteenth century, political evaluations of population growth changed once again as empirical data appeared that seemed to refute the Malthusian pessimism. Not only had unprecedented population growth not been accompanied by emiseration and economic stagnation, the economy had never grown so fast nor individual prosperity increased so rapidly. Ricardo, Nassau Senior, and J. S. Mill, among others, suggested that the onset of diminishing returns might be significantly delayed by advances in agricultural technology. In an industrial society, moreover, the advent of a stable state might be delayed almost indefinitely through technological progress, greater human skills deriving from better education, and the possibility of obtaining raw materials from abroad.[23] There was evidence, furthermore, that population growth was starting to decline of its own volition in association with rising standards of living, and it was hoped that the spread of better birth control methods and devices—the new Malthusianism—would serve to eliminate the old Malthusian specter.

In contrast to Malthusianism, Marxian economic-population theory is optimistic and pronatalist. Marx criticized Malthus and the latter's concern for overpopulation, asserting that there is no abstract "law of population" but that each historical period has its own law dependent on the form of the relations of production. The only population law explicitly treated by Marx was the capitalist law according to which,

> the laboring population . . . produces, along with the accumulation of capital produced by it, the means by which itself is made relatively superfluous, is turned into a relative surplus population.[24]

In other words, Marxian theory holds that capital equipment tends to displace labor, creating unemployment; further, Marx

[22]United Nations, *Determinants and Consequences*, pp. 40–41.
[23]Ibid., pp. 42–46.
[24]Karl Marx, *Capital*, vol. 1, trans. from the 3rd German ed. by Samuel Moore and Edward Aveling (Chicago: Charles H. Kerr and Co., 1915), p. 692.

contended that this mechanism is a necessary condition of capitalism for it keeps wages low and permits capital accumulation. While Marx did not formulate the socialist law of population, his denunciation of capitalism endowed his disciples with a sense of optimism regarding the ability of a socialist economy both to induce and support a growing population. Through the influence of rising standards of living on mortality, the rate of population growth would increase; moreover, the socialist mode of production would enable the economy to absorb the additional population into the productive work force. Lenin, in particular, repudiated the idea of diminishing returns under conditions of technological progress and appeared to think that a growing population would be helpful to the economy.[25] There is evidence today, however, that the similarity of demographic trends in both socialist and capitalist countries is forcing socialist demographers and economists to reexamine some of their assumptions about the causes of population growth.[26]

Population and the Role of the State

Notwithstanding the association, real or perceived, between population and national power and prosperity, it is probable

[25]The belief that a growing population would be beneficial to a socialist economy appears to be only implicit in Lenin's writings. See, for example, "The Agrarian Question and the 'Critics of Marx,'" *Selected Works*, 12 (New York: International Publishers, 1938), pp. 51–63. See also the discussion in John R. Knarr, "Population Politics and the Soviet Polity," unpublished Ph.D. dissertation, University of California, Los Angeles, 1976, p. 105. An explicit statement of this point was made by A. Y. Popov in 1953 and cited in William Peterson, *Population*, 2nd ed. (New York: The Macmillan Co., 1969), p. 635.

[26]See, for example, Vladimir Srb, "On the Issue of Population Laws of Socialism and Communism," *International Demography Symposium, Zakopane, 1964* (Warsaw: Państwowe Wydawnictwo Naukowe, 1966), pp. 51–56.; Boyarsky, 1970, cited in Heer, "Recent Developments," p. 259; Timon Ryabushkin, "Social Policy and Demography in the Soviet Union," *Population and Development Review* 4, 4 (December 1978), pp. 715–20, reprinted from *Social Sciences Today* (Moscow, 1978); and Urlanis, 1971, cited in Knarr, p. 103. Earlier Marxists who expected population growth rates to decline with the improved status of women and the rising prosperity of the socialist state included August Bebel, *Woman and Socialism* (New York: Schocken Books, 1971, first published in Moscow in 1894); and S. G. Strumilin, cited in Knarr, pp. 106–7.

that the most significant determinant of population policy is the role of the state in a society. Although it can be argued that military strength, international influence, and economic growth are of universal importance to a nation, the historical record shows that past governmental efforts to influence demographic trends have been undertaken exclusively by strong, centralized, and somewhat monolithic states. In contrast, more pluralistic states which have practiced limited government have been much less prone to intervene in what they considered to be the private affairs of individual citizens. In short, the role of the state in a society and the relations between the citizen and the state go far to explain variations in the propensity of governments to introduce population policies.

The association between population policy and monistic, centralized states can be traced at least as far back as the classical period. The functions of the Greco-Roman city-state were, in Leslie Lipson's words, "everywhere considered to be co-extensive with society."[27] In Greece the economy was subject to political control in the public interest, religion consisted in state worship of the Olympic pantheon and the local patron hero or deity, and the arts were produced under the influence of state demand. "The state was the paramount social institution when and where it chose to intervene."[28] Similar conditions obtained in the city-state of Rome and continued throughout the Republic and the Empire despite the more pluralistic government structure which evolved out of the need to govern a diversity of peoples of different religions and cultures. Citing Lipson again:

> The governmental tradition associated with the name of Rome was and is authoritarian. The major concepts that typify the Roman contribution to politics are expressed in these Latin-derived words: power—*potestas*, authority—*auctoritas*; empire—*imperium.*[29]

Roman pronatalist policies remained in force for a full two centuries after Augustus and did not start to erode until Constantine's conversion to Christianity brought Christian ideas of marriage and procreation into the heart of the Roman state. Not

[27]Leslie Lipson, *The Great Issues of Politics* (New York: Prentice-Hall, 1954) p. 403.
[28]Ibid., p. 157.
[29]Ibid., p. 230.

that Christianity was opposed to marriage; many passages in the New Testament commend the institution of marriage and the founding of a family. Rather, while the founding of an earthly family was seen to be good in that it furnished a legitimate outlet for the temptations of the flesh, the condition of celibacy was thought to be better as it provided fewer distractions from the preparation of the soul for the life of the world to come. Francesco Nitti, an Italian statesman who studied the teachings of the major religions, concluded in 1894 that "among all the religions of civilized people, Catholicism is the least favorable to fecundity."[30]

Influential as were Christian beliefs on the course of population policy, it is possible that even greater significance attaches to the fact that Constantine, upon his conversion, entered into articles of agreement between the Roman state and the Church. In so doing, he opened the doors to a thousand years of church-state dualism which undermined the authority of the state and attempted to divide the management of societal affairs between the spiritual and temporal realms.[31] Not until the Renaissance and the emergence of the national state based on the theories and philosophies of Bodin, Machiavelli, and Thomas Hobbes, among others, did governments once again feel it incumbent on themselves to attempt to influence population trends in the interests of the state. The mercantilist era was, however, preeminently one of state intervention in economic affairs. Government policies regulated prices and wages, exports and imports, discouraged the export of specie, and provided a range of incentives and subsidies for setting up new industries. Imaginative measures were also introduced to stimulate population growth through the reduction of mortality, the encouragement of marriage and childbearing, and the regulation of emigration and immigration.[32] Spengler observes, moreover, that mercantilist population policies were most elaborate and most forcefully im-

---

[30]Strangeland, p. 83.

[31]For a discussion of the history of church-state dualism during this period, see Lipson, pp. 161–73; for an extended discussion of the evolution of political philosophy during the period, see George H. Sabine, *A History of Political Theory* (New York: Henry Holt and Co., 1937), pp. 159–313 passim.

[32]Spengler, "Mercantilist and Physiocratic Growth Theory," p. 29; Glass, *Policies and Movements*, pp. 92–94.

plemented in Spain and Germany, both of which had both suffered serious depopulation during the sixteenth and seventeenth
centuries.[33] As mercantilism declined, pronatalism gave way to
laissez-faire policies which expressed in concrete terms the philosophies of individualism, economic liberalism, and limited
government that underlay the relationship of the citizen to the
state throughout the nineteenth century and beyond.

Under the stimulus of low fertility and declining population
growth, European governments have started once again to con-
template the need for explicit policies to encourage a higher
birth rate. During the 1920s and 1930s a number of Western
European governments enacted legislation designed to increase
fertility through the medium of severe penalties for abortion and
restricted access to contraceptives and birth control information.
Only in Nazi Germany, however, and to a much lesser extent in
Mussolini's Italy, was the government able to muster the political will to enforce the measures and to support them with incentives to marriage. Only in Germany was there such a barrage of
pronatalist propaganda designed to foster psychological acceptance of the repressive measures. During the 1960s and 1970s,
likewise, it has been the socialist states of Eastern Europe, with
their commitment to centralized planning as well as their more
monolithic structure of government, that have acted most decisively to formulate and implement comprehensive population
policies.

Contemporary Views

As Europe enters a period of stable or declining population
growth, intellectual ideas about the relationships between population and national power, economic prosperity, and the role of
the state are in a state of flux. The simple understanding of
national power as being dependent on military strength has
given way to a broader conception of the bases of power. Modern students of international relations define national power in
terms of a nation's ability to manipulate its international environment and, in particular, to withstand the unwelcome influ-

---

[33]Spengler, "Mercantilist and Physiocratic Growth Theory," p. 30.

ences of other nations.[34] Nevertheless, although the basis of power is now seen to reside in a complex of factors that includes the technological capacity of the nation, the quality of its people, its organizational ability, political stability and legitimacy, international moral standing, and structure of alliances, there is still a belief among many academic and governmental analysts that population size is of prime importance. It is argued, for example, that while every large nation may not be a great power, every great power must be a large nation. In 1964 Organski and Organski estimated that a population of forty-five million was the minimum that would enable a nation to develop and support the educational and technological capacity to design, produce, and deploy sophisticated weapons systems; they argued further that as weapons systems became more sophisticated, the minimum size of the necessary population base would increase.[35]

During the past two decades, however, many have questioned the relationship of population size to national power as it has been realized that the large and growing populations of Third World states impede their economic development and diminish their influence in world affairs. Organski, Lamborn, and des Mesquita have bridged the apparent gap between those who argue for and against population size as a source of national power by showing that what counts is the capacity of the state to mobilize the human resources of the nation. In the opinion of these scholars, the present advantage enjoyed by more developed nations with smaller actual but larger "effective" populations will be lost as currently underdeveloped nations gradually attain comparable levels of effective use of human resources. When Third World countries reach this state of development,

---

[34]See, in particular, A. F. K. Organski, Bruce Bueno des Mesquita, and Allen Lamborn, "The Effective Population in International Politics," in U.S. Commission on Population Growth and the American Future, *Research Reports*, vol. 4, *Governance and Population* (Washington, D.C.: Government Printing Office, 1972), p. 237; Morgenthau, p. 126; Wright, *Study of International Relations*, p. 362; Ray S. Cline, *World Power Assessment: A Calculus of Strategic Drift* (Boulder, Colo.: Westview Press, 1975).

[35]Katherine Organski and A. F. K. Organski, *Population and World Power* (New York: Alfred A. Knopf, 1961), p. 13. By 1972 Organski had increased the minimum size to 50 million.

population size will emerge once again as directly related to national power.[36]

The relationship between population growth and economic prosperity has been questioned once more in the light of the decline of European economic growth and the simultaneous fall in the birth rate. The belief that population growth is necessary, or at least very helpful, for economic growth has pervaded elite opinion ever since it was advanced by Keynes, Hansen, and other "stagnation thesis" economists as a partial explanation for the Great Depression.[37] Nevertheless, the paucity of contemporary economic analysis under conditions of population decline has left policy-makers without clear scientific guidance. Reviewing the "scant" literature on population-economic relations, Thomas Espenshade concluded in 1978 that "the health of a nation depends far more on the wisdom of its economic policies than on its underlying demographic trends."[38] Espenshade hastened to add, however, "it needs to be stressed that this conclusion ignores the possibility of long-term decline, and that this is the real concern in some societies."[39] In sum, the present state of the art suggests that governmental policy-makers will tend to receive inadequate and conflicting advice from their economic advisers and are therefore likely to place more reliance on their own perceptions and judgments when coming to population policy decisions.

The relationship of the individual to the state in contemporary Western liberal democracies is also somewhat ambiguous. As is the case in the socialist countries of Eastern Europe, there has been a steady increase during the twentieth century in both the size of government and in its intervention in areas which were formerly thought to be the private domain of individuals. State regulation of all aspects of the economy and the provision of health, social security, education, and numerous welfare pro-

[36]Organski, Bueno des Mesquita, and Lamborn.

[37]See, for example, Keynes and Alvin H. Hansen, "Economic Progress and Declining Population Growth," *American Economic Review* 29 (March 1939), pp. 1–15.

[38]Thomas J. Espenshade, "Zero Population Growth and the Economics of Developed Nations," *Population and Development Review* 4, 4 (December 1978), pp. 645–80.

[39]Ibid., p. 667, fn. 36.

grams by governments of all political hues have multiplied the points of contact between the citizen and the state and greatly enhanced the ability of the state to influence the lives of individuals.[40] Along with this growing power of control by the state, however, there has been a parallel expansion in the commitment of the state to protection of the personal rights of individual citizens. Significantly, from the perspective of population policy, women have been successful in claiming the right of control over their own bodies. While the state *may* reserve to itself the right to intervene in the reproductive affairs of private individuals should this be required in the "interests" of the society and the state,[41] many if not most private citizens regard procreation as supremely a personal matter.

[40]For an extended discussion of the many ways in which state regulation can be achieved short of centralized planning, see Robert A. Dahl and Charles E. Lindblom, *Politics, Economics, and Welfare* (New York: Harper Torchbooks, 1953).

[41]See, for example, the remarks of the former French Minister of Health, Mme. Simone Veil, at the IUSSP Population Conference held in Mexico City, August 1977, "Human Rights, Ideologies, and Population Policies," trans. David B. Doty, *Population and Development Review* 4, 2 (June 1978), pp. 313–21.

III

THE RISE OF TWENTIETH-CENTURY PRONATALISM

The Political, Economic, and Intellectual Context of Population Policy

The first systematic efforts by modern governments to raise the birth rate took place in Western Europe during the 1920s and 1930s under the stimulus of fertility that had fallen to sub-replacement levels. It was not fertility decline alone that evoked in governments a pronatalist sentiment unparalleled in intensity since the mercantilist era; rather, it was the combination of low fertility with military and economic imperatives, as perceived by the governments of the day, that convinced them of the need to reverse the demographic trend. In a period of serious economic depression and mounting international tension, and in the context of a belief that population size and national power are intimately related, low fertility was seen by many national leaders as a threat to national survival.

Subreplacement fertility made its appearance in country after country at a time when there was much less knowledge about population laws and trends than there is today. The concept of demographic transition had yet to emerge, and there was little or no understanding that what was occurring was a transition from one relatively stable rate of population growth character-ized by high levels of fertility and mortality to another character-ized by low fertility and mortality rates. There was less recogni-tion than there is today that "stability" in population terms implies long- and short-term swings and oscillations around a relatively constant mean level. The implications of the new and sophisticated fertility measures that were developed during the 1930s were not completely understood, and it was generally assumed that birth rates would continue to fall unless the decline was halted by some successful intervention. The projections made by demographers during this period all led eventually to a decrease in population, the only differences being in the time of the onset and the speed of the decline.[1] One can only speculate, moreover, on what was the significance for demographers, government officials, and other elites in the early years of the century of the pervasive trend in intellectual thought which saw in the "love of luxury" and reluctance of European women to bear children signs of the degeneration and decay of Western Civilization?[2] Some writers drew parallels between Western Europe's low birth rates and the low fertility that had afflicted Rome at the time of its greatness and which, for many, had come to symbolize its decline.

Among the countries that experienced low fertility during the interwar years, none reacted more strongly than France and Germany. Sweden also reacted with a sense of alarm to its low fertility, but its ultimate response was very different from those of France and Germany. The policy measures adopted by these three countries differed in their design, and even more so in their implementation, but all have left distinctive marks on national attitudes toward population today. It is appropriate, therefore, to examine separately the development and implementation of the population policies of the 1930s in each of the three countries.

Fear of Depopulation in France

The demographic transition

One of the most enduring and significant elements in French perceptions of low population growth, the close association that

---

[1]Alexander M. Carr-Saunders, *World Population: Past Growth and Present Trends* (Oxford: The Clarendon Press, 1936), pp. 27–28, fig. 26 on p. 28.

[2]See, for example, Oswald Spengler, *Decline of the West*, trans. C. F. Atkinson (New York: Alfred A. Knopf, 1926–28); Arnold J. Toynbee, *A Study of History* (London: Oxford University Press, 1934–39). Numerous further examples are summarized and discussed in Pitirim A. Sorokin, *Social Philosophies of an Age of Crisis* (Boston: Beacon Press, 1950).

is made between declining fertility and declining national power, originates in the unusual form taken by the demographic transition in France. In most European countries mortality started to fall prior to or simultaneously with the decline in fertility, thereby triggering a considerable spurt of rapid population growth. In France, by contrast, the birth rate started to fall well before standards of living and health care rose sufficiently to effect an improvement in mortality. France, therefore, experienced only a small and short-lived growth spurt which occurred principally in the second part of the eighteenth century. France thus fell behind in the "population race," and its population structure aged in comparison with those of its neighbors. For over a century French perceptions of the nation's problems of international relations and economic development have been linked to these demographic circumstances. In the words of Alfred Sauvy, the most renowned and influential demographer in France:

> This difference between France and other countries, this drying up of the sap at the moment of great expansion, is the most important fact of all her history; it has determined all subsequent development and is still in action today.[3]

Although the start of the demographic transition in France occurred before the introduction of national population censuses and before the registration of vital events was complete, it seems to be established that mortality fell between 1750 and 1800 mainly because the period was free of the plagues and famines that had scourged the population intermittently throughout the seventeenth and early eighteenth centuries.[4] It was this fall in mortality that allowed the population of France to grow from an estimated 24.5 million in 1750 to 29.1 million in 1800,[5] leaving behind the populations of Germany with 25 million, Italy with 18 million, and Great Britain with 16 million. Only Russia, with 37 million, exceeded the population of France; but Russia was

---

[3]Alfred Sauvy, *La prévention des naissances: "Birth Control"* (Paris: Presses Universitaires de France, 1962), p. 13.

[4]Louis Henry, "The Population of France in the 18th Century," trans. Peter Jimack, in *Population in History*, ed. David V. Glass and David E. C. Eversley (London: Edward Arnold, Ltd., 1965), pp. 434–56.

[5]Louis Henry and Yves Blayo, "La population de la France de 1740 à 1860," *Population* (Special Issue: Démographie Historique), November 1975.

considered weaker in all important respects because of its lack of development.[6] The level of mortality in France remained relatively stable throughout this period, and the death rate did not commence its regular decline until around 1870. Thereafter the fall in mortality, though steady, was slow for the next two decades. Even after that, death rates, especially among men, remained high for an industrialized nation.[7]

Fertility started to fall, it is thought, around 1770 and thereafter declined steadily. In his study of the evolution of the French population since the eighteenth century, Jean Bourgeois-Pichat calculated that the Gross Reproduction Rate (GRR) must have fallen from around 2.39 in the period 1771–75 to approximately 2.01 thirty years later.[8] Using rather different methods of analysis, van de Walle has recently concluded that by the start of the nineteenth century, fertility in several *départements* had "already by then reached a level that most administrative units elsewhere in Europe would only approach a century later."[9] Three *départements* in Normandy actually had birth rates not much above 20 per 1,000 as early as the period 1801–5, a level not experienced by the United States until more than a century later.[10] While it is not yet certain to what extent the start of the decline was the result of the use of contraception within marriage rather than of widespread postponement of marriage, evidence has appeared from a number of small communities[11] that lends support to earlier geneaological evidence of resort to contraception by aristocratic families during the eighteenth century.[12] Van de Walle concludes that the conti-

[6] Philip M. Hauser, ed., *Population and World Politics* (Glencoe, Ill.: The Free Press, 1958) p. 117.

[7] Jean Bourgeois-Pichat, "Evolution de la population française depuis le dixhuitième siècle," *Population* 6, 4 (October-December 1951), pp. 652–53.

[8] Ibid., p. 644, table 6.

[9] Etienne van de Walle, "Alone in Europe: The French Fertility Decline until 1850," in *Historical Studies of Changing Fertility*, ed. Charles Tilly (Princeton, N.J.: Princeton University Press, 1978), p. 260.

[10] Ibid., p. 263.

[11] References for these studies will be found in ibid., p. 263.

[12] Claude Levy and Louis Henry, "Ducs et pairs sous l'ancien régime: caractéristiques démographiques d'une caste," *Population* 15, 4 (October-December 1960), pp. 807–30; Louis Henry, *Anciennes familles génevoises*, INED, Travaux et Documents, Cahier no. 26 (Paris: Presses Universitaires de France, 1956).

nued decline of fertility from the low levels that had already been reached by 1801–5 could not have occurred without the widespread use of contraception within marriage, not only by a privileged segment of the population but also by the peasants and "small folks" of the rural sector.[13]

From this early start fertility fell steadily throughout the nineteenth century from an estimated GRR of about 2.5 in 1870 to about 1.00 in 1935.[14] After 1935 the birth rate started to rise slowly and, after an interruption during the early years of the war, turned sharply upward to reach its highest level in 1947–48, with completed fertility of nearly three children per woman on the average. Even the somewhat lower level of 2.7 attained between 1953 and 1958 was higher than any level reached between 1905 and 1947.[15] The most significant feature of the demographic transition in France is the fact that because of the peculiar relationship between the curves of mortality and fertility decline, the population grew only slowly. On no less than twenty-four occasions between 1884 and 1939, including a stretch of six successive years after 1933, there was an excess of deaths over births.[16] When the first postwar population census was taken in 1946, the population was found to be nearly one and a half million smaller than it had been in 1936, only 250,000 of the loss being military casualties.[17]

Intellectual reactions to low fertility

Serious concern over France's slow demographic growth did not develop until the middle of the nineteenth century.[18] For one

[13]van de Walle, pp. 262–63.

[14]Glass, *Policies and Movements*, p. 177, gives the GRR as 1.004 and the NRR as .866 in 1935. The large difference between these figures indicates the relatively high mortality in France at the time. INED cites a TFR of approximately 3.5 for 1870 which fell to about 2.35 in 1914 (*Natalité et politique*, pp. 5–6).

[15]INED, p. 6.

[16]Joseph J. Spengler, *France Faces Depopulation* (Durham, N.C.: Duke University Press, 1938), p. 112; Colin Dyer, *Population and Society in Twentieth Century France* (New York: Holmes and Meier Publishers, Inc., 1978), p. 83.

[17]Dyer, pp. 132, 127.

[18]Spengler, *France Faces Depopulation*, p. 111. Spengler's work has been drawn on extensively in this section. In addition to his own cogent analysis, Spengler provides an extensive bibliography.

thing, it had become apparent toward the end of the eighteenth century that contrary to popular belief at the time, the annual number of births was increasing and the population was growing.[19] For another, even after it was realized in the 1820s and 1830s that fertility was declining and that the rate of population growth was slower than in other countries, the generally Malthusian and liberal tenor of social thought predominant at the time prevented the arousal of alarm. According to Spengler, a majority of intellectuals saw in the slow rate of population growth evidence of the prudence and forethought of the French people and a sign that France would remain free of mass poverty and the pressure of population on subsistence.[20] For those of a more nationalistic turn of mind, France under Napoleon had brilliantly demonstrated its military supremacy over Europe and confidence in the invincible quality of the French army remained high right up to 1870, despite occasional warnings that it was falling behind the armies of other nations, especially that of Prussia.[21]

Even the Church remained silent. The antireligious, anticlerical spirit that accompanied the revolution of 1789 undermined

---

[19]Spengler notes that while it was commonly believed during the eighteenth century that the population was declining, both Messance (1766) and Moheau (1778) demonstrated that the number of births was increasing and that the population was growing. See *France Faces Depopulation*, p. 106.

[20]Ibid., pp. 108–9.

[21]The French general, Louis Trochu, created a furor with his book *L'armée française en 1867* (Paris: 1867), in which he demonstrated that the French army was becoming outdated because its officers were inadequately educated and its soldiers too "individualistic." He argued that traditional French élan could not be relied on to win a war against a modern adversary and called for thoroughgoing reform. The French military attaché in Berlin, Baron Eugéne Stoffel, sent several dispatches warning of the dangers of French "ignorance and presumption" in ignoring the growing strength, discipline, education, and organizational ability of the Prussians. See *Rapports militaires écrit de Berlin de 1866 à 1870* (Paris, 1871), 17, pp. 321–22. Despite these warnings and the shock of the Prussian victory over the Austrians at Sadowa in 1867, funds were not forthcoming for any reform of the army mainly because, in the opinion of Koenraad Swart, those who were aware of the weakness of France were opposed to increasing the budget, since they feared that this would bolster the tottering regime of Louis Napoleon. See *The Sense of Decadence in Nineteenth-century France* (The Hague: Martinus Nijloff, 1964), pp. 120–122. However, neither of these warnings contained references to the *size* of the army and its relation to low population growth.

both the Church's moral authority and its physical presence. John T. Noonan has observed that as late as 1815, 13,000 French parishes were without priests; moreover, instruction given by Rome to French bishops and priests was extremely tolerant of *coitus interruptus*.[22] Not until the rise of the birth control movement in Western Europe after 1875 did the attitude of Rome toward birth control harden somewhat, and then only in those countries with substantial numbers of Catholics.[23]

The belief that France's international position was declining on account of the failure of her population and her wealth to grow started to find expression around 1850. Public discussion continued throughout the next two decades both within and outside the legislature; but right up to the eve of the Franco-Prussian War, liberal-economic and Malthusian views predominated, and the tone of the debate remained calm.[24] In January 1870 a proposal to implement some pronatalist measures was introduced in the Senate but was defeated, members asserting that the real cause of low population growth was the high infant mortality rate, and that in any case population growth was desirable only if the necessary capital was available to make the larger population more productive.[25]

The surprise and humiliation of the defeat by Prussia in 1870 greatly intensified France's alarm over its low population

[22]The decline of moral theology in France antedates the revolution by a considerable margin. Noonan dates its origin at around 1762, when some 6,000 Jesuits responsible for over 200 colleges were expelled from France by Louis XV. The Order was entirely suppressed by Pope Clement XIV in 1778. See *Contraception* (Cambridge, Mass.: Harvard University Press, 1965), p. 395. Noonan attributes the rapid spread of contraception throughout France to the "spiritual malaise" that followed the revolution. The Church was officially supported but privately rejected, and "contraception could only be controlled where there was spiritual allegiance" (pp. 389–90).

[23]Noonan, p. 414. In addition to its long tolerance of birth control, Rome has only recently started to speak out against abortion. The Conseil permanent de l'épiscopat français notes that Popes Pius XI, Pius XII, and John XXIII, made formal statements on abortion only eight times in the thirty-five years between 1913 and 1958. More recently Pope Paul VI intervened more than thirty times in fifteen years. See *Faire vivre: l'Eglise catholique et l'avortement* (Paris: Editions du Centurions, 1979). Reviewed in *Le Monde*, April 24, 1979, p. 14. The antiabortionist position of Pope John Paul II is well known.

[24]Spengler, *France Faces Depopulation*, pp. 111–20.

[25]Ibid., p. 120.

growth. As a consequence of the war and the Communard revolution that followed, the demographic balance of Europe was altered, much to the disadvantage of France.[26] Deaths exceeded births by more than half a million in 1870–71, to which must be added the population lost through the cession of Alsace and Lorraine to Germany.[27] Between 1870 and 1939 a flood of books, newspaper articles, and pamphlets appeared that theorized about the causes of the fertility decline and proposed measures to reverse the trend.[28] Depopulation was frequently the topic of discussion at meetings of learned societies, and in 1896 a large and well-supported organization, the National Alliance for the Growth of Population, was founded to sponsor scientific research and to act as a pressure group for legislation to deal with the issue. Somewhat earlier, numerous small regional associations had started to spring up in support of large families, and in 1921 most of them came together to form a national association, the Federation of Associations of Large Families in France.[29] Pronatalist associations were formed in the Chamber

[26]Spengler observes that Levasseur pointed out the changed demographic balance as early as 1872. Ibid., p. 121, n. 2.

[27]Spengler notes that the population in 1872 numbered 1,956,000 fewer than in 1866 mainly owing to the loss of territory. He cites the estimate of Bodart (1916) that losses during 1870–71 were as follows: military losses from war and disease, 500,000; excess deaths among the civilian population, 600,000 approximately; losses during the Commune, 50,000. Ibid., p. 121, n. 1.

[28]Almost everything was blamed for the fall in fertility, from inheritance laws and "social capillarity" to the riding of bicycles by women and the coddling of poodles. Frederick Le Play, *La réforme sociale en France* (Paris: E. Dentu, 1867) pointed out that under the Napoleonic code, parents were required to divide their property in specified proportions among all their children. He argued that owners of land restricted the size of their families in order to prevent fragmentation of the land. Arsène Dumont, *Dépopulation et civilization: étude démographique* (Paris: Lecrosnier et Babe, 1890) argued that "social capillarity"—the desire and opportunity to rise in social and economic status—had become very strong since the revolution, which had created equal political rights that were not accompanied by economic and social equality. Very similar theories are advanced today to account for fertility decline in developing countries. Spengler, *France Faces Depopulation*, pp. 135–74, provides a good discussion of contemporary French theories of fertility decline.

[29]The fundamental purpose of the family associations was to protect and further the rights and welfare of large families. Though often in sympathy with measures proposed by the National Alliance, the objectives of family associations were based on the principles of equity and justice rather than pronatal-

of Deputies in 1914 and the Senate in 1917, and in 1919 the High Council on Fertility was created under the aegis of the Ministry of Health, to examine questions relating to fertility and mortality.[30]

The alarm over low population growth, or depopulation as it was erroneously called, sprang principally from an intense nationalism that became much more widespread in the society after the events of 1870–71. For the first time, people of all intellectual traditions, liberals as well as conservatives and Catholics, spoke about the inevitable loss of military, political, diplomatic and colonial power that would ensue if France's population continued to decline relative to the populations of other European nations. It was feared that France would lose its cultural integrity if it were forced to admit large numbers of foreign immigrants to compensate for labor shortages.[31] The Church, finally protesting the practice of birth control, combined nationalistic arguments with its moral and religious appeals.[32] Many intellectuals also feared that population stagnation would lead to a failure of economic development, a decline in the spirit of enterprise, and a general economic disequilibrium that would result in unemployment and a lowering of living standards.[33]

---

ism. For a discussion, see Jean Bourgeois-Pichat, "France," in *Population Policy in Developed Countries*, ed. Bernard Berelson, p. 547. According to Glass, *Policies and Movements*, p. 150, the Federation was responsible in 1927 for founding the International League for Life and Family as a response to and attack on the first international world population conference held in Geneva at the instigation of Margaret Sanger. The federation correctly believed that the conference was intended to spread the gospel of birth control. See also Richard Symonds and Michael Carder, *The United Nations and the Population Question* (New York: McGraw-Hill Book Company, 1973), pp. 11–15.

[30]Glass, *Policies and Movements*, p. 150.

[31]Spengler, *France Faces Depopulation*, pp. 121–34; Swart, p. 174. Spengler, pp. 130–33, summarizes anticipated consequences of fertility decline under ten headings: military; political and diplomatic; colonial; foreign penetration; economic development; spirit of enterprise; progress; economic equilibrium and well-being; and biological and social.

[32]The Swiss cardinal Gaspard Mermillon, for example, in a Bastille Day speech at Beauvais in 1872 said: "You have rejected God and God has struck you. You have, by hideous calculation, made tombs instead of filling cradles with children; therefore you have wanted for children." Cited in Noonan, p. 414.

[33]Swart, p. 174; Spengler, *France Faces Depopulation*, pp. 123–24.

Despite the constant stream of populationist propaganda and the bills introduced in parliament, no legislation intended to stimulate the birth rate was passed by the National Assembly prior to World War I. The unexpected ease with which France had paid the enormous indemnity exacted by Germany, the splendor of the great international expositions of 1878 and 1889, and the success of French colonial expansion after 1888 all served to raise the morale of the people, although their hopes were still fixed on the "blue line of the Vosges"—the distant mountains that marked the territories lost to Germany.[34]

There were also some more immediate factors at work to delay the passage of legislation to stimulate fertility. The organized birth control movement was slow to get under way in France, but in 1896 an organization to promote birth control, the League for Human Regeneration, was formed under the leadership of Paul Robin.[35] Robin was a member of the First International, and the League was supported by many socialists who felt that the pronatalist movement was a plot to assure a supply of cheap labor.[36] Many liberals, on the other hand, despite their concern over population, felt that state intervention to manipulate reproduction was essentially socialistic. They felt that the real imperative for France was to prevent the spread of socialism and the attendant risk of increased state controls. They still maintained that only a regime of free competition could ensure a continuation of economic growth and guarantee the welfare of the mass of citizens.[37]

[34]Spengler, *France Faces Depopulation*, p. 123.

[35]Glass, *Policies and Movements*, pp. 161–62. Glass comments that the League never exerted much political influence. It suffered from internal dissention and in 1908 split into several factions. Glass considers, however, that the activities and propaganda of the League may have delayed the passage of legislation to encourage fertility.

[36]Swart notes that on the eve of World War I, even the socialists began to revise their opinions. Victor Griffuelhes, the syndicalist leader, touring the deserted French countryside, exclaimed: "The Malthusians have gone too far. So much effort to build a just and brotherly city in which no one will live." In like vein the distinguished socialist economist Charles Rist remarked: "France is an island of sugar that is melting." He proposed that the ideal solution would be for each worker to have no more than two children and each bourgeois at least four. Cited in Swart, pp. 174–75.

[37]Ibid., p. 174.

The evolution of pronatalist policy

The first pronatalist measures were enacted in 1920 and 1923 on the recommendations of the newly created High Council on Fertility, which was attached to the recently established Ministry of Hygiene, Assistance, and Social Providence.[38] The new laws were "repressive," having the twin objectives of preventing contraception and punishing abortion. The law of 1920 provided fines and prison sentences for divulging, offering to divulge, or facilitating the use of methods to prevent conception. The law of 1923 reduced the penalties for abortion in the hope of getting more convictions. Prior to 1923 the abortion laws of France derived from the Penal Code of 1912, which provided for five to ten years penal servitude for both the woman concerned and the person procuring the abortion.[39] For many years the number of prosecutions under the act had been very small, and the number of convictions and sentences smaller still, largely because juries were not prepared to punish women for offenses their own wives had committed. The law of 1923 classified abortion as a misdemeanor and considerably reduced the penalties, thereby eliminating the need for a jury.[40] However, neither of the two laws was very effective in increasing the birth rate. Condoms, which were not classified as contraceptives but as means of protecting against disease, and other hygienic devices that could be used as contraceptives although that was not their primary purpose were still freely available. After the 1923 act the number of convictions for abortion increased somewhat, but the number of abortions procured remained high.[41] Notwithstanding their lack of effectiveness, the two laws remained in force until the mid–

[38]Bourgeois-Pichat, "France," p. 549.

[39]Glass, *Policies and Movements*, p. 157. Glass reports, pp. 160–61, that if the abortion was procured by a physician, pharmacist, or other health worker, the punishment was increased to a sentence of from five to twenty years of hard labor and involved transportation to a penal colony. Many abortionists were midwives, whose profession was overcrowded.

[40]The penalties remained severe nevertheless. For the woman they involved a period of one to six months in jail and a fine of 100 to 2,000 francs; for the abortionist the penalty was prison for one to five years and fine of 500 to 10,000 francs. See Glass, *Policies and Movements*, pp. 160–61.

[41]Glass, *Policies and Movements*, pp. 163–64, gives a careful assessment of the impact of the abortion law in France.

1960s, restrictions on the distribution of contraceptives even being increased in 1939.

Positive measures to support families with children were introduced rather earlier than the repressive measures, under private rather than governmental auspices and without, it would seem, any pronatalist intention. As early as 1884 a small number of industrialists established funds to grant additional pay to employees who were fathers. During the ensuing thirty years the idea spread to other industries and to some grades of workers in the employ of central government. According to David Glass, who has provided a thorough discussion of the evolution of family allowances in France, the scheme was started and supported by industry because in a time of rising prices, it was cheaper to give additional pay only to those who were most in need.[42] There is some evidence, in addition, to suggest that employers also believed that the payment of allowances would prevent the cooptation of married workers by the radical trade union movement.[43] Under pressure from the National Alliance and the family associations, the scheme spread very rapidly during the 1914–18 war among industrial and commercial firms and to all workers in central government.[44]

Although the family allowances initially had no pronatalist intention, as they came to be applied more widely throughout the society, they received the strong support of pronatalist groups. During the 1920s and 1930s, the state found itself obliged to take a more active role in regulating the funds, encouraging the provision of additional benefits and services—for example, maternity care and benefits, allowances for mothers who were breast-feeding, holiday camps for children—and equalizing payments among the regions. Local government workers were gradually brought into the scheme, and funds were established to serve the agricultural sector. However, prior to 1932, the state was not involved financially except in the case of its own employees.

In January 1939 the government took the first step in developing a comprehensive population policy, establishing a high-level committee closely linked to the centers of power to stimu-

[42]Ibid., pp. 94–144, 212–18.
[43]Ibid., p. 103.
[44]Bourgeois-Pichat, "France," pp. 150–51.

late and coordinate action within government departments. Based on the committee's recommendations, the Code de la Famille was promulgated in July 1939. The Family Code was a complex policy that combined incentives to childbearing with a series of "welfare" measures intended to protect and further the health, social, and legal status of mothers and children. Under the Family Code family allowances were extended to additional occupational groups and were made to increase in amount for successive children. The allowances were still small, however; a family with four children received the equivalent of 49 percent of the average wage paid in the *département* of residence. In addition to family allowances, birth premiums were introduced, and a supplementary allowance equal to 10 percent of the average wage was paid to the *mère au foyer*[45] in urban areas. A different approach to maintaining the birth rate was the introduction of interest-free marriage loans to young couples in the agricultural sector as part of an effort to retard the "flight from the land." Rural fertility was still higher than urban fertility, and the government was anxious to encourage this useful differential. On the whole, however, although the Family Code did represent the first systematic effort to formulate a comprehensive population/family policy, the transfers were small and did not compensate for the additional costs of children. Throughout the war years the provisions of the code were applied and augmented by the Vichy government, which made the family one of the foundations of its regime.[46]

Population policy after 1945

The collapse of France in 1940 signaled the start of a new stage of French pronatalism. For many if not for most French people, a fundamental reason for both the military defeat and the political betrayal of the country was to be found in the ineffective

---

[45]A useful French phrase that does not translate well into English. It is used to refer to mothers who remain at home and do not go out to work. Literally, "mother in the home."

[46]Nicole Questiaux and Jacques Fournier, "France," in *Family Policy: Government and Families in Fourteen Countries*, ed. Sheila B. Kammerman and Alfred J. Kahn (New York: Columbia University Press, 1978), pp. 119–20.

leadership of France's aged generals and politicians.[47] This in turn was attributed to the country's long history of demographic weakness which, coupled with the serious loss of life during the 1914–18 war, had left the country in the hands of tired old men incapable of innovative planning or decisive action.[48] In addition, the severe deficiency of births during the earlier conflict meant that there were few young men to send to the front in 1939 and 1940; instead, the defense of the country was in the hands of veterans of 1914–18 who had little enthusiasm for war.[49] In 1945 it was generally agreed that the first requirement for reconstruction was the rejuvenation of the population. General de Gaulle, as leader of the provisional government, asked the people to produce "in ten years, twelve million beautiful babies."[50]

In a climate of opinion supportive of positive population policy and, ironically, accompanied by a rising birth rate, one of the first acts of the new government was the establishment, in April

[47]According to Colin Dyer, a rough count of France's top military leadership shows the mean age to have been 67. Marshal Pétain was 84, Weygand was 73. By contrast, Hitler was 51 in 1940 and the mean age of the German leadership was 50. See, Dyer, pp. 93–94. In the years after World War II there was a flood of books and articles by scholars and statesmen in France that lamented the age of the French population and called for an increase in the birth rate. A good example is Robert Debré and Alfred Sauvy, *Des Français pour la France* (Paris: Gallimard, 1946). The most persistent campaigner for a younger population has been Alfred Sauvy; there is barely a single publication in his extensive bibliography that does not contain a section on the consequences of what he has termed "perfidious senescence." But see particularly *La prévention des naissances: "Birth Control"*; *La montée des jeunes*; *A General Theory of Population*, trans. by Christopher Campos (New York: Basic Books, Inc., 1969); and, the most recent, Sauvy's contribution in *La France ridée*, by Gérard-François Dumont, et al. Almost all the respondents in the present study commented on the age-structure of France and its role in precipitating the defeat of 1940.

[48]Of 8.5 million men mobilized in France during World War I, 1.4 million, or 16.5 percent, were killed. This is the highest proportion of dead suffered by any of the major combatants. See Dyer, p. 140.

[49]The crude death rate, which was 18.2 per 1,000 in 1913 and 17.9 in 1914, fell to 9.5—its lowest point—in 1916 and was still only 12.6 in 1919. See Dyer, p. 150. The attitude of the French people during the 1930s toward the approaching war is brilliantly conveyed in Jean-Paul Sartre's trilogy *Roads to Freedom*, especially the third volume, *Iron in the Soul*, trans. Gerard Hopkins (London: Hamish Hamilton, 1950).

[50]Dyer, p. 132.

1945, of a High Consultative Committee on Population responsible directly to the Prime Minister. Within six months the committee, several times presided over by de Gaulle himself, had elaborated formulas designed to complete the existing measures in support of the family. The committee laid down a framework within which family policy became an integral part of a global social security program that also included sickness and old-age insurance schemes. In order to ensure the availability of relevant information, the committee also recommended at this time the creation of two research institutes, the Institut national d'Etudes démographiques (INED) and the Institut national d'Hygiène.[51]

The family-oriented population policy introduced in 1945 followed the pattern established by the Family Code of 1939 and pursued both populationist and welfare goals with a series of measures designed to serve both ends. There were still some efforts to influence fertility directly by means of the laws on contraception and abortion and by the payment of "windfall" premiums for births that occurred within certain time limits. For the most part, however, the effect of fertility and population growth was intended to be indirect. Among other things, measures were introduced to protect the health of pregnant women, to reduce infant and child mortality, and to provide financial support for dependent children. As the years went by, the pronatalist objective tended to decline in importance, and the welfare or "social justice" goal came to predominate.[52]

As originally enacted, the family allowances were not only generous but were indexed to a series of occupation-specific basic wages. Within a year, however, under the pressure of inflation and rising prices and wages, the indexing scheme was abandoned and has never again been taken up.[53] As a result there has been a

[51]Bourgeois-Pichat, "France," p. 552. The thrust of the work carried out by INED has changed somewhat since the institute was founded. In 1964 the Institut national d'Hygiène was reorganized under the name Institut national de la Santé et de la Recherche médicale (INSERM).

[52]The best short discussion in English of the 1945 family policy and its evolution over the years is to be found in Jacques Doublet and Hubert de Villedary, *Law and Population Growth in France*, Law and Population Monograph Series, no. 12, the Fletcher School of Law and Diplomacy, Tufts University (Medford, Mass., 1973). The discussion is both analytical and substantive.

[53]Jacques Doublet, *L'Aide aux familles* (Geneva: International Labor Organization, 1975).

constant erosion of the real value of the allowances, starting in the early 1950s and continuing well into the 1970s. To a certain extent the decline has been offset by the introduction through the years of a variety of additional benefits, including significant housing allowances and substantial deductions in income tax for dependent children. Despite the additional benefits, however, the proportion of social security funding allocated to family policy declined continuously in relation to old-age and sickness insurance.[54] Nevertheless, throughout the whole period from 1945 until today, France's family policy has remained by far the most generous in Western Europe.[55]

National Socialist Expansionism in Germany

Reactions to fertility decline

Concern over low population growth is of much shorter duration in Germany than in France but immediately prior to 1945 was probably no less intense. Throughout most of the nineteenth

[54]The proportion of social security funding allocated to family policy declined from 37 percent in 1958 to a little over 20 percent in 1970, while the proportions devoted to old age and sickness increased from 31 to 44 percent in the same period. See Jacqueline Hecht, "La politique familiale française depuis 1939," in *La France et sa population aujourd'hui*, Les Cahiers Français, no. 184, January-February 1978 (Paris: La Documentation Française), p. 51. The tendency for funds properly intended for the family to be used to make up deficiencies in other social security programs was referred to in the recent discussions of the deficit in social security funding, *Le Monde*, December 13, 1978, p. 45. Sauvy has commented that the High Committee on Population in 1945 spoke out very clearly against transferring all social benefits through the same agency. "We will see," the committee had said, "the resources for children pass to the old and sick." See, "La necessité d'une nation jeune," *Le Figaro*, April 27, 1979, p. 2. See also, Paul Paillat, "Economic and Social Assistance to Families," in Kirk et al., eds., p. 78.

[55]In 1970, for instance, while the ratio of total social benefits to national income varied little among the six member states of the European Economic Community, family allowances accounted for 21 percent of total social benefits in France, 20 percent in Belgium, 14 percent in Italy and the Netherlands, and 8 percent in the Federal Republic of Germany. See Gérard Calot and Jacqueline Hecht, "The Control of Fertility Trends," in *Population Decline in Europe*, ed. Council of Europe (New York: St. Martin's Press, 1978), p. 191, n. 10.

century the population of Germany grew steadily, almost doubling between 1843 and 1913 despite substantial net emigration.[56] As in most of Western Europe, the birth rate did not start to fall until the last quarter of the nineteenth century; indeed, there is still some doubt whether the onset of the German fertility decline occurred in the late 1870s or twenty years later.[57] Once it started, however, the decline was more rapid in Germany than in France, the crude birth rate falling from 39.2 per 1,000 in 1876–80 to 14.7 in 1933.[58] Reflecting the rapid decline in mortality as well as fertility, the GRR and NRR fell from 2.46 and 1.45 in 1881–90 to 0.800 and 0.698 in 1933.[59]

Reactions to the slower rate of population growth appeared very soon after the birth rate started to fall. As early as 1898 one writer observed that the German government showed "a good deal of concern over this issue, although . . . population growth in Germany is not especially small."[60] While French deputies in the National Assembly made frequent reference in military debates to the growing population differential between France and

---

[56]Overseas emigration from Germany was heavy at times even prior to the unification of Germany, over 2 million Germans arriving in the United States alone between 1820 and 1870. Between 1870 and 1914, net *overseas* emigration exceeded 2.5 million, being heaviest between 1880 and the early 1890s and declining somewhat after the fertility decline got firmly under way. See, John E. Knodel, *The Decline of Fertility in Germany, 1871–1939* (Princeton: Princeton University Press, 1973), pp. 189–91. It should be noted that these figures exclude emigrants to other parts of Europe.

[57]Knodel, pp. 56–57. There was a considerable rise in the number of births for several years after the Franco-Prussian War, and some scholars are of the opinion that the decline that appeared in the 1880s was simply a return to the former, prewar level. Their argument is supported by reference to a period of relatively constant fertility between 1883–90 which suggests to them that the regular decline did not start until around 1900.

[58]Glass, *Policies and Movements*, pp. 69–70.

[59]The series of GRRs and NRRs for the period is as follows:

	1881–90	1924–26	1931	1933
GRR	2.459	1.116	.862	.800
NRR	1.448	.924	.748	.698

Sources: Robert R. Kuczynski, *The Measurement of Population Growth* (London: Sidgwick and Jackson, Ltd., 1935), pp. 122 and 212; Glass, *Policies and Movements*, p. 270.

[60]de Bliokh, p. 131.

Germany, German delegates in the Reichstag made increasing allusion to Russia's huge population and military potential.[61] According to Glass, moreover, there was already, prior to 1914, "a considerable literature on the subject," and widespread discussion in the press canvassed various types of intervention to halt the decline in births.[62] In 1913 the German Catholic bishops issued a pastoral letter which echoed the nationalistic tone of the French bishops after 1870 by reminding the faithful that the chief end of marriage was procreation "in order to secure the continuation of the Church *and the state.*"[63] Not surprisingly, the level of concern grew during the war: a number of municipalities awarded cash prizes to mothers of large families; the issue was fully debated in the Reichstag; and in 1917 the first German association for the promotion of large families, the Vereinigung Kinderreicher Familien und Witwen, was established.[64]

After the war pronatalist sentiment continued to find both official and private expression, and in 1921 a national union of already existing large-family associations was formed, which had some success in disseminating information through mass rallies and popular publications.[65] The practical effect of these movements was undermined, however, by the rapid spread of the birth control movement, which set up a national network of clinics to distribute low-cost contraceptives and advice to working-class women. The birth control movement started in Germany in 1889, rather earlier than in France, with the foundation

[61]Wright, *A Study of War*, p. 1136. The differential perceived by French deputies was in both size and growth. Dyer, p. 6, cites the French scholar Huber on the relative size of the two populations in 1871 and 1911 as follows:

	1871	1911	% increase
German Empire	41.1	64.9	57.8
France	36.6	39.6	9.7

[62]Glass, *Policies and Movements*, pp. 270–72. My account depends heavily on Glass's detailed work, by far the best source available in English. Unfortunately, Glass's book was published in 1940, prior to the full development of "repressive" legislation in Germany.

[63]Noonan, p. 421. The emphasis is mine.

[64]Glass, *Policies and Movements*, p. 272; see also, Adelyne More, *Fecundity versus Civilization* (London: Allen and Unwin, n.d.), pp. 25–28. The catalogue of the British Museum Reading Room gives a date of 1916 for this book.

[65]Glass, *Policies and Movements*, p. 272.

of the Sozial-Harmonischer Verein.[66] Unlike the Ligue de la Régénération in France, with its Socialist International associations, the Sozial-Harmonischer Verein was a middle-class intellectual movement, modeled on the British Neo-Malthusian League. It was bitterly opposed by the Social Democratic leadership on orthodox Marxist grounds and "because of the needs of the Social Democratic army in its battle against capitalism."[67] Later, however, the movement received the strong practical support of the trade unions; and in the more democratic political climate of the Weimar Republic, workers' birth control associations were formed all over the country. Most of these associations maintained permanent birth control clinics, and many of them even ran mobile clinics that traveled from place to place in less densely populated areas.[68] In the immediate post war years, Glass notes, contraceptive use was also increased by the creation of a number of commercial birth control associations founded by manufacturers for the specific purpose of creating a market for their products.[69] Thus, prior to the establishment of the Third Reich, modern methods of contraception were readily available and, as the birth rate suggests, freely used.

It was under pressure from the left-wing parties that the abortion law, which derived from the Penal Code of 1872, was modified. Prior to 1926 a punishment of up to five years' penal servitude was prescribed for both the woman and the abortionist;

[66]Ibid., p. 276, cites 1892 as the date of founding of this organization. However, More, p. 11, and Noonan, p. 406, both give 1889.

[67]The paternalist and intellectual tone of the Malthusian movement in Britain and other Western countries is clearly conveyed in the report of a conference called in London in 1922. See *Report of the International Neo-Malthusian and Birth Control Conference, (Fifth) London, 1922*, ed. Raymond Pierpont (London: William Heinemann, Ltd., 1922), especially the statement of Max Hausemeister of Germany, pp. 12–15. August Bebel, the German Social Democratic leader was particularly antagonistic to the neo-Malthusian movement. Bebel anticipated that fertility would decline under socialism because of the improved status of women. See *Woman and Socialism*. Bebel also believed that the party would take control of the Reichstag "toward the year 1898" and apparently believed that the birth control movement might delay the revolution. See his remarks to the Reichstag in 1892, cited in More, p. 33.

[68]Glass, *Policies and Movements*, p. 277.

[69]Ibid., p. 276.

under the new law penal servitude for up to fifteen years was retained for the abortionist who took money for his services, but the punishment was reduced in the usual case to simple imprisonment. In spite of the change, the punishment was still severe, and socialist organizations continued their pressure for further reform until the National Socialists were elected in 1933. Moreover, despite the law, the number of abortions remained large.[70]

Nazi population policy

The population policy that emerged in Nazi Germany embodied and expressed three of the most fundamental values and myths of the National Socialist state: a belief in the innate superiority of the "Aryan race"; a political philosophy that placed the needs of the state and the community above the desires of the individual; and the doctrine of the polarity of the sexes—the idea that men and women belong innately to different social spheres.[71] The first of these basic principles underlay the Nazi drive to increase the number of Germans of Aryan stock while it justified the elimination of the hereditarily unfit and "racially impure." Belief in Aryan superiority also justified the apparently contradictory drive for "living space" for the future generations of Aryans, even if the coveted space was already occupied by

---

[70]Glass, pp. 278–79, cites several sets of data from sickness benefit funds in different cities to show that the ratio of abortions to live births changed from 85:100 to 113:100 between 1929 and 1932. It is not clear from Glass's account if the figures for live births comprise all the births in the area or only those whose mothers were entitled to claim benefits from the funds. Another possible source of error is the inevitable omission from the abortion tally of clandestine abortions in the area. Thus the ratios can only be understood to imply that abortions were still frequently and openly procured at this time.

[71]In his analysis of the family under National Socialism, Alfred Meusel viewed population policy as the core of National Socialist racial policy. See "National Socialism and the Family," *Sociological Review* 23 (April-October, 1936), p. 178. Leila J. Rupp, *Mobilizing Women for War* (Princeton, N.J.: Princeton University Press, 1978), pp. 11–50, furnishes an interesting discussion of Nazi ideology as it related to women. The doctrine of separate and complementary spheres of men and women was most fully elaborated by Alfred Rosenberg, *Der Mythus des 20. Jahrhunderts: Eine Wertung der Seelischgeistigen* (Munich: Hoheneichen-Verlag, 1930).

other nationalities. Second, the political philosophy expressed in the slogan "Gemeinnutz vor Eigennutz,"[72] which placed the needs of the state first, was used to legitimize the coercion of couples to bear children for the state. Men and women of Aryan stock were encouraged to beget additional illegitimate children by racially pure mates, and divorce was encouraged in cases where a marriage proved to be sterile.[73] Finally, the doctrine that there is a separate, complementary, but subordinate sphere proper to women underlay the use of propaganda to spread the idea that women's fulfillment was to be found in the kitchen and the nursery rather than in the factory or office.[74]

Pronatalist policy was an integral part of the measures designed to establish the tone and character of the new National Socialist state. Plans for the introduction of a eugenic policy were actually made in 1932, the year before the National Socialists took office; and an act for the prevention of hereditary diseases was placed on the statute books in July 1933, only a short time after their accession to power.[75] Also in place from

[72]The interest of the community before selfish interest, or "Community before self."

[73]A discussion of the many pressures on Aryan Germans to procreate which were outside of legislated policy measures is given in Hans P. Bleulel, *Strength Through Joy: Sex and Society in Nazi Germany*, trans. Maxwell Brownjohn (London: Seker and Warberg, 1973), pp. 148–79.

[74]Rupp, p. 34, comments that, while Nazi *ideology* proclaimed the reconstruction of the family and the significance of a women's role as mother, housewife, and guardian of racial purity after what National Socialists perceived to have been their destruction by liberal-socialist individualism and feminism, Nazi *policy* tended to pull the family apart and minimize the role of women (my emphases). See also, Meusel, pp. 395–98 and 406. In this connection a memorandum from Martin Bormann discussing the future implementation of Hitler's plan for making up war losses by increasing fertility through a system of plural marriages is presented in Oran J. Hale, "Adolf Hitler and the Post-War German Birth-Rate: An Unpublished Memorandum," *Journal of Central European Affairs* 17, 2 (July 1957), pp. 166–73.

[75]The text of the Nazi sterilization law and a justification for it are to be found in Rudolf Frercks, *German Population Policy* (Berlin: Terramare Publications, no. 5, 1938). It should be borne in mind that the Nazis were not alone in enacting legislation for the compulsory sterilization of the hereditarily unfit. In Sweden government reports on compulsory sterilization were presented in 1929 and 1933, and in 1934 legislation was passed that permitted the compulsory sterilization of the insane and mentally defective provided each case satisfied an additional eugenic (the disease was hereditary) or social (the individual

the start was a vigorous propaganda campaign intended to create a new image of German society and of women's place in it.[76] At first, some of the measures introduced were intended as much to ameliorate the effects of the Depression as to further the ideological ends of National Socialism. For example, the program of marriage loans, introduced in 1933, had the dual objective of encouraging childbearing and reducing unemployment. Under this scheme young couples who could satisfy certain racial, eugenic, character, and conduct criteria could apply for interest-free marriage loans to help them establish a home. In order to qualify for a loan, the bride had also to show proof that she had been employed in one of certain specified categories of work for at least six months prior to the date of application for the loan. Furthermore, she had to agree not to take up paid work again unless her husband's income fell below a specified level. The loan was paid in the form of coupons that could be used to buy furniture and household equipment; it was calculated that each loan would provide work for two men: the job vacated by the woman and an additional position that would be generated by the increased prosperity of the industries producing household goods.[77]

The pronatalist objective of the marriage loan scheme, which in Glass's opinion was initially of only secondary importance, gradually took on greater significance and, once preparations for war had eliminated unemployment, became the main purpose of the program. The scheme was financed from the start by means of a special tax on all unmarried men and women whose incomes were not less than 75 marks per month, and repayment of the loan was canceled by 25 percent at the birth of each child within the eight-year repayment period. Once the scheme was

---

was incapable of caring for a child) criterion. See Alva Myrdal, pp. 212–16. Compulsory sterilization of the hereditarily unfit was commonly advocated by scholars and public figures during the 1920s and 1930s. For an example, see the remarks of Dr. Horatio Pollock at the International Birth Control Conference (Fifth), London, 1922.

[76]Bleuel and Rupp both give a good feeling for the content and form of this propaganda addressed to women. See also George Mosse, *Nazi Culture: Intellectual, Cultural and Social Life in the Third Reich* (New York: Grosset and Dunlap, 1966), especially pp. 39–47, and Otto Helmut, *Volk in Gefahr* (Munich: J. S. Lehmanns Verlag, 1933).

[77]Frercks, p. 6.

well established, the sums repaid were used to finance a variety of additional grants and allowances for large families. They were never as generous as the French allowances, however, and for the most part the first four or five children were not eligible. As was the case with marriage loans, recipients of any grant had to show proof of racial and eugenic purity and evidence of good conduct and character.[78]

"Repressive" measures restricting access to means of family limitation were introduced deceptively slowly in Nazi Germany. Until 1941 contraceptives were available, and the existing abortion law, that of 1926, was even "liberalized" to allow abortion to prevent the birth of "hereditarily diseased" offspring. Nevertheless, the government acted strongly against birth control using means other than punishment. Almost immediately after taking office, the Nazis authorized a vigorous police action to close all birth control clinics and to seek out and prosecute abortionists. This action had the effect of eliminating the organizations that provided low-cost contraceptives and advice to thousands of working- and lower middle-class women. At the same time, penalties were introduced for the display or advertisement of abortifacients as well as for offering to assist in procuring abortion. Thus, while contraception and the sale of contraceptives were legal, in practice contraceptives were virtually unobtainable by the majority of ordinary women. Women were forced to stay at home without work and were subject to a barrage of propaganda informing them of their duty to procreate. Notwithstanding these and other measures which closed off most means of family limitation, Glass notes that until 1937 there was no significant increase in the number of persons accused of criminal abortion. He was of the opinion that the increase that occurred in 1937 and 1938 may have reflected an increase in the number of abortions being procured rather than more vigorous prosecution of offenders by the police.[79]

Not until 1941 was a complete ban on all "methods, materials, and instruments for the prevention or interruption of pregnancy" promulgated under a Himmler police ordinance, which also banned irradiation or injection for the purpose of prevent-

---

[78]Glass, *Policies and Movements*, pp. 287–89.
[79]Ibid., pp. 285–86.

ing pregnancy. The ordinance was incorporated into law in March 1943 in a revision of the Penal Code. The revision provided for penal servitude for these offenses and for anyone who willfully destroyed or substantially damaged the procreative faculty in himself or others. The death penalty was introduced for cases in which the accused was "found guilty of continually prejudicing the vital power of the German people."[80]

With the exception of the propaganda campaign that constantly reminded women of their duty to procreate, the pronatalist and family policy adopted by the Nazis was, until 1943, not so very different from that of France. Prior to the Himmler police ordinance of 1941, not formally enacted into law until 1943, the *legislation* in Germany was somewhat less repressive than that of France; and the positive incentives, though probably smaller on balance than those of France, were nevertheless substantial. The difference lay in the determination and rigor with which the repressive legislation was implemented in Germany and the extension of the German measures into the field of racial policy. Despite the harsh enforcement of the Nazi birth control laws, there is little evidence that the overall effect on fertility in Germany was either more or less than the effect of French family policy in France.

National Socialist population policy nevertheless had unexpected and unfortunate consequences for German society after World War II. Negative attitudes toward birth control that had been inculcated in both the police and the medical profession were slow to change, and the repressive apparatus of control proved harder to dismantle in practice than in law.[81] More seriously, the revulsion felt by the German people for "population

---

[80]Hans Harmsen, "Notes on Abortion and Birth Control in Germany," *Population Studies*, 3, 4 (March 1950), pp. 402–3.

[81]Ibid. Harmsen notes that one of the social problems faced by Germany immediately after the cessation of hostilities was a large number of cases of rape and assault on German women. This gave rise to a heavy toll of mental breakdown among young women, and even mortality from clandestine abortion. When the authorities repealed the abortion legislation in the hope of alleviating these unfortunate consequences, the police refused to recognize the repeal, contending that the Himmler Police Ordinance was still in effect. Furthermore, the medical profession in the three Western occupation zones continued to act in accordance with the severe abortion law. According to Harmsen, the legislative changes were respected only in the Russian zone.

policy," which was indelibly associated in minds of the people with the racial policy and worst excesses of National Socialism, has seriously undermined the ability of the society to deal with its present demographic problems. For many years after the war demography and population issues fell into disrepute, the training of demographers and population specialists was abandoned, and little or no research on population questions was undertaken. Only within the last decade has it gradually become possible to speak again of population policy, to commence the training of demographers, and to establish an institute for population research.[82]

Population and Social Welfare in Sweden

Demographic transition and overpopulation

In contrast to the situation in France and Germany, where there is still uncertainty about the start of the demographic transition, the course of fertility and mortality decline in Sweden can be traced from its beginning. Even before the earliest signs of regular demographic change appeared, Swedish mercantilists had introduced a system of compulsory population registration that has resulted in the compilation of an unbroken series of population statistics of remarkable accuracy for every year from 1749 until the present. On the basis of this record it is known that Sweden provides a textbook example of demographic transition of the type characteristic of Northwest Europe.[83] By 1749 the crude birth rate had already fallen to around 33 per 1,000, mainly through the postponement of marriage.[84] Within mar-

[82]These points are elaborated in Chapter 6.

[83]John Hajnal, "European Marriage Patterns in Perspective," *Population in History*, Glass and Eversley, eds., pp. 101–43.

[84]Alva Myrdal, pp. 29–30. Although marriages were not recorded by age prior to 1860, an approximate distribution made by the Swedish demographer Sundbärg around 1900 permits one to estimate that the average age at marriage for women was between 26 and 27. It can also be estimated that approximately 60 percent of marriages occurred when the bride was between 20 and 24. It can be inferred, therefore, that a substantial proportion of marriages could not have taken place until the bride was considerably older than 26–27. Sundbärg's distribution also suggests that 10 to 11 percent of women never married. See Sweden, Royal Ministry of Foreign Affairs, *The Biography of a People* (Stockholm, 1974), p. 37.

riage fertility remained high, the average woman giving birth to about eight children, of whom four or five survived to adulthood. In the mideighteenth century mortality varied around an average level of 27 per 1,000. Between 1750 and 1810 mortality and fertility fluctuated around these average levels but sometimes in opposite directions, so that in several years deaths exceeded births.[85]

The demographic transition proper got under way about 1810, with an improvement in mortality, uneven at first but gradually becoming a continuous decline that has continued until today. Birth rates remained at pretransition levels for a further sixty years, starting to fall only during the decade from 1871 to 1880. Once fertility started to decline, however, it continued to do so without interruption, even gaining momentum after the turn of the century. By 1935 the crude death rate had fallen below 12 per 1,000, and the crude birth rate had reached its nadir of 14 per 1,000. At this time both the gross and net reproduction rates had reached their lowest levels of 0.811 and 0.729.[86] Throughout the period the age of marriage remained high and the proportion married continued low. In the census year 1930 some 20 percent of Swedish women reaching age 50 had never married, compared with only 10 percent in France.[87]

In marked contrast to the feeble rate of population growth in France, the most significant consequence of Sweden's demographic transition was a lengthy growth spurt which gave rise to overpopulation. Despite occasional years of excess mortality prior to 1810, the population grew at an average rate of 0.8 percent per annum between 1749 and 1850, doubling in size from 1.7 to 3.5 million. The annual rate of growth increased to nearly 1.0 percent by 1815, and after 1850 natural increase was in excess of 1.0 percent until the start of the twentieth century.[88]

The period of rapid population growth in Sweden coincided with the rise of economic liberalism under the influence of which profound changes were made in the form of agricultural production. The first half of the nineteenth century witnessed the grad-

---

[85]Sweden, *Biography of a People*, pp. 18–19.
[86]Alva Myrdal, p. 21; Glass, *Policies and Movements*, p. 314.
[87]Alva Myrdal, p. 35.
[88]Sweden, *Biography of a People*, pp. 55–79.

ual evolution of the enclosure movement, a concurrent loss of rights to the use of common land, and the creation of a landless rural proletariat in a society in which industrialization had barely begun. Well before the middle of the century, the capacity of the still almost entirely agricultural economy to absorb the population increase was seriously overburdened, and there were problems of unemployment and impoverishment in the rural areas.[89] As in other European countries during the nineteenth century, the Swedish response to overpopulation was emigration. After 1840 the success of liberal ideas in the Riksdag resulted in the gradual lifting of the old mercantilist barriers to out-migration and paved the way for the great waves of emigration that took place between about 1860 and the first years of the twentieth century.[90] The outflow of Swedish people, especially to the United States, was massive, at first affecting whole families but later becoming more selective of young people in the prime working ages.[91] It has been calculated that while the population actually increased to 6.1 million by 1930, the figure would have been 8.5 million had there been no emigration. Of the 2.4 million deficit, just over one million was a direct consequence of out-migration; the balance is accounted for by the absence of children who would have been born in Sweden had there been no emigration.[92]

Public interest in population issues started to appear toward the end of the nineteenth century, stimulated by the defense needs of the country and a perceived lack of labor in both agriculture and industry. The deficiency in the number of young men became obvious in the course of a reorganization of Sweden's system of national defense and became a cause for alarm in the atmosphere of growing international tension after 1900. In response to what they considered to be Sweden's poten-

[89]Ibid., pp. 56–62, 66–68.

[90]Ann-Sofie Kälvemark, "Swedish Emigration Policy in an International Perspective, 1844–1925," in *From Sweden to America*, ed. Harold Runblom and Hans Norman (Minneapolis: Minneapolis University Press, and Uppsala: Acta Universitatis Upsaliensis, 1976), pp. 96–100.

[91]Runblom and Norman, see also Sweden, *Biography of a People*, pp. 68–71.

[92]Erland Hofsten and Hans Lundström, *Swedish Population History* (Stockholm: National Central Bureau of Statistics, 1976), pp. 76–77.

tial military weakness, conservative groups started to call for a reduction in the flow of emigrants out of the country. Conservative demands were supported by spokesmen for agricultural interests who alleged that there was a shortage of labor in agriculture; in addition, liberal groups believed that the lack of workers in the cities was delaying the progress of industrial development. Although by this time the period of heavy out-migration was over, the movement led to the appointment in 1907 of an Investigating Committee on Emigration.[93] The Committee addressed itself principally to rural conditions in employment and living standards, and its report, released in 1913, recommended thorough reform of agricultural production to alleviate serious poverty in the rural areas.

Another issue that helped to bring the population question to the fore was birth control. In marked contrast to its success in Germany, the birth control movement was slow to get under way in Sweden. Neo-Malthusian ideas were introduced to Sweden in the early 1880s, primarily by Knut Wicksell, later to become a leading economist. While still a student, Wicksell became convinced that Sweden's poverty could only be overcome by voluntary restriction of childbearing, and he traveled the country preaching birth control.[94] The idea of intervening in a natural— almost religious—function provoked a strongly negative reaction, expressed in moralistic terms, among the middle and upper classes of society. The outcry appears to have had some success in preventing the spread of modern methods of birth control. It was not until 1911 that the first Swedish branch of the Malthusian League was established,[95] and in 1922 Wicksell reported to a birth control conference in London that the few branches that had later been formed had exerted little political influence and were already, to the best of his knowledge, extinct.[96] Not until the depression years of the 1920s did Malthusian ideas become widely known and accepted within the working class.[97] In 1910, however, the anti-birth controllers succeded in getting legislation

---

[93]Kälvemark, "Swedish Emigration Policy," pp. 103–12.
[94]Alva Myrdal, pp. 24–25.
[95]Noonan, p. 407.
[96]Report of the Fifth International Birth Control Conference, p. 11.
[97]Glass, *Policies and Movements*, p. 320.

passed prohibiting the public sale of contraceptives and dissemination of birth control information.[98]

"Qualitative" population policy

The population policy adopted by Sweden in the 1930s and 1940s differed from those of France and Germany in three important respects. First, the policy was introduced by a socialist government more concerned with improving the social and economic status of the people than in developing the military strength of the nation. Second, the proposed measures were based on thorough study of demographic trends and analysis of their implications for the future well-being of the society. Third, for the first time, efforts to stimulate the birth rate were linked with liberal policy on birth control.

Like other Western nations, Sweden suffered an economic depression in the early 1920s, and in 1923 the birth rate, already below replacement level, became the lowest in the world, a position it was to retain until 1934.[99] The significance of this event did not escape population statisticians and economists. In 1926 Professor S. D. Wicksell, son of the earlier Wicksell, published a series of population projections based on different assumptions of mortality and fertility, some of which forecast an absolute decrease in population size.[100] During the late 1920s and early 1930s, moreover, a number of commissions were established to investigate aspects of unemployment and socioeconomic conditions in both urban and rural areas. From the work of these commissions, the country was learning with some surprise of the deprived conditions under which the mass of Swedes were living. After the election to office of a minority Social

---

[98]Alva Myrdal, p. 24; Glass noted in 1939 that the law had in general only been used against peddlers selling contraceptives in public markets. However, by 1937 there were still only five clinics in the entire country that offered birth control advice. Moreover, the number of patients seen for any reason amounted to fewer than 3,000 in 1937–38, and most of them were in Stockholm. See "Population Policy," in *Democratic Sweden*, ed. Margaret Cole and Charles Smith (New York: The Greystone Press, 1939), pp. 286–87, 299, n. 1.

[99]Alva Myrdal, p. 26.

[100]Glass, *Policies and Movements*, p. 315.

Democratic government, the Agrarian Party started to cooperate with the government in a massive program to reduce unemployment. In 1931 the two issues of population decline and poverty were linked in the Riksdag when the Conservative leader introduced a motion requesting modification of the tax structure in favor of married couples with children. Despite the amount of concern over both issues, the motion was unsuccessful.[101] In 1934 the Conservatives again took up the population question in parliament, advocating measures to relieve the economic burden of children on young couples. At the same time, the Agrarian Party cited the higher fertility of rural couples as a reason for increasing allocations for rural housing. Notwithstanding the growing sympathy for social reform, neither of these conservative initiatives succeeded.[102]

The breakthrough for population policy came with the publication in 1934 of a book, *Kris i Befolkningsfrågan* (Crisis in the Population Question), coauthored by Gunnar and Alva Myrdal, two prominent Social Democrats.[103] The book closely examined demographic trends and drew the conclusion that unless strenuous action was taken, the population must inevitably decrease in size. The end result would be economic stagnation, lowered morale, and cultural disintegration. Judging that modern conditions and ways of life ruled out the possibility of a return to population growth, the Myrdals recommended that the nation attempt to prevent an absolute decline in population numbers by adopting public policy intended to raise fertility to replacement level. Taking account of mortality, involuntary sterility, and Swedish patterns of nuptiality, even this limited goal would require the inculcation of a four-child norm among fertile married couples.[104]

[101]Ann-Sofie Kälvemark, *More Children of Better Quality?*, Studia Historica Upsaliensis, no. 115 (Uppsala: Acta Universitatis Upsaliensis, 1980), p. 51.

[102]Ibid., pp. 51–52.

[103]In the preface to her book *Nation and Family*, published in the United States in 1941, Alva Myrdal notes that it was intended by Gunnar Myrdal and herself as a substitute for an English translation of *Kris i Befolkningsfrågan*. The first nine chapters of *Nation and Family* contain a summary of the Swedish book, while part 2 (chs. 10–22) contains a discussion of the work of the commission and the legislation recommended and passed. Certain aspects are also elaborated in Gunnar Myrdal.

[104]Glass, in 1939, cited what appears to have been Myrdal's original estimate of the necessary fertility level as 2.8 children per family. See "Population

The innovative quality of the Myrdals' work is found in the way the two authors were able to combine two apparently contradictory objectives: the stimulation of fertility and the creation of a nationwide network of birth control clinics that would make contraceptive advice and services available to the entire public. The Myrdals were at pains to disavow the existence among Swedes of a spirit of nationalism, pointing out that Sweden had for more than a century relinquished any territorial ambitions outside its own borders. It was their thesis that a democratic nation could only countenance a pronatalist policy if it were based on the principle of voluntary parenthood. Thus the policy advocated by the Myrdals aimed at the creation of a society in which economic, social, and medical obstacles to childbearing would be eliminated, and in which couples would also be given the means of realizing their chosen size of family, whether that was large or small.[105] The list of suggested reforms included measures to provide free mental, physical, dental, and maternity health services; housing and rent subsidies; reduced food costs for children; free education from preschool to university; reduced cost of clothing for children; subsidized recreational facilities; greater economic and occupational security for parents, including women; and public responsibility for children in handicapped families.[106]

The Myrdals' book quickly became a bestseller and created an unprecedented amount of interest in the population question.[107] In 1935 another Conservative motion, this time requesting the establishment of a Population Commission, was accepted by the Riksdag. Nonetheless, opinion was divided; on the extreme right the National Group, a short-lived party formed from the breakaway youth wing of the Conservative Party and im-

---

Policy," p. 285. Gunnar Myrdal, p. 176, and Alva Myrdal, p. 106, both give the larger figure which is based on the calculation made by C.-E. Quesnal for the Population Commission's *Report on the Sexual Question*, published in 1936.

[105]Gunnar Myrdal, pp. 195–202; Alva Myrdal, pp. 113–53.

[106]Alva Myrdal, pp. 131–32.

[107]Gunnar Myrdal notes that he and Mrs. Myrdal assembled a collection of over 10,000 press clippings, several thousand letters, and more than 200 pamphlets and articles, all stimulated by *Kris i Befolkningsfrågan*. See Gunnar Myrdal, pp. 83–84.

bued with National Socialist ideas, called for a "qualified" population policy structured along racial lines.[108] This group later succeeded in getting a proposal for a program of marriage loans, consciously patterned on the German model, adopted by the Riksdag.[109] At the other extreme, the Communist Party claimed that the real objective behind the proposed pronatalist policy was to ensure a plentiful supply of military conscripts and cheap labor.[110] Glass observes, moreover, that many working-class people who had come to regard family limitation as a sign of prudence and forethought were disturbed by the pronatalist theme; large families came to be sneeringly referred to as "Myrdal's families," and a new verb, "to myrdal," meaning "to copulate," made a temporary appearance in the language.[111] More significantly, the main body of the ruling Social Democratic Party remained distrustful of the pronatalist objective. In a much quoted remark made at a party congress in 1936, for example, Gustav Moller, the Minister for Social Affairs, said,

> I must say that I will not hesitate to frighten no matter how many Conservatives, Farmer's Unionists and members of the Liberal Party with the threat that our people will otherwise die out, if with this threat I can get them to vote for social proposals I put forward. This is my simple view of the population issue and it is good enough for me.[112]

In the four years of its existence the Population Commission of 1935, whose members included a number of "experts" including the Myrdals themselves, produced seventeen research reports and many recommendations. Only a few of the latter were adopted by the Riksdag, and their impact was diminished by the small sums allocated for their implementation. Moreover, some of the most important proposals adopted by the Riksdag originated elsewhere and were only endorsed by the Population Commission. In the judgment of one student of the commission, these measures would have been introduced anyway, even with-

---

[108]Alva Myrdal, pp. 159–60; Kälvemark, *More Children*, pp. 51–52.
[109]Kälvemark, *More Children*, p. 67.
[110]Ibid., p. 55; Alva Myrdal, pp. 163–67.
[111]Glass, "Population Policy," p. 292.
[112]Sweden, *Biography of a People*, p. 115.

out the Commission.[113] As indicated above, the program of marriage loans was initiated by the Nazi-inspired National Group. Another of the significant measures introduced, a substantial program of rent subsidies and state loans to communities for the construction of family housing, originated in the Social Committee for Housing. The membership of this committee, established in 1933, included both the Myrdals, and there was an obvious carry-over to the work of the Population Commission.[114] Finally, while the Population Commission recommended the repeal of the anticontraceptive law of 1910, its recommendation on abortion was more restrictive than that of the Abortion Committee, which had been referred to the Population Commission for comment. The Population Commission's proposal, which was adopted by the Riksdag, legalized abortion for therapeutic, eugenic, and "ethical" (mainly rape) reasons but excluded abortions on social and economic grounds. In order to improve the social and economic conditions that might give rise to applications for abortion, the Population Commission instead advocated a large program of maternity bonuses, payable to most mothers, and an additional system of maternity grants for those in special need.[115]

Despite the introduction of these and other measures, the Myrdals' proposals were not fully adopted by the Commission or the Riksdag. Several reasons can be advanced for their lack of success at this particular time. For example, one of the basic principles underlying the Myrdals' proposals was that transfers should be made as far as possible in kind rather than cash.[116] The creation of the large administrative structure that would

---

[113]Ann-Katrin Hatje, *Befolkningsfrågan och Välfärden: Debatten om Familjepolitik och Nativitetsökning under 1930– och 1940–talen* (Stockholm, 1974), English summary, pp. 237–45; see also Alva Myrdal, p. 206. In *Befolkningsfrågan* Hatje refers to the 1935 Population Commission as the "Population Committee," a more correct translation of the Swedish term. She uses the term "commission" to distinguish the 1941 committee. Since the sources available in English usually employ the term "commission" to refer to the 1935 committee, I have followed this usage. I refer to to the 1941 committee, which is less well known to English readers, as "committee" in order to distinguish the two.

[114]Kälvemark, *More Children*, p. 109; See also Alva Myrdal, p. 206.

[115]Kälvemark, *More Children*, ch. 4, especially pp. 85–89.

[116]Alva Myrdal, pp. 133–53.

have been needed to implement the program must have seemed extravagant in the context of impending war. Even more importantly, it appeared unnecessary in the light of the spontaneous increase in the birth rate after 1935. After careful study of contemporary sources, moreover, Ann-Sofie Kälvemark is of the opinion that because of his pronatalist position, Myrdal was not fully accepted within the Social Democratic Party and had difficulty carrying his ideas.[117] As Europe prepared for war, the entire program came to a halt in order to release funds for defense. In the long run, however, the Myrdals' "qualitative" and "democratic" policy proposals constituted a new concept of pronatalist policy founded on voluntary parenthood that provides the framework within which pronatalism is understood throughout the West today.

In the early years of the war, the birth rate resumed its decline, and the population issue reached the political agenda once again. This time, in the midst of the world conflict, fears for national security generated a more strongly pronatalist sentiment among people of all political persuasions. In 1941 the wartime coalition government responded to the public clamor and established a new Committee on Population. Like the earlier commission, the committee concerned itself with housing, but it also paid more attention to conditions in the home and to the family. As the war came to an end and defense expenditures were reduced, large sums were allocated for programs that were similar to some of those earlier advocated by the Myrdals.[118]

Notwithstanding the underlying consensus on both the desirability of raising the birth rate and the need to spend money on a comprehensive program of social reform, political factors and ideological differences profoundly influenced the shape of the legislation that emerged from the work of the committee. In the 1940s, as earlier, the Social Democrats took a less natalist stance than the Conservatives. By adroitly ensuring that their representative on the committee was of outstanding ability, the Social Democrats managed to curb the more extreme pronatalist demands of the Conservatives for the creation of a state agency to manage population affairs and to conduct a pronatalist propa-

[117]Conversation with Dr. Kälvemark, Ann Arbor, October 23, 1979.
[118]Hatje, p. 238.

ganda campaign.[119] The Social Democrats were forced to compromise on the issue of income redistribution, to which they attached great importance. Thus the family allowance scheme introduced in 1948 applied to all families irrespective of income, and the amounts payable did not increase with the birth order of the child. On the other hand, some equalization was achieved through the abolition of the right to claim tax deductions for dependent children which, owing to the highly progressive Swedish income tax scales, unduly favored the rich.[120]

Demographic Effects of Population Policies in the 1920s and 1930s

The above discussion indicates that notwithstanding marked differences among the three countries, there are fundamental similarities both in the ways pronatalist policies evolved in France, Sweden, and West Germany and in the actual policies that were implemented. In all three countries pronatalist sentiment was associated with a belief in the need for population growth as a source of national power which, in turn, was primarily associated with conservative political views. In all three countries socialist and liberal opinion acted as a brake on the adoption of pronatalist policies, socialists basing their opposition on the rights of women to control their own lives, in reproduction as in other spheres, liberals on opposition to state controls in general. Only in Sweden, and then only briefly, were the socialists able to find a way to combine social-liberal ideology with the "need" of the state for more babies. Once a decision was made to intervene, attempts to regulate fertility directly by restricting access to birth control soon gave way in France and Sweden to efforts to influence reproductive behavior indirectly through broadly based social policies. In introducing the latter policies, the two governments were motivated as much by a desire to further the ends of social welfare and equality as to create a society in which the bearing and rearing of children would be facilitated. Only the

---

[119]Hatje notes that the principal Social Democratic representative on the committee was Tage Erlander, undersecretary for social affairs, an outstanding politician who was later to become prime minister. See Hatje, p. 240.
[120]Ibid., p. 242; Sweden, *Biography of a People*, p. 99.

fascist regime of Nazi Germany, which openly asserted the subordination of the individual to the state, actually implemented restrictive policies on contraception and abortion; and even the National Socialists placed considerable emphasis on social policy for both socioeconomic and pronatalist reasons.

It is worthy of note that the reactions and policy responses of France and Sweden were echoed in all the major nations that experienced very low fertility during the 1920s and 1930s, with the exception of Italy. Thus Belgium's population policy and the manner in which it was implemented mirrored that of France, while Norway and Denmark to a lesser degree adopted the stance taken by Sweden.[121] Neither the United States and Britain, nor any of the British Dominions, seriously considered introducing pronatalist measures, despite official investigations of the population question in both countries.[122] All these countries introduced broadly based social welfare policies before or after World War II, but for nondemographic reasons. Only Mussolini, whose pronatalist policy was the model on which Hitler's was based, actually enforced repressive measures—though to a much lesser extent than did Hitler.[123]

How effective were these policies in raising the birth rate, and how useful are they as models for governments today? It is not easy to answer these questions as there has been little in the way of rigorous assessment of the impact of the policies of the 1930s and 1940s. As in other areas of social policy evaluation, there are enormous conceptual and methodological problems yet to be resolved before such investigation can be undertaken with confidence. Problems arise from the absence of precise knowledge of the determinants of fertility and from the lack of techniques for ruling out the effect of causal factors other than policy initiatives.[124] There is also the problem of determining at what

[121]Glass, *Policies and Movements*, pp. 314–43 passim.

[122]The National Resources Committee in the United States and the Royal Commission on Population in the United Kingdom were both established to examine the population trend and make recommendations. See United States, *The Problems of a Changing Population* (Washington, D.C.: Government Printing Office, 1938); and United Kingdom, *Report*.

[123]Glass, *Policies and Movements*, pp. 219–68 passim.

[124]Fuller discussions of these points are to be found in Paolo de Sandre, pp. 149–54.

point combined demographic and social objectives shade off into purely social aims—and when social policies start to carry demographic intent.

The evaluations that do exist, whether impressionistic or rigorous, indicate that the impact of pronatalist policy on fertility tends to be felt in the short rather than the longer term. In 1934–35, for example, the German birth rate showed a rise that exceeded by a considerable margin the simultaneous rise in other European countries. This differential created a great deal of interest among demographers who were following the impact of Nazi policies.[125] Ten years later Hajnal showed that the increase was primarily a "catch-up" phenomenon. Because marriages that already existed in 1933 had produced abnormally few children, birth rates in later years were inclined to rise. The long-term trend was a slow and gradual decline in completed family size accompanied by widely fluctuating annual fertility rates.[126] In Sweden, likewise, the marked upswing in fertility during the 1940s, when the crude birth rate reached its highest level since the early years of the century, was caused almost entirely by changes in the timing of births rather than in the lifetime fertility of the average family. Indeed, no Swedish cohort after the birth cohort of 1890 has succeeded in replacing itself.[127] For France also, Calot and Hecht give the impression that they consider the increase in fertility in the 1930s to have been a catch-up phenomenon, at least in part. In general, however, they estimate that about 10 percent of French fertility in the 1940s and 1950s, about 0.2 child per woman, can be attributed to pronatalist family legislation.[128]

Evaluations of the effect of specific measures are even fewer than impressionistic assessments of overall policies. Glass, who made a careful study of the impact of French family allowances

[125]Glass, *Policies and Movements*, pp. 304–5; P. K. Whelpton, "Why the Large Rise in the German Birth Rate?", *American Journal of Sociology* 41, 3 (November 1935), p. 299.

[126]John Hajnal, "The Analysis of Birth Statistics in the Light of the Recent International Recovery of the Birth-Rate," *Population Studies* 1, 2 (September 1947), p. 150.

[127]Eva Bernhardt, *Trends and Variations in Swedish Fertility: A Cohort Study*. URVAL no. 5 (Stockholm: Central Statistical Bureau, 1971) pp. 12 ff.

[128]Calot and Hecht, pp. 191–92.

prior to the 1939 Family Code, concluded that "any effect that family allowances may have had on fertility has not been strong enough to prevent a general decline of fertility, especially after 1933."[129] In Nazi Germany the introduction of marriage loans in 1933 was accompanied by a rise in the number of marriages. Some of the increase preceded the introduction of the loans; and Burgdörfer, Germany's leading demographer, believed that most of the additional marriages would have taken place in any case owing to returning confidence after the election to power of the National Socialists.[130] The increase in the number of births that first appeared in Germany in 1934 and 1935 was analyzed by Burgdörfer, who concluded that while some of the additional births were the result of the larger number of marriages, some were the consequence of a genuine increase in fertility. Since most of the positive pronatalist measures had not yet been extended to the mass of the population, Burgdörfer considered that the increase in births was the result of the "psychic rebirth" of the German people.[131] On the other hand, an American demographer, after weighing the evidence, thought that the additional births were more likely to have been a consequence of the antiabortion policy. A reduction of only one-third in the estimated annual number of abortions procured in earlier years would have sufficed to account for the rise in the birth rate.[132]

In an impressionistic assessment of Sweden's pronatalist policy, Paolo de Sandre attributes the greater increase in postwar fertility in Sweden, relative to the increase in Norway, to the larger and more widely distributed Swedish family allowances.[133] A detailed evaluation of the impact of the marriage loan program in Sweden recently undertaken by Ann-Sofie Kälvemark reached a different conclusion. Analysis of the individual fertility records of a sample of the women who received the loans after 1942 showed that the average number of children born to women whose marriages were assisted by the loans was lower than the number born to Swedish women in general. Moreover, the number was so low as to render it unlikely that the loans

---

[129]Glass, *Policies and Movements*, p. 202.
[130]Ibid., pp. 306–7.
[131]Ibid., p. 310.
[132]Whelpton, "Why the Large Rise?"
[133]de Sandre, p. 159.

exerted any pronatalist effect at all.[134] Discussing possible explanations for these surprising findings, Kälvemark suggests that
the politicians concerned and their advisers did not appreciate
the extent to which Swedish couples were already regulating
their fertility by means of birth control rather than by delaying
marriage. They therefore imposed conditions for the granting of
the loans—evidence of employment or other means of repaying
the loan, evidence of good character and thriftiness—that unwit-
tingly built into the program a bias in favor of those individuals
who were most likely to plan their families.[135] If Kälvemark's
hypothesis is correct, this case illustrates the great difficulty of
designing programs intended to modify individual behavior in a
time of rapid social change.

On the basis of the limited evaluations that have been made,
it seems that Western European couples in the 1930s and 1940s
responded to pronatalist policies much as couples in Eastern
Europe are doing today. Except, perhaps, in France, where the
postwar policy was especially vigorous, the larger numbers of
children born each year appear to have been a consequences of
short-term changes in the timing of births rather than signs of a
real change in lifetime fertility. Some of the increase may have
occurred even without specifically pronatalist measures, as
couples decided to have the children they had postponed during
the Depression.

Despite the lack of evidence of long-term changes in reproduction following the introduction of pronatalist policies, the
policies may not be without value. Even a short-lived boost to
the birth rate will be followed by recurrent "boomlets" as the
larger cohorts reach the age of reproduction and may suffice to
prevent the growth of population from falling into a self-
perpetuating downward spiral. Thus, in a contracepting population whose reproduction is closely attuned to transient fluctuations in social and economic conditions, a government that can
master the art of offering timely incentives at critical moments
may have found a way to achieve at least a stationary, if not a
growing, population.

[134]Kälvemark, *More Children*, pp. 75–78.
[135]Ibid., pp. 82–84.

IV

FRANCE: THE MYTH OF PRONATALISM

For over a century the slow rate of growth of France's population has given rise to a fear of low fertility, justified, in the minds of many Frenchmen, by the military defeats of 1870 and 1940. Throughout this period discussion of population issues has been dominated by the pronatalist views of those who have attributed many of France's ills to her poor demographic performance, and who have urged successive governments to take steps to encourage the birth of more children. The sheer volume and eloquence of the pleas for pronatalist policy have overshadowed the views of a large segment of the population that has looked much more favorably on low fertility. From 1870 almost until the present, adherents of the political left have been content merely to refute the pronatalist arguments of the right; only with the emergence in the 1960s of the conservationist-ecological movement, and its alliance with militant feminist groups, has this party to the debate advanced a positive argument for low or stable population growth.

While public debate has centered on the supposedly deleterious consequences of low fertility and low population growth, governments in France have for the most part been unable to translate pronatalist sentiment into pronatalist policy. Not until 1939 was a consensus reached over the need for a comprehensive public policy to stimulate fertility. The consensus grew during the war years and found expression in a vigorous pronatalist policy elaborated by the Provisional Government in 1945. By 1946, however, the resolve of only a year earlier was starting to falter, and some of the most important measures were never implemented, or were implemented in a less wholehearted way than was originally intended. What emerged in the long run was a family policy with both welfare and pronatalist objectives, but in which the pronatalist elements were gradually permitted to deteriorate.

Declining birth rates in recent years have once again stirred dormant fears of national decline and stimulated expressions of pronatalist sentiment in some sectors of the population. Signs of pronatalism have also appeared in certain parts of government. In an important policy speech in 1975, President Giscard d'Estaing spoke of

> This elementary fact: the biological future of the society in which our children and grandchildren will live depends on the family. If families do not fulfill their biological function of keeping alive the French population, if the number of our children no longer suffices to ensure the replacement of the elders by the young, our country will become weakened, enfeebled and dull.[1]

In 1975, also, the Central Planning Council, meeting under the chairmanship of the president to consider the demographic situation in connection with preparations for the Seventh Plan (1976–80), adopted a demographic objective: "a stable fertility rate close to, and preferably slightly higher than, one needed to ensure the replacement of cohorts."[2] The council requested the National Institute for Demographic Studies (INED) to prepare a report on the relative effectiveness of measures that might be capable of halting the decline of fertility.[3] Following receipt of the report, the Council of Ministers announced the introduction of a "global family policy" that incorporated several of the suggested measures.[4] Despite both the obvious intention to address the problem of low fertility and the numerous pronatalist moves that have been made since 1976, it is argued in the following

[1]Speech at La Bourboule, July 13, 1975. Abstracted and reprinted in *Une politique pour la famille*, supplement to Actualités-Service, no. 306 (Paris: Service d'Information et de Diffusion, n.d.), pp. 6–7.

[2]Cited in Calot and Hecht, p. 190. It should be borne in mind that the plans of the Central Planning Council are indicative and bind neither the government nor the private sector. Nevertheless, they give a sense of direction.

[3]The report was published under the title *Natalité et politique démographique*.

[4]*Le Monde*, January 2, 1976, p. 16.

pages that France is unlikely to implement a strong and coordinated pronatalist policy in the near future.

The Demographic Situation

In the years following the end of World War II, fertility in France has known a series of wide fluctuations unprecedented in the country's modern history. A sharp increase in the number of babies born between 1945 and 1949, when fertility reached a maximum of nearly three children per woman on the average, was followed by a period of fluctuation and an eventual downward plunge, starting in 1965. The fall in the birth rate was most precipitous between 1972, when 878,000 infants made their appearance in the world, and 1976, when there were only 720,000 births, a decrease of 18 percent in only four years.[5] The Total Fertility Rate (TFR), 2.90 in 1965, declined to 2.47 in 1970, remained poised in 1971–72, and then fell to 1.8 by the end of 1975. Since then it has stabilized, oscillating between lows of 1.83 in 1976 and 1978 and highs of 1.87 and 1.86 in 1977 and 1979.[6] While a comparison of the period and cohort fertility rates shown in Figure 3 indicate that a substantial part of these swings can be attributed to changes in the timing of births, the cohort rates also show that there has been a real and substantial decline in completed family size since the mid–1950s among cohorts that have completed their fertility. By 1978, indeed, deaths exceeded births in 30 of 95 *départements* and in three out of 22 entire regions.[7]

What are the implications of recent fertility trends for population growth and age composition in the coming years, and how will they offset the development of the economy and society? A series of official projections, based on the 1975 census figures, allows us to picture the evolution of the population from the present until the year 2050 under different fertility assumptions.[8]

[5]France, Ministry of Labor and Participation, *Neuvième rapport sur la situation démographique de la France* (Paris, 1980), p. 2, table 2.

[6]Gérard Calot, "La baisse de la fécondité depuis quinze ans," in Ministry of Labor and Participation, *Colloque national sur la démographie française* (Paris, 1980), p. 29.

[7]*Le Figaro*, December 4, 1978.

[8]Jacques Desabie, "Projections démographiques à moyen terme (2000) et à longue terme (2020, 2050) pour la France," *Colloque national*, pp. 84–88.

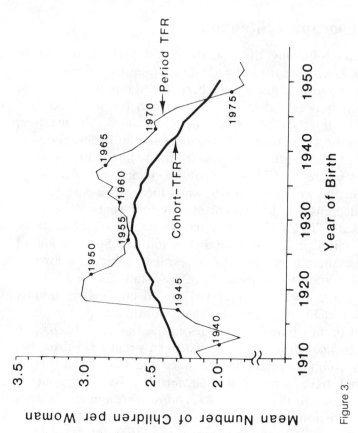

Figure 3.

Period and cohort total fertility rates, 1910–79.

Source: Gérard Calot, "La baisse de la fécondité depuis quinze ans," Ministry of Labor and Participation, *Colloque national sur la démographie française* (Paris, June 1980), p. 30.

The "central" projection adopted by the National Institute of Statistics and Economic Studies (INSEE) is based on the assumption that fertility will rise gradually to around the year 2000, reaching a completed family size of 2.1 children per women for the cohorts born in 1970 and thereafter. A second projection assumes a very slight fall in fertility from present levels to a cohort TFR of 1.8 children per woman, prior to stabilization at that level. Fertility of this level would generate a rate of population growth 14 percent below that required for replacement. Mortality assumptions are the same for both projections and envisage a slow decline in infant mortality from 13.6 per 1,000 live births in 1975, as well as reductions of 4–10 percent in the mortality of most other age groups. Both projections assume a slight increase in mortality in the population between 10 and 20 years of age due to a rise in the number of deaths from accident. Taken together, these assumptions add up to an increase in the expectation of life from 69.0 to 69.8 years for men, and from 77.1 to 77.8 for women between 1975 and 2000. Finally, the migration assumption for both projections anticipates a net balance of zero throughout the projection period. It should be noted that while both fertility and mortality are assumed to stabilize in the year 2000, perfect stabilization is extremely unlikely to occur in a real population. The assumption of stabilization, however, allows one to understand the underlying implications of specific population trends.

As Table 2 shows, under the replacement fertility assumption (TFR=2.1) the total population will continue to grow throughout the projection period, increasing from 53.6 million in 1980 to 61.8 million in 2030 and stabilizing thereafter. Under the lower fertility assumption (TFR=1.8), growth will cease somewhere between the year 2000 and 2010, and the population will decline at an accelerating rate to reach 48.6 million by 2050 (Table 3). Of greater significance for policy-makers with responsibility for planning the distribution of public services are the likely changes in the age composition of the population under different fertility assumptions. Taken overall, Tables 2 and 3 show a considerable aging of the population, especially under the subreplacement assumption. With fertility at replacement level, the youngest age-group, 0–19, will remain relatively constant in size, fluctuating between 16 and 17 million throughout

Table 2

Evolution of the Population by Age-group, 1975–2050, TFR = 2.1
(in thousands)

									Age-group
Year	Total	0–19	(%)	20–59	(%)	60+	(%)	75+	(%)	Annual rate of growth (%)
1975	52,600	16,888	32.1	26,040	49.5	9,672	18.4	2,656	5.1	+.41
1980	53,597	16,355	30.5	28,147	52.5	9,095	17.0	3,061	5.7	+.44
1985	54,829	16,174	29.5	28,925	52.8	9,730	17.7	3,336	6.1	+.46
1990	56,085	16,246	29.0	29,625	52.8	10,214	18.2	3,474	6.2	+.43
1995	57,262	16,333	28.5	30,303	52.9	10,626	18.6	2,918	5.1	+.38
2000	58,240	16,709	29.7	30,775	52.8	10,757	18.5	3,315	5.7	+.29
2010	59,788	16,422	27.5	31,744	53.1	11,622	19.4	3,803	6.4	+.24
2020	61,127	16,513	27.0	31,533	51.6	13,080	21.5	3,574	5.8	+.17
2030	61,826	16,668	27.0	31,177	50.4	18,982	22.6	4,527	7.3	+.05
2040	61,985	16,559	26.7	31,693	51.1	13,733	22.2	4,823	7.8	+.02
2050	62,065	16,718	26.9	31,567	50.9	13,779	22.2	4,748	7.7	+.01

Source: Adapted from French Ministry of Labor and Participation, *Colloque national sur la démographie française,* June 1980, tables 1–4 and 6, pp. 96–99 and 101.

the period. Even with replacement fertility, however, this group will comprise only 27 percent of the total population in 2050, compared with 32 percent in 1975. With a TFR of 1.8 the 0–19 year age-group will cease to grow between the years 2000 and 2010 and will decline in both numbers and proportion, from nearly 17 million in 1975 to below 11 million in 2050.

Under both fertility assumptions, the relative contribution of the active population aged 20–59 will remain more or less stable, increasing from 49.5 percent in 1975 to between 53 and 55 percent in the early years of the twenty-first century and stabilizing at around 51 percent by 2040. Despite the constant proportions, the absolute numbers in this age-group behave very differently under the two assumptions. With fertility at replacement level, this age category grows steadily, from 26 million in 1975 to 31.6 million in 2050. With total fertility at 1.8, the growth trend will reverse around 2010, and the population will

Table 3

Evolution of the Population by Age-group, 1975–2050, TFR = 1.8
(in thousands)

		Age-group								Annual rate of growth (%)
Year	Total	0–19	(%)	20–59	(%)	60+	(%)	75+	(%)	
1975	52,600	16,888	32.1	26,040	49.5	9,672	18.4	2,656	5.1	+.41
1980	53,534	16,292	30.4	28,147	52.6	9,095	17.0	3,061	5.7	+.32
1985	54,351	15,697	28.9	28,925	53.2	9,730	17.9	3,336	6.1	+.27
1990	55,046	15,206	27.6	29,625	53.8	10,214	18.6	3,474	6.3	+.23
1995	55,622	14,693	26.4	30,303	54.5	10,626	19.1	2,918	5.2	+.17
2000	56,005	14,536	26.0	30,712	54.8	10,757	19.2	3,315	5.9	+.08
2010	56,029	13,688	24.4	30,719	54.8	11,622	20.7	3,803	6.8	−.08
2020	55,285	12,868	23.3	29,337	53.1	13,080	23.7	3,574	6.5	−.20
2030	53,743	12,260	22.8	27,501	51.2	13,982	26.0	4,527	8.4	−.39
2040	51,300	11,531	22.5	26,089	50.9	13,680	26.7	4,823	9.4	−.53
2050	48,574	10,920	22.5	24,695	50.8	12,959	26.7	4,748	9.8	−.57

Source: See Table 2.

decrease to below 25 million by the end of the projection period. It should be borne in mind, however, that while the proportion of total population in the potentially active age-group may remain more or less constant throughout the projection period, the numbers of producers relative to the numbers of dependents may be significantly modified by changes in the age of retirement and the number of women who work.[9]

A closer look at the projections by age-group in Tables 2 and 3 indicates some of the difficulties that will confront policymakers as they attempt to adapt the economy and society to anticipated population changes. Under the lower fertility assumption, the steady decline in the number of younger people under 20 years of age suggests declining enrollments in schools

[9]Hervé le Bras and Georges Tapinos, "Perspectives à longue terme de la population française et leurs implications économiques," *Population* 34, special number (December 1979), pp. 1391–1451.

and redundancies among teachers and other professionals serving the needs of the young. These redundancies will become a constant fact of life throughout the entire projection period unless fertility increases again at some point. From a planning perspective the problems associated with a steady decline may be easier to deal with than the fluctuations in the size of the 0–19 age-group that will appear under the replacement fertility assumption.

By far the most dramatic change, and the one that will be the most difficult to provide for, will be the growing number and increasing age of the oldest of the three large age-groups, those aged 60 and over. As Table 4 shows, the initial sharp increase in the relatively active and healthy group aged 60–64 is almost over, and this group will grow by less than 850,000, or about 34 percent, between 1975 and 2020, when it reaches its maximum. By contrast, the over–75s will increase by nearly 80 percent, from 2.65 million to 4.75 million, and the over–85s by 140 percent, from 498,000 to 1.2 million, by the end of the projection period. These large increases in the number of very old people will place unprecedented demands on the society for expensive health and social services. As we stated above, all the individuals in the over–75 age-groups have already been born, and their numbers cannot be affected by changes in fertility until after the end of the projection period.

Explaining the Fertility Decline

Social scientists in France, like their counterparts elsewhere, are unable to determine with any exactitude the reasons for the sudden fall in fertility. By the same token, they are uncertain whether the recent stabilization signifies the end of the decline or whether it is merely a pause before a resumption of the downward trend. In contrast to the earlier decline in the 1920s and 1930s, the more recent low fertility trend was set in motion at a time of exceptional economic prosperity; ironically, the decline has halted at a time when European nations face the worst recession of the postwar period.

One reason often advanced by pronatalists in France for the decline of fertility is the legalization of abortion that was introduced for a provisional five-year period in November 1975 and

Table 4

Evolution of the Elderly Population, Aged 60 and Over, 1975–2050

a) *Population* (in thousands)

Year	Age-group 60–74	75+	85+
1975	2,623	2,656	498
1980	1,608	3,061	580
1985	2,889	3,336	683
1990	2,859	3,474	788
1995	2,852	2,918	843
2000	2,613	3,315	865
2010	3,495	3,803	857
2020	3,520	3,574	944
2030	3,461	4,527	862
2040	3,022	4,823	1,158
2050	3,056	4,748	1.191

b) *Proportion of total population* (in %)

TFR =	1.8	2.1	1.8	2.1	1.8	2.1
1975	5.0	5.0	5.1	5.1	0.9	0.9
1980	3.0	3.0	5.7	5.7	1.1	1.1
1985	5.3	5.3	6.1	6.1	1.3	1.2
1990	5.3	5.2	6.3	6.2	1.4	1.4
1995	5.3	5.1	5.2	5.1	1.5	1.5
2000	4.7	4.5	5.9	5.7	1.5	1.5
2010	6.2	5.8	6.8	6.4	1.5	1.4
2020	6.4	5.8	6.5	5.8	1.7	1.5
2030	6.4	5.6	8.4	7.3	1.6	1.4
2040	5.9	5.0	9.4	7.8	2.3	1.9
2050	6.3	5.7	9.8	7.7	2.5	1.9

Source: Adopted from *Colloque national sur la démographie française*, pp. 100–2, tables 5–7.

enacted permanently into law in December 1979. For at least two reasons this argument appears to be fallacious. For one thing, fertility was already approaching its lowest point before the abortion law was liberalized. For another, in-depth analysis of abortion trends after the act suggests that the legalization simply enabled a switch from clandestine to open abortions, without a significant increase in the number of abortions obtained.[10] As the following statistics indicate, moreover, the fertility decline has been accompanied by a switch from traditional to more effective methods of contraception, made possible by the passage of the Neuwirth Act in December 1967.[11]

	1961–62 %	1975 %
Withdrawal	66	30
Rhythm	21	9
Condom	4	8
Mechanical/Chemical	3	2
Pill	—	36
IUD	—	14

This act authorized the manufacture and sale of contraceptives for the first time in France. However, although modern methods of fertility regulation are much more reliable than traditional methods, they are unlikely to increase the *motivation* for family limitation. Furthermore, even in 1975 French use of the most effective methods still lagged behind their use in other developed countries like the United States and Great Britain.

As Table 5 indicates, declining fertility has been accompanied by an increase in labor force participation by married women of all ages. It is not easy to interpret these statistics, however, as scholars have not yet been able to satisfactorily explain the nature of the relationship between women's labor force participation and fertility. It is still unclear whether women have fewer children because they work, or whether they work because they have fewer children. Recent research has suggested that while in

[10]Chantal Blayo, "Les interruptions volontaires de grossesse en France en 1976," *Population* 34, 2 (March-April 1979), pp. 307–42. Although the number of legal abortions reported for 1976 totaled only 135,000, it was thought that there had been serious underreporting. Primarily by making geographical comparisons of fertility rates and trends with reported abortions, Blayo estimated that the true number of abortions must have been in the region of 250,000. Since 1976 the total number of reported and unreported abortions is thought to have been similar. INED researchers have also estimated that prior to the abortion reform, illegal abortions must also have numbered about 250,000 annually. See *Neuvième rapport*, pp. 39–40.

[11]Adapted from *Neuvième rapport*, p. 18.

Table 5

Activity Rates of Married
Women

Age-group	1968 (%)	1975 (%)
20–24	51.2	62.3
25–29	43.1	56.2
30–34	37.0	49.6
35–39	35.5	46.2
40–44	37.4	49.3
45–49	39.1	41.5

Source: Louis Roussel, "Changements démographiques et nouveaux modèles familiaux," *Colloque national,* p. 70.

the short run the causal link may run from fertility to employment, in the longer term the dominant effects may run from employment to fertility.[12] The question is still far from settled; nevertheless, if the research just cited is valid, there is every reason to believe that the rise in women's employment may have determined part of the fall in the birth rate.

Changes in family formation

Of the three hypotheses just discussed, only the rise in women's labor force participation provides a convincing, if partial, explanation for the falling birth rates of recent years. The fertility decline has also been accompanied by changes in the patterns of family formation which appear to signify that the preference for small families is only one aspect of a profound change emerging in the concept of the family. As far as fertility is concerned, the decline has occurred mainly at the third and higher birth orders, leading the Director of INED, Gérard

[12]See, for example, James C. Cramer, "Fertility and Female Employment: Problems of Causal Direction," *American Sociological Review* 45 (April 1980), pp. 167–90.

Calot, to affirm that the large family will from now on be a species near extinction.[13] At the same time, there is no indication in France that children and families are going out of favor. As in other developed countries, the number of couples with only one child has declined, and couples that voluntarily remain childless have almost disappeared.[14]

Along with these changes in reproductive behavior there have been significant alterations in the pattern of nuptiality. After a steady increase during the 1950s, the proportions of both men and women entering into first marriages have fallen slowly since 1964, attaining in 1977 levels that were somewhat lower than those of around 1950. This fall in the number of marriages in France parallels the decline in nuptiality observed in Great Britain and Belgium but falls far short of the speed and size of the decline in Sweden and Denmark.[15] Along with the decline in first marriages, the frequency of divorce has increased, from 11 divorces for every hundred marriages in 1960 to nearly 25 per hundred in 1979.[16] This means, of course, that the number of persons "at risk of marriage," including widowed and divorced persons available for remarriage, has also increased.[17]

Very recently, after nearly forty years of almost constant decline, the average age of first marriages for both sexes started to rise slightly in 1974.[18] Part of the explanation for this trend may be the rather sudden increase in the number of young couples cohabiting prior to marriage. Very little is yet known about this new custom; but a French study undertaken in 1977 found that among young married couples under age 30, some 31 percent had cohabited with their spouse before their marriage. The duration of the period of cohabitation varied from around three months to approximately three years, the average liaison lasting

---

[13]*Le Figaro*, April 26, 1978, p. 2. "La fin des grandes familles."

[14]Alain Girard and Louis Roussel, "Fécondité et conjoncture. Une enquête d'opinion sur la politique démographique," *Population* 32, 3 (May-June 1979), pp. 567–88.

[15]France, INED, *Septième rapport sur la situation démographique de la France* (Paris, 1978), pp. 33–42.

[16]Michel Louis Levy, "Divorces et divorcés," *Population et Sociétés* 144 (February 1981).

[17]*Septième rapport*, pp. 43–45.

[18]Ibid., p. 40.

approximately eighteen months.[19] Only two years earlier, fewer than 21 percent of newly married couples admitted to cohabiting prior to marriage.[20] The 1977 study also showed that among persons between 18 and 29 years of age, approximately 10 percent of both sexes were cohabiting, many of them with a clear intention of legalizing their union at a later date. Fewer than 10 percent of these couples had already had a child, and a large majority indicated either that they would not have a child outside of marriage or that they had not discussed the question. Very few intended to have a baby outside of marriage.[21]

The practice of living together prior to marrying and starting a family has had the effect of slightly raising the age of first marriage and therefore reducing the length of time available to couples for childbearing. The length of the childbearing period has also been reduced by a new tendency for most women to complete their childbearing by age 30 or soon after. Together these changes are likely to exert a significant downward effect on the number of children born to couples. On the other hand, the growing number of remarriages may have a countervailing effect to the extent that men and women desire a child from the new match.

To the extent that expressions of opinion can be taken as indicators of future patterns of family formation, attitude surveys undertaken regularly since the 1950s give some idea of possible developments. Over the past twenty years the surveys have clearly demonstrated the gradual adoption of a two or three child norm for "ideal" family size. In 1974, for the first time, the percentage of respondents preferring two equaled the number selecting three, and since then the number preferring two has gradually increased.[22] In December 1978, however, when public discussion of the fertility trend had become intense, there was once again a reversal in favor of the three-child family. At this time the percentage selecting three as the ideal "in general" reached just over 51 percent, a level that had not been attained since 1965. Predictably, the number choosing

[19]Louis Roussel, "La cohabitation juvénile en France," *Population* 33, 1 (January-February 1978), p. 16.

[20]Ibid., p. 17, n.2.

[21]Ibid., p.35.

[22]See, for example, INED, pp. 66–76.

three as ideal "for themselves" was smaller, but still slightly in excess of those selecting two.[23] In 1978, moreover, some 65 percent attributed the low birth rate to general economic conditions and the fear that they would not improve within the next year or two. Three years earlier the same proportion had attributed the fertility decline to more permanent societal trends: "permissiveness," the mother wished to continue working, and abortion. Finally, in 1978, 59 percent of respondents thought it desirable that the state should intervene in an attempt to raise fertility. In 1975 only 39 percent thought this way, although a majority felt some additional assistance to the family was necessary.[24] In sum, while it is impossible to judge to what extent the rise in "ideal family size" reflects a true change in attitudes toward fertility, it seems that a pronatalist policy would meet with greater approval than in 1978.

Perceptions of Low Fertility and Low Population Growth

Discussions of low fertility in France almost invariably start with some reference to France's unusual fertility history and the strong pronatalist sentiment to which it gave rise. A number of respondents in this study mentioned the total lack of "Malthusianism" in France, a term that appears to denote both an exclusively or predominantly economic approach to reproduction and the Anglo-Saxon and Scandinavian "obsession with contraception." It would be a mistake, however, to attribute to the French an undifferentiated attitude of intense pronatalism. Although the French as a nation may display less tolerance of a low birth rate than the Swedes or British, those who take a strongly pronatalist position probably constitute quite a small minority drawn mainly from the older members of the society. Nevertheless, virtually all the policy-makers and influentials interviewed for this study considered the present birth rate too low and anticipated serious consequences for the nation if it should continue.

[23]Girard and Roussel. INED surveys routinely ask respondents to answer certain questions in two forms: (a) for themselves, i.e., "in your own milieu"; and (b) for others, i.e., "in general".

[24]Ibid., pp. 579–80; INED, p. 31.

Age structure and aging

Undoubtedly the problem weighing most heavily on the minds of policy-makers is the escalating cost of pensions and health and social care for the aged. This problem was mentioned by virtually all the persons interviewed as the most pressing for the government to deal with. Already for some years, the health and old age insurance Funds,[25] contributed largely by employers and workers, have been falling more deeply into debt despite successive increases in the contributions exacted. The situation will worsen as larger numbers of elderly dependents reach the advanced age of 75 or more and start to make heavy demands on expensive medical services. The perilous financial status of the social security system has been aggravated in recent years by a marked increase in unemployment that has reduced contributions to the Funds at a time of rapidly rising costs. In December 1978, for example, the Council of Ministers approved an increase in the size of contributions that was expected to correct the imbalance between revenue and expenditures for at least three years.[26] Within six months a further deficit had appeared and was expected to reach about 2.4 billion francs by the end of the year. According to the ministry, two-thirds of the new deficit was a consequence of unanticipated increases in expenditure, while one-third was a result of reduced revenue as a consequence of higher unemployment.[27] Despite efforts to patch up the social security system, deficits were recorded for each year between 1978 and 1981. By the end of May 1981 it was estimated that the accumulated deficit would reach a total of 5 billion francs by the end of the year.[28]

[25]The capitalized term "Fund/s" is used here to translate the French term "Caisse/s" used to denote the national and local organizations responsible for administering the monies allocated to the various branches of the social security system. For example, "Caisse Nationale d'Allocation Familiale."

[26]*Le Monde*, December 13, 1978, p. 45.

[27]*Le Monde*, June 28, 1979, p. 38; July 1, 1979, p. 1. See also Jean-Pierre Dumont, "Social Security: Balancing the Ins and Outs," *Manchester Guardian Weekly*, July 5, 1979, p. 14. FF 2.4 billion was approximately equal to U.S. $370 million in July 1979.

[28]*Le Monde*, May 29, 1981, p. 2.;

Michel Debré, former Gaullist prime minister and vigorous spokesman for a strong pronatalist policy, returned repeatedly to this theme during the course of a short interview. Several times Debré reiterated his belief that "unless something is done in the next five years, France will not be able to pay the bill for pensions and old people."[29] Pointing out that the social security budget, which is administered by special Funds outside the formal government structure, is now larger than the regular state budget, Debré has stressed the need for it to be controlled by parliament.[30] However, the present system of financing is popular with the unions, which have a large say in the way the social security funds are administered.

Another constantly recurring theme, especially among older respondents, can be traced to the traumatic effect of the events of 1940, when the French defeat at the hands of the Germans was commonly attributed to the age of France's military and political leaders. Because of this experience the French are unusually sensitive to what are perceived to be unpleasant psychological effects of an aging population. References to the uninteresting society that will eventuate if the population does not rejuvenate itself are often included in the calls of political elites for a higher birth rate.[31] Gérard Calot, in particular, observed that many people are oppressed by the dullness, the lack of vitality and gaiety they experience when visiting one of the areas with a high proportion of elderly and dread the thought of an even older society. Calot also took up a theme that appears from time to time in the press—fear of a growing resistance on the part of the working population to additional taxes for pensions and social services for the elderly. Pointing out that the financial cost of the shift in the balance of dependence from the young to the old will depend on whether the cost of an old person is greater or less than the cost of a youth, Calot remarked,

[29]Michel Debré, Interview, May 31, 1978.

[30]Michel Debré, "La menace démographique et politique," *Le Monde,* April 21, 1978, p. 9.

[31]See, for example, Giscard d'Estaing's speech at Le Bourboule, which has already been cited. See also Monique Pelletier, minister for women's conditions, "Des lieux de bonheur et de sociabilité," *Le Figaro,* April 26, 1979, p. 2. The same theme recurs in much of the work of Alfred Sauvy.

Even if the cost is about the same, the psychological costs are different. For children you spend your own money and get a good return in pleasure. The cost of the elderly is met by social transfers which are anonymous and felt as burdensome and unpleasurable.[32]

Psychological costs apart, it has been estimated that the public cost of an elderly dependent in France is approximately twice the cost to the state of a young dependent.[33]

Less often mentioned in interviews but also recognized as serious consequences of continued low fertility are dislocations arising from, or aggravated by, rapid age-structural change. Prominent among them will be the decline in career opportunities for the growing number of young people who will be entering the labor force between now and the end of the century. The teaching profession provides an illustration of one area in which this problem will be especially acute. Because of poor planning during the baby boom, the teaching profession has a grossly unbalanced age structure; at the present time 60 percent of all primary school teachers are under 30 years of age. Unless the population of school-age children starts to grow once again, promotion possibilities will be severely reduced and, moreover, entry to the profession will be seriously restricted. One estimate indicates that while one applicant in seven is currently accepted for teacher training, the ratio may have to drop to one in seventy in the future.[34] Similarly, the depopulation of the rural areas and the rapid aging of the rural population will put additional difficulties in the way of providing satisfactory social services and facilities in the rural areas.[35]

[32]Interview, June 9, 1978. See also Dominique Bidou, "Le débat est politique," *Le Monde* December 29, 1978, p. 2.

[33]Jean Bourgeois-Pichat, "La transition démographique: vieillissement de la population," in *Population Science in the Service of Mankind*, papers presented at the Conference on Science and Life, Vienna, 1979 (Liège, Belgium: IUSSP, 1979), pp. 211–39.

[34]Evelyne Sullerot, Interview, July 6, 1978. See also Sullerot's *La démographie de la France: bilan et perspectives*, report presented to the Economic and Social Council, June 1978 (Paris: Journaux officiels and La Documentation Française, 1978), pp. 129–34.

[35]Ibid., pp. 147–52. The aging of the rural population has been very rapid since the 1960s because of massive rural-urban migration. See Paul Paillat, "Le vieillissement de la France rurale. Intensité, évolution, diffusion et typologie." *Population* 32, 6 (November-December 1976), pp. 1147–88. According to this

Population numbers, national power,
and cultural integrity

In the late 1970s political elites and influentials in France displayed, albeit in attenuated form, many of the same preoccupations that concerned their forefathers earlier in the century. Invited to give their views of the long term *economic* consequences for the society, the persons interviewed for this study expressed themselves in vague and generalized terms in which national and international, economic and noneconomic aspects of power appeared to be fused.[36] Nowhere was the global concept of France's world status more evident than in the remarks made by M. Debré following the announcement by Chancellor Schmidt of increases in family allowances and changes in Germany's investment policy. "The day I have been waiting for has come . . . , " wrote Debré,

> Let us take some of the same seed if we do not want history to repeat itself. Whatever turn present events in Europe may take, a France without investments, without children, in a state of permanent inflation, must bow before German superiority, with the well-known consequences of that situation.[37]

---

study the number of *cantons* in which persons aged 65 and over amounted to more than 20 percent doubled, from 173 to 393, between 1962 and 1968.

[36]A list of terms used to describe long-term consequences of low fertility culled from the responses of policy-makers and speeches by President Giscard d'Estaing and Prime Minister Raymond Barre, as well as from articles in the press, includes the following: "disastrous," "catastrophic," "etiolation," "decay," "loss of strength," "devitalization," "the slope that leads to effacement," "moral danger," "collective suicide," and "decline of the West." See, especially, *Le Figaro*, February 7, 1978, p. 10; March 22, 1979, p. 2; April 6, 1979, pp. 1–2; *Le Monde*, October 18, 1978, p. 12. An exception to the tendency to dismiss long-term consequences in vague generalizations were the remarks of Pierre Fournier, of the Division of Population and Migration in the Ministry of Labor. Fournier remarked that the ministry is well aware that there will be changes in the structure of consumption and demand to which the economy will have to adjust. He added, however, that they would appear only "in the long term, the very long term, around the turn of the century." Interview, June 7, 1978.

[37]See, "Ce jour que j'attendais . . . , " *Le Monde*, August 12, 1978, pp. 1, 6.

It was also clearly seen in President Giscard d'Estaing's stated ambition that France should overtake Germany in economic power and international leadership and his perception of demographic decline as a cause of decadence.[38]

More generally, however, the policy-makers and influentials interviewed noted that France's historical concern over her security has greatly diminished since World War II. As one respondent put it, "Anxiety about declining power has mitigated greatly. France has no threatening neighbors." This official, chargé de mission in the Division of Population and Migration between 1972 and 1975, pointed to another anxiety felt by France—not the military potential of Germany but fear of immigrant invasion by Arab populations from North Africa.

> To the extent that France is concerned about its security, the integrity of its culture, and so on, it is the Maghreb it fears. All Europe fears the Maghreb, but France particularly so because its links are closer—politically and geographically—and it is to France that the North Africans look. They are also very populous.[39]

There is no doubt that many people in France are concerned about the growing numerical strength of the peoples of the Maghreb, not for reasons of military security in the strict sense but from fears that France's empty territories will be "invaded" by the excess populations of North Africa and the Middle East. Such an influx, it is thought, would lead to unbearable racial tensions, loss of cultural integrity, and an indirect diminution in France's international influence.[40] Once again it was Michel Debré who expressed most clearly his anxiety over the Maghreb. Drawing attention to Algeria which, with a population barely one-fourth the size of France's has as many children as France, Debré spoke of the great rapidity with which the ethnic

[38]The president's ambition and his views about demographic decline as a cause of decadence were clearly expressed in his television interview with Jean-Jacques Servan-Schreiber on October 16, 1978. See *Le Monde*, October 18, 1978, pp 12–13; also the article by René Dabernat, "Le 'Questionnaire' de M. Giscard d'Estaing: La référence allemande," ibid., pp 1, 42.

[39]Interview, April 25, 1978. The Division of Population was at that time located in the Ministry of Labor, Employment, and Population.

[40]It will be recalled from Chapter 3 that this fear of being overrun by alien peoples has long been a feature of French attitudes to depopulation. See, for example, Spengler, *France Faces Depopulation*, especially pp. 131, 209–10.

balance can change; he cited Lebanon, where only thirty years ago Muslims and Catholics were equal in numbers, but where today Muslims outnumber Catholics by seven to three. "Within twenty years," he added, "the Mediterranean basin will be divided into two camps: France, Italy, and Spain, ranged against Africa and the Middle East."[41]

Fears of being swamped by foreigners of markedly different ethnic origin, and of the growing racial tensions that might ensue, underlaid the determination of both the Pompidou and Giscard administrations to reduce the number of foreigners in the country. In turn, the closing of the door to the immigrants, who for over a century have helped to compensate for France's inability to meet her own needs for labor, lent additional force to the arguments in favor of a pronatalist policy. Because of the magnitude of France's historical dependence on migrant labor and the radical nature of the change in the attitudes of government officials toward immigration after the oil price rises of the 1970s, it is appropriate to pause briefly to consider the part that immigration has played in the French economy.

Immigration and immigration policy in France

Since the middle of the nineteenth century, a growing stream of immigrants has served to compensate for France's low fertility and feeble rate of natural increase. According to Spengler the flow began to develop around 1840, gradually increasing until, by 1920, immigrants were arriving at the rate of 200,000 a year.[42] Between 1920 and 1930 the flow continued, over 2 million registered and unregistered immigrants entering the country during the decade. In 1931 the number of registered foreign workers reached 1.6 million, exclusive of dependents, not far short of the 1.9 million present in 1975.[43] Some of these immigrants returned home after a time but the majority, around 70 percent, remained permanently in France, adding significantly

[41]Interview, May 31, 1978. See also, Michel Debré, "Donner des Français à la France," *Revue des Deux Mondes* (December 1976), pp. 514–24.

[42]Spengler, *France Faces Depopulation*, pp. 194–95.

[43]France, Ministry of Labor and Participation, Secretariat of State for Immigrant Workers, *La nouvelle politique de l'immigration*, n.d. (circa 1978).

to the country's population growth. Compared with a natural increase of approximately 2 million between 1850 and 1930, immigration contributed about 3.5 million in the same period. With the onset of the Great Depression, however, the government made strenuous efforts to restrict further entry of immigrants and to encourage the return home of unemployed migrant workers already in the country.[44] In Spengler's judgment these efforts, highly reminiscent of the Giscard regime's efforts to reduce the number of foreigners in the country, were relatively successful.[45]

At the end of World War II, a significant level of immigration was deemed necessary for both economic and demographic reasons—the latter because it was thought that the higher fertility of foreigners would assist France's demographic recovery. It was soon realized that immigrants rapidly adopt the fertility norms of the host country, and the demographic objective of immigration policy was gradually abandoned.[46] Large-scale immigration continued to be encouraged for economic reasons until around 1968–70, when the first signs of unemployment appeared and racial tensions increased. According to Fournier, director of the Division of Population and Migration in the Ministry of Labor and Participation, in 1978

> Migration policy has not been determined by either demographic or economic motives in recent years. It has been dominated entirely by social and racial factors and the fear of being swamped by too many people who are very foreign and different from Frenchmen.[47]

---

[44]Spengler, *France Faces Depopulation*, p. 195.

[45]Ibid., pp. 220–2.

[46]This point was made by Jacqueline Hecht, of INED, in an interview on April 21, 1978, and by Jacques Doublet, Conseiller d'Etat (Honorary), in an interview on June 6, 1978. Doublet's involvement with population policy stems from 1939 when he was appointed secretary-general of the High Committee on Population. After 1945, Doublet served as a member of the committee. He has maintained his close interest in population policy throughout a long career in related fields. Doublet has also served as president of the governing board of INED.

[47]Interview, June 7, 1978. In the view of the government, the hardening of French attitudes toward foreigners arises from four sets of factors all of which take on additional significance in the context of high and rising unemployment

In response to deteriorating economic conditions, an effort was made during the early 1970s to reduce the number of immigrants entering the country. At first an attempt was made to close the loophole that permitted the "regularization" of immigrants brought in as tourists by contractors without passing through the formal immigration channels. Despite these efforts, by 1974 there were 4.13 million foreigners resident in France, comprising 7.7 percent of the total population and 8.5 percent of the active population.[48] In July 1974, therefore, France, like other Western nations, suspended immigration following the oil crisis and ensuing recession. This move virtually eliminated the inflow of new workers. At the same time, the government started to expel small numbers of unemployed migrants under existing legislation that permitted deportation if the approval of the court was obtained. Some time later immigrant workers were offered a grant of 10,000 francs if they voluntarily returned home; however, relatively few took advantage of this offer. In 1979 proposals were placed before the National Assembly that would have permitted cancellation, by administrative means without the courts' approval, of the residence permits of immigrants who had remained unemployed for a specified period. These proposals met with strong opposition from immigrant groups, trade unions, and parties of the left, as well as from leading members of the government, including the minister of justice.[49] Despite the uproar, similar proposals were later passed, and many unemployed workers were deported. In May 1981, however, within a few days of taking office, the Mitterrand administration announced the immediate but provisional end of expulsions, save in cases where public order is threat-

---

and growing competition for jobs. These are identified as: (a) the heavy concentration of immigrants in certain towns and quarters; (b) the perceived delinquency of immigrants; (c) the tendency of immigrants to isolate themselves from French society as a means of assuaging their own sense of insecurity; and (d) frank racism built on stereotypes. See France, *La nouvelle politique de l'immigration*, pp. 28–32.

[48]Ibid., p. 12.

[49]*New York Times*, May 31, 1979, p. A5; *Le Monde*, June 2, 1979, p. 31; June 15, 1979, p. 10. The government's position is outlined in an article by the then secretary of state for immigrants, Lionel Stoleru, "Entre le bouc et l'autruche," *Le Monde*, June 15, 1979, p. 38.

ened. Making the announcement, the new minister of the interior added that restrictions on admissions would not be lifted. "Realism," said the minister, "communist vigilance, and the demands of French workers urge the government to maintain the controls."[50]

Even under the Giscard administration, policy-makers in France, unlike a majority of their counterparts in Sweden and West Germany, favored a relaxation of the restrictions on immigration as soon as economic conditions improved. Indeed, concurrently with the imposition of restrictions in 1974, efforts were made to facilitate the integration or assimilation of immigrants already present. Thus families were still permitted to join their husbands and fathers, requirements for naturalization were simplified, and social policies were introduced, albeit to a minimal degree, to hasten the integration process.[51] In 1980, in connection with preparations for the Eighth Economic Plan, 1981–86, the High Committee on Population advocated a resumption of immigration as soon as the state of the economy warrants it. In making this recommendation the committee took account of the important and growing contribution made by immigrants to population size, through naturalizations as well as through marriages with French citizens and childbearing.[52] In the present conditions of economic recession and high unemployment, however, it is generally recognized that proposals to ease the controls on worker immigration would be politically inept, even though indigenous workers may be reluctant to undertake the "socially undesirable" tasks usually allotted to foreign workers.

Even in the longer term, forces are developing that may encourage both government and industry to attempt to reduce

[50]*Le Monde*, May 28, 1981, pp. 1, 18 ("La France est leurs pays").

[51]Full assimilation has been one of the principles underlying French immigration policy since 1945. The need for migrant labor became so great, however, that the authorities closed their eyes to the practice whereby prospective guest workers were brought in illegally by contractors and acquired work permits by the process of "regularization." This practice led to considerable exploitation of immigrants in terms of salary, living conditions, and general social status. See Bourgeois-Pichat, "France," pp. 582–83.

[52]For statistics on these contributions, see France, Ministry of Labor and Participation, *Rapport de synthèse travaux du Haut Comité de la Population* (Paris, 1980), pp. 71–74. See also Michel Louis Levy, "Les étrangers en France," *Population et Sociétés* 137 (July-August 1980).

their dependence on immigrant labor. For one thing, with lower rates of population growth and higher levels of industrialization, several of the traditional sending countries of southern Europe no longer encourage their citizens to seek employment abroad. Immigrant workers, therefore, are increasingly likely to come from geographically and culturally more distant Third World countries whose citizens are more difficult to integrate into advanced European societies.[53] There is a growing risk, therefore, of racial and ethnic tensions between indigenous and immigrant groups. Second, it is becoming apparent that immigrant workers in Europe are no longer cheap workers. Working and social conditions of immigrants are increasingly mandated by international conventions that exert pressures toward the continual evolution of costly social and educational programs to facilitate the integration of foreign workers.[54] Moreover, as soon as immigrant workers are joined by their wives and families, demands are made on the social services provided by the host society that far exceed demands made by immigrant workers themselves. Thus employers are coming to appreciate that the rationalization of industrial processes may be more cost-effective than continued reliance on foreign labor. And, as one official involved in population policy formulation remarked in an interview, "it is more sensible to try to raise the birth rate rather than to leave oneself entirely dependent on immigration."

Population Policy Formulation in France

The previous section has indicated that low fertility was generally viewed with some concern by political elites, policy-makers, and influentials involved with population issues in France. It has suggested that current perceptions of low fertility and its consequences have been shaped in large measure by recollections of

[53]It will be recalled that in 1978, Fournier stated that immigration policy had recently been based on racial rather than economic considerations. The increase in unemployment that occurred since then appears to be responsible for the stronger deportation measures that were later implemented.

[54]Several international organizations in Europe, including the ILO, the OECD, and the Council of Europe, have been active in furthering the social, civic, and political rights of immigrant workers and their dependents.

the nation's recent historical experiences with low fertility, particularly the disasters attributed to aging. In this section the discussion will turn to a consideration of the four aspects of the policy-making system that appear to have relevance for the formulation of population policy: (a) the amount and quality of demographic information available to government; (b) the political ideology of the ruling party or parties; (c) the mechanisms for coordinating policy among ministries; and (d) existing commitments that limit the government's freedom of action, including, importantly, the relationship of the citizen to the state in the society.

Demographic information

At the end of World War II, the High Consultative Committee on Population and the Family showed its appreciation of the need for a continuing flow of high-quality demographic information by recommending the creation of a government demographic research institute attached to the ministry responsible for population. Since its establishment in 1945, INED has become the leading population research institution in France—even in Europe—and has earned an enviable reputation for first-class demographic research of great methodological sophistication and thoroughness. Along with the census office,[55] INED is the principal provider of population statistics and demographic analysis for government. Despite the excellence of of its work and the high esteem in which it is held internationally, INED is not without its critics. It is argued by some knowledgeable individuals that the institute's concentration on basic demography has caused it to abandon its mandate to assist in the process of policy formulation. Invited to comment on INED's influence on government thinking on population issues, one long-time observer who asked not to be identified replied, "It is not influential at all. INED's reports are just not read in the ministries; they are written in such a way that no one can understand them." The respondent maintained that there has been a vast change in the character of INED's research since the early days when the analysis of specific policy problems was often under-

[55]The National Institute for Statistics and Economic Studies (INSEE).

taken along with basic demographic studies. "Nowadays," he remarked, "they write only for themselves and other academics in Europe and America."[56] This respondent later acknowledged that INED studies are occasionally taken up by the press and thus reach a wider audience.

A somewhat different criticism was advanced by two non-INED demographers who commented to the author that INED's approach is too narrowly demographic to be capable of illuminating so complex a phenomenon as reproductive behavior. They felt that INED is unwilling to risk its reputation by undertaking research that might call for methodologies that are not highly developed and are therefore less sophisticated than those commonly employed by INED researchers. They observed that the government has been reluctant to support such research either by INED or in the universities.[57] Even the press has remarked indirectly on INED's narrow focus. Reporting on a recent demographic conference, one journalist cited with approval several studies emanating from French and foreign universities which had employed less traditional economic and psychological approaches to the study of fertility. "Though not always convincing," the author wrote, "the explications had at least the merit of carrying French demography away from the simple analysis of population phenomena to which it tends to confine itself."[58]

Notwithstanding these criticisms, the close relationship be-

[56]A perusal of the early volumes of *Population*, the journal of demography published every two months by INED, indicates that in the early years a significant part of INED's work was addressed to the analysis of policy-related problems like tuberculosis, infant mortality, alcoholism, that contributed to France's high mortality rate and thus, it was thought, to the low rate of population growth. After the first few years the broadly social analyses no longer appear and the purely demographic studies become both more numerous and more sophisticated. In the present writer's judgment that in very recent years, say from 1978, there has been an increase in the numbers of articles of direct policy relevance. Some of these papers, on such subjects as economic implications of age-structure changes, have been cited in this chapter.

[57]Interviews, June 30, 1978. Interviews with knowledgeable observers outside of France also gave the impression that the government had deliberately chosen to encourage INED's "narrowly demographic" focus.

[58]Jean-Marie Dupont, "Faut-il encourager la reprise de la natalité?" *Le Monde*, May 2, 1979, p. 28.

tween INED and the ministry responsible for population[59] constitutes an effective mechanism for keeping the government abreast of current developments in demographic trends and analysis. Less than two years after the first downturn in the birth rate, for example, President de Gaulle personally presided over two meetings of the High Committee on Population at which the outline of a policy intended to raise the birth rate was formulated.[60] The implementation of this policy was prevented by the political disturbance of 1968 which eventuated in the overthrow of de Gaulle. These events also coincided with the rise of a militant women's movement dedicated to the repeal of the restrictive legislation on contraception and abortion. Although de Gaulle's initiative proved abortive, the governmental response in 1967 came several years before similar actions in other Western European countries and argues the existence of timely and effective advice from the research organization.

Also useful and influential among those most closely responsible for formulating population policy are the attitude and opinion surveys carried out every two or three years since 1945. Although many scholars argue that survey techniques do not capture the important unconscious motivations for reproduction, the French have found that reproductive aspirations reflected in this series of directly comparable surveys have accorded well with actual reproductive behavior. The findings of the most recent survey, undertaken at the request of the government after the Central Planning Council had adopted a fertility goal in 1975,[61] were constantly mentioned by policymakers interviewed by me. It is clear that the findings of the survey with regard to policy measures that would be acceptable

[59]The ministry responsible for population changes varies from time to time. During the Giscard presidency it was the Ministry of Labor and Participation. President Mitterrand has placed the Division of Population and Migrations within a newly created Ministry of National Solidarity. This appears to mean that population matters are to be related to broad social policy rather than to labor market policy.

[60]The meetings were held in October and December 1967. See "Le haut comité de la population," an unsigned, undated document produced by the Division of Population and Migration, Ministry of Labor and Participation, circa 1975.

[61]INED, *Natalité et politique*.

to the general public formed the basis of changes in family policy in 1977 and 1978.[62] In recent years efforts have been made to close the communication gap between INED demographers and government officials. Under a decree of 1968 INED is required to submit to the government an annual report on the demographic situation. These reports, each on a different topic, succinctly summarize and analyze the latest findings of INED's basic research in a format that should prove comprehensible and useful.[63] In addition, the transfer of information from INED to the policy-making system is facilitated by the presence within the Division of Population and Migrations of a staff member who is a demographer with special responsibility for liaison with INED.

Turning to the second criticism, it seems indisputable that France, like other countries, has a long-term need for basic research on the psychological/economic/motivational aspects of the determinants of fertility. A *conseiller technique* in the Division of Population and Migration, admitted in 1978 that the government does not have sufficient information of this sort to design an effective pronatalist policy. Elaborating on his personal judgment that the ministries were consciously attempting to raise the birth rate despite official statements at that time to the contrary, this official added:

> The research we have is not sufficient to allow us to isolate any one factor that definitely influences demographic trends and events. Therefore, we can only institute a range of social and policy measures that look as though they may help.

[62]Specifically, while public opinion favored greater financial assistance to families in general, it repudiated measures that were seen as coercively pronatalist. Such measures included special allowances for children that were born within a specified time after the marriage of their parents or the birth of a previous child and special benefits for large families. The government acted quickly to remove these measures from the statutes. Most women said that the opportunity to take part-time work and to find their old job waiting for them after a year or two at home with a new baby would be the measures most likely to encourage them to have an additional child.

[63]The High Committee on Population, meeting in 1980, recommended that in the future, the first part of these reports should follow a standard format from year to year, thus facilitating their use. See France, *Rapport de synthèse*, p. 96.

On the other hand, there is no reason to assume that specifically French research in these areas would make the picture any clearer. Despite the large amount of research on the determinants of fertility that has been carried out around the world, and to which French scholars have access, there is still no precise understanding of specific policy measures that would definitely influence fertility trends.

While the demographic information provided by INED may suffer from a lack of breadth, this disadvantage may be offset by the efficiency with which the information reaches the policy-making centers of government. In addition, the research information generated by INED is of internationally recognized quality and has a continuity and comparability that might be difficult to obtain from university-based research. A more significant information gap may be the apparent lack of research on the economic implications of low fertility. This is an area of research that has just begun to develop in any country but which seems to be especially underdeveloped in France. In the course of writing this book, I found only two works by French economists on this subject.[64] Moreover, two recent and extensive reviews of the economic literature on low population growth cite only three articles by French scholars, all of whom are demographers.[65] Finally, the impression that there is a paucity of research information on the economic implications of low fertility was confirmed by Michel Debré, who commented that French economists have only recently started to display an interest in population.

Political ideology

For well over one hundred years there has existed in France a marked left-right ideological split over the need for population growth. Where political conservatives, in alliance with the military and the Church, have viewed the welfare of the state and the sanctity of the family as closely associated with or dependent

---

[64]Le Bras and Tapinos; Jean-Didier Lecaillon, *L'économie de la sous-population*, (Paris: Presses Universitaires de France, 1977).

[65]Espenshade, "Zero Population Growth"; Thomas J. Espenshade and William J. Serow, eds., *The Economic Consequences of Slowing Population Growth* (New York: Academic Press, 1978).

on a large and growing population, liberals and socialists have attached more importance to individual welfare and fulfillment. These liberal values, it is felt, have little to do with population growth and, indeed, are more likely to be attained under conditions of stable population growth. Despite the deluge of pronatalist rhetoric that poured from the pens of conservative intellectuals and politicians after 1870 and the many attempts in the National Assembly to introduce pronatalist legislation, it was not until the late 1930s, as was shown in Chapter 3, that France managed to introduce a pronatalist policy. After the war, despite the national *prise de conscience* over the ultimate cause of France's defeat in 1940, pronatalist fervor soon started to fade, and the strong thrust of pronatalist policy was lost. Thus only rarely, at times of great national crisis, has there been a consensus great enough to support a vigorous pronatalist policy.[66]

Ideological differences have played a significant role in shaping population-related policies during the past fifteen years and are an important factor underlying the Giscard government's hesitation to introduce a comprehensive pronatalist policy. The women's movement, increasingly militant after the mid–1950s and strongly supported by the Socialist and Communist parties, succeeded in 1967 in securing the repeal of the restrictive 1920 law on contraception and its replacement by a more liberal law, the Neuwirth Act, which has already been mentioned. In November 1974, after a long struggle, the women's movement, with the support of environmentalists and the left, was successful in forcing the passage of one of the most liberal abortion laws in Europe. Liberalization of abortion was bitterly opposed by the Church, members of the legal and medical professions, and right-wing nationalists of the Gaullist party, the Rassemblement pour la République (RPR), for whom Michel Debré is a leading spokesman.[67] The successful bill, drawn up and guided

[66]Jacques Doublet, whose involvement with population goes back to the 1930s, observed that in his view the pronatalist policy of the 1930s was made possible only because the measures advocated by the Conservatives for pronatalist reasons were in accordance with the measures espoused by the Front Populaire under Léon Blum to improve conditions for agricultural workers. Interview, May 31, 1978.

[67]For a succinct discussion of the emergence of the abortion issue, see Bourgeois-Pichat, "France," pp. 558–72.

through the political process by the then minister of health, Simone Veil, had the unusual distinction of receiving the unanimous support of the left-wing opposition parties while being condemned by the right-wing and Catholic deputies of the government majority parties. Feeling was so strong that the new law was introduced for only a trial period of five years.

In 1979, as earlier in the decade, the contentious and bitter debate over abortion involved all sectors of the community. Feminists, supported by left-wing parties and trade unions as well as by environmentalists and other radical groups, were sharply critical of the geographically uneven and niggardly way in which the law had been implemented. They charged that certain regional and administrative restrictions on the availability of legal abortions, plus the cost of the operation, still drove many poorer women into the hands of clandestine abortionists, at serious risk to their health and life. These groups demanded the removal of all remaining restrictions, including the charge levied for the operation.[68] These criticisms and demands were incorporated into a bill introduced to the National Assembly by the Socialist Party in June 1979.[69] More conservative elements of the population, including the right-to-life group "Let Them Live," called for the law to be repealed.[70] Earlier in the year the Permanent Council of Catholic Bishops in France had published a White Book on abortion which spoke of the termination of pregnancy as "an act of death, a serious fault, and a societal ill"—although the statement was somewhat less condemnatory than previous Church statements as far as non-Catholics are concerned.[71] The

[68]For a short article describing the law as it had been implemented prior to the second debate in 1979, see Claire Brisset, "La loi française," *Le Monde*, April 26, 1979, p. 14.

[69]Proposition de Loi, no. 1224, introduced by the Socialist Party, June 20, 1979.

[70]Claire Brisset, "Le débat sur l'avortement," *Le Monde*, October 9, 1979, pp. 1, 16.

[71]Le Conseil Permanent de l'Episcopat Français, *Faire vivre: l'Eglise catholique et l'avortement* (Paris: Editions du Centurion, 1979). The White Book is discussed in several articles in *Le Monde*, April 24, 1979, p. 14. It is of interest to note that a number of leading Jesuit thinkers have in recent years questioned whether abortion can always be thought of as an act of homicide. See, for example, Philippe Roqueplo in *Informations Catholiques Internationales* 453 (April 1, 1974); Bruno Ribes in *Etudes* (January 1978); and Patrick Ver-

political nature of the debate is highlighted by the changing positions adopted by many right-wing deputies between the general elections of 1978 and the abortion debate in 1979. A poll of deputies taken during the election campaign of 1978 indicated that a majority of RPR deputies did not think it worth risking political division between the nonsocialist parties (UDF and RPR) in order to modify the law, and only a small minority were actively committed to repeal.[72] In 1979, with no election in the offing, a majority of the RPR deputies voted against the abortion bill. After an emotionally charged debate lasting a full three days, the government's abortion bill, with only slight modifications of the original 1975 text, was again adopted by the National Assembly on the strength of the unanimous vote of the Socialist and Communist opposition parties. As was the case in 1975, the bill was rejected by a majority of deputies in the government coalition. Of the 154 RPR deputies who voted, only 24 were in favor of the bill, and 130 were against it; in the UDF 45 deputies voted for the bill and 76 against it.[73] In November 1981 the Mitterrand government approved plans for a publicity campaign to inform women about contraception and the means available to them for realizing their "ideal" family size.[74]

Political/ideological differences are also evident in the continuing debate over family policy. Frequently couched in budgetary terms, the discussion is centered on the role of women and the place of the family in society. The National Union of Family Associations (UNAF)[75] and other traditional elements are anx-

spieren in *Laennec* 2–3 (Winter 1978–79); all cited by Alain Woodrow, "Crime et Châtiment," *Le Monde*, April 24, 1979.

[72]Claire Brisset, "L'avortement, tabou de la campagne électoral," *Le Monde*, March 8, 1978, p. 15.

[73]The existing text was adopted definitively by the National Assembly on November 30, 1979. *Le Monde*, December 1, 1979, pp. 1, 8.

[74]*Le Monde*, November 12, 1981, p. 5.

[75]UNAF, the National Federation of Family Associations, enjoys a position of privilege with regard to the formulation of family policy. Although its political base is small in comparison with the unions, for example, UNAF is entitled to be consulted by government on all matters concerning the family. Moreover, UNAF is the only channel through which family associations may make representations to government. Originally limited to associations of large families and closely linked with the Catholic Church, UNAF has recently attempted to broaden its base. See Nicole Questiaux and Jacques Fournier, "France," pp. 133–34.

ious to see more realistic opportunities for women to stay at home with young children without suffering economic hardship; more radical elements of society want to create the possibility for women to participate equally with men in the labor market. A proposal to create a "maternal salary," put forward in 1973 by UNAF and introduced as a bill to the National Assembly over the signature of 112 members of the government majority, was strongly contested by the trade unions and the more militant women's groups.[76] The basic objection of the left was that the measures would encourage women to stay at home against their true interests. Feminists and their supporters would prefer to see a more lavish provision of crèches, nursery schools, and day-care centers which would, they feel, enable women to further their independence and development. Both policies would be costly. In 1978 the cost of a maternal salary was estimated to be approximately 25 billion francs each year if the salary were made equal to 50 percent of the minimum wage; but studies have shown that day care is also extremely expensive because families cannot be expected to pay fees that reflect the real cost.[77] The high cost notwithstanding, Michel Debré has pushed hard for the creation of a special fund that would lay the foundation for introducing a maternal wage for mothers with three or more children, arguing that the nation cannot afford to neglect the mothers of its future citizens.[78] The Giscard government preferred, however, to steer clear of the political and fiscal issues involved and adopted instead an additional family benefit to cover some of the costs of child care. Parents may therefore decide for themselves whether to patronize a crèche, employ a baby sitter, or provide the service themselves.[79]

The new family policy introduced by Veil in readiness for the Seventh Plan, 1976–81, included an intention to ease the strain of combining motherhood with paid employment, an area of

[76]Ibid., p. 178.

[77]Questiaux and Fournier, pp. 151–52, 178–79. FF 25 billion was approximately equal to U.S. $5.8 billion in 1979. The High Consultative Committee on the Family has advocated that the maternal salary should be fixed at 75 percent of the minimum wage.

[78]See, for example, "Pour un Grenelle des familles," *Le Monde*, December 14, 1978, p. 1.

[79]Questiaux and Fournier, pp. 179–80.

intervention which, as Veil pointed out, had not previously been considered part of family policy.[80] The implementation of this policy required the government to walk a political tightrope between the wishes expressed by a majority of women and those of the militant minority. While most women have asked for more flexible working hours, more part-time work, longer postmaternity leave, and similar measures, the more militant women's groups and labor unions are determined to protect what they perceived to be the "real" interests of women—a "genuine" opportunity to become economically independent through participation in the labor force. In general these groups do not favor the introduction of special labor force legislation for women, fearing that such measures will encourage employers to discriminate against women. In the context of high unemployment, moreover, the government was itself extremely cautious in implementing policy changes that might foster such discrimination. To defuse political opposition when the right to two years' unpaid postmaternity leave was introduced for women in large industrial enterprises, a clause was inserted permitting the leave to be taken by either parent. While reducing the discriminatory appearance of the legislation, the clause provoked an outcry from the right, one deputy referring to it as a "crime against civilization."[81]

In recent years the labor unions have used the "demographic crisis" as a source of additional leverage in their battle for the adoption of a shorter working week, not solely for mothers but as a universal standard. A reduction in working hours, it is contended, would give parents more time with their children and obviate the need for the potentially discriminatory measures proposed by government. As unemployment has increased, the argument has also been made that a 35–hour week would help spread the available work among more workers. The proposal was strongly opposed by employers, who called it "economic suicide," and was resisted by the government of President Gis-

[80]See, especially, Veil's press conference on December 31, 1975. This is excerpted in *La France et sa population aujourd'hui*, supplement no. 4, Cahiers Français 184 (Paris: La Documentation Française, 1978), under the title "A propos de politique familiale."

[81]Information supplied by Jacqueline Hecht in an interview on April 21, 1978.

card d'Estaing.[82] One of President Mitterrand's first acts on taking office was to announce his intention of working toward a 35–hour week—for all employees and not only for parents of large families.[83]

It is important to stress that the evidence of political conflict over specific population policy proposals is not intended to give the impression that there are important differences among the parties over the desirability of encouraging the birth of more children. Many older socialists who lived through the demographic decline of the 1920s and the humiliations of 1940 differ little from members of the right and center in their attitudes toward low fertility. The distinguished demographer and prominent socialist Alfred Sauvy, for example, has long emphasized the contribution made by a young population to the health and vitality of a nation. Likewise, in a National Assembly debate on the Seventh Plan, François Mitterrand, still in opposition, found himself in agreement with Michel Debré in his belief that "a pronatalist policy must be one of the prime features of any government's program." Mitterrand observed that in a declining population,

> No social policy and no economic policy will be possible any longer. And, of course, France's independence and impact on the world stage will also be a thing of the past if the Government of France, whatever kind of government it is, does not look this problem straight in the face.[84]

It is possible, indeed, that there is less conflict over demographic goals in France than in the other two countries in this study. Evelyne Sullerot, another influential socialist and currently a member of the High Committee on Population, remarked to the author that "not a single political party in France is Malthusian." She explained that while the right is interested in stimu-

---

[82]For a discussion of this issue, see the series of articles prepared by Jean-Pierre Dumont, "La réduction du temps de travail," parts 1–3, *Le Monde*, May 31–June 2, 1979.

[83]See Jean-Pierre Dumont, "Innovation et précipitation," *Le Monde*, May 29, 1981, p. 7. See also *Le Monde*, May 28, 1981, p. 9. In November 1981 the Council of Ministers announced the government's intention of reducing the workweek to 36 hours by September 1, 1983. *Le Monde*, November 6, 1981, p. 24.

[84]Cited in John Murray, "Population Policies in Europe," paper presented at the Conference of the Population Geography Study Group of the Institute of British Geographers, Durham, England, September 1978, p. 9.

lating the birth rate for nationalistic reasons, the parties of the left are, in general, more concerned about the social consequences of population decline. Sullerot's report, *La Démographie de la France*, which she prepared for the Economic and Social Council, lays out a number of the social consequences of continued low fertility. It suggests measures that might be taken to enable women to have the number of children they say they desire but which, it is claimed, economic or social conditions cause them to postpone or to avoid altogether.[85]

The difference in attitudes toward a shorter working week, just discussed, exemplifies the difference between socialists and the center-right coalition in their approaches to low fertility. While the outgoing government tended to focus its efforts on measures addressed to families with children, and especially the large family, the incoming socialist government appears to regard the low birth rate as evidence of deficiencies in the society at large. In a bill placed before the National Assembly in 1976, for example, the Socialist Party stressed the need to go beyond financial incentives in an attempt to "resolve the problems where they are found, in industry and in the cities."[86] This would involve confronting the problems posed by women's right and desire to work; it would also call for the development of new ways to adapt communities and cities to the needs of families and children.[87]

A statement of his demographic policy prepared by Mitterrand during the presidential election campaign prudently offered something for everyone but moved away from the Giscardian emphasis on the third child. The future president insisted that he would follow a "noninterventionist" approach that would "allow for the full exercise of the freedom of couples in regard to their

---

[85]Sullerot, feminist and founder of the French Family Planning Movement, told me that she had written her report for the Economic and Social Council (of which she is a member) because she saw in the pronatalism of the political parties "the most serious existing or potential threat to all that has been achieved by feminism over the years." Interview, July 6, 1978.

[86]Proposition de Loi, no. 2536, placed before the National Assembly by the Socialist Party on July 10, 1976.

[87]See, for example, the 1976 response of the Socialist Party to a letter from the newly formed Association for a Demographic Renaissance, seeking the party's support for certain measures proposed by the association. The correspondence is reprinted in Gérard-François Dumont et al., pp. 449–59.

demographic plans."[88] The measures discussed by Mitterrand included a 50 percent increase in family allowances—long sought by the Communist Party—and eligibility to start with the first child rather than with the second, as hitherto. In addition, Mitterrand promised to introduce changes in the method of calculating the tax exemption for families with children which would reduce the advantage currently accruing to upper-income families; a simplification of the complicated system of family benefits to make it easier for individuals to know and exercise their rights; the creation of an additional 300,000 places in day-care centers; and a stepping-up of the priority attached to the construction of housing "on the basis of social need."[89] The social and economic program announced by the president in May-June 1981 makes it clear, however, that these measures, intended as they are to improve the economic situation of families with children, are viewed as an integral part of a much wider plan to raise the quality of life for all workers, irrespective of family size.[90] Over and above the "demographic measures" mentioned by the president, the broader program also includes a 10 percent increase in the minimum wage; an increase in the allowance for the handicapped, which will be brought up to the same level as the pension for the old; and the creation of 60,000 new jobs, more than 54,000 of them in the public sector and local communities.[91]

Formulation and coordination of policy

Even more than most aspects of social life, demographic trends emerge as a function of a diversity of influences: social, eco-

[88]"President Mitterrand on Population Policy in France," statement prepared for the National Alliance Against Depopulation, translated and reprinted in *Population and Development Review* 7, 3 (September 1981), pp. 568–69.

[89]Ibid.

[90]An unidentified French official recently told a *New York Times* reporter, "There is a charming anachronism in the family allowance. There is no population problem now . . . . The family allowance is the most sacred of all our political sacred cows." *New York Times*, November 30, 1981, p. 4 ("France Takes Aim at Social Security").

[91]*Le Monde*, June 4, 1981, p. 1. "Social Measures Decreed by the Council of Ministers."

nomic, biological, psychological, and political. Because of this, policies capable of regulating demographic trends call for measures in a variety of substantive and ministerial domains. The formulation and implementation of a comprehensive pronatalist policy is therefore dependent on the existence of mechanisms which encourage consultation, cooperation, and coordination of policy among interested ministries. Except for a brief period immediately before and after World War II, it is doubtful if the arrangements for coordinating pronatalist policy in France have ever been such as would foster the sort of cooperation needed to formulate and implement a broadly based policy. Since the early postwar years, in particular, responsibility for population policy has come to be located at a distance from the centers of governmental power. Paradoxically, since the recent fertility decline started to develop momentum, the scope of population policy has been more narrowly defined. Only in 1979 were there signs of a growing resolve to strengthen once again the mechanisms for formulating a more comprehensive pronatalist policy.

Before attempting to discuss the arrangements for population policy formulation and its coordination among ministries, it is necessary to clarify some unusual aspects of French government administration that give an impression of instability and confusion. To the outsider many ministries appear to be in a perpetual state of flux, the formal designation of ministerial portfolios changing as administrative divisions (*directions*) acquire or lose ministerial or quasi-ministerial status, or even migrate for a while to other ministries.[92] In order to understand the mechanisms for coordinating policy within an issue area, it is important to appreciate that for historical reasons, a French government ministry is a somewhat less unified structure than the ministries of most other countries. Because there was already in existence a highly developed administrative structure

[92]By this I mean that from time to time, particular administrative divisions are placed directly under the responsibility of the minister or, occasionally, of a secretary of state. In the first instance the name of the ministry may change to reflect the increased importance attached to the function of a division. For example, when Veil was given direct responsibility for the family in 1978, her designation and the name of the ministry were changed from Health and Social and Security to Health and Family. The functions of the ministry were unchanged.

long before the appearance of democratic institutions in France, ministries are frequently simple agglomerations of administrative services that have been brought together under a minister on the basis of the general relatedness of their traditional functions and responsibilities. Because many of these services were developed by specialized technical "corps" with traditions of administrative autonomy that go back in some cases to the Napoleonic era or beyond, they are held in high esteem and jealously guard their administrative independence. There has been resistance to the introduction of a civil service position comparable to the British permanent secretary, for example, standing between the divisional directors and the minister.[93] Thus the coordination of policy within and among ministries is achieved at the level of the minister and his personal cabinet and, in the opinion of students of French government administration, has to overcome the special problem posed by the tendency to divisional independence.[94]

At the level of central government, policies are formally adopted by the Council of Ministers at meetings chaired by the

[93]Since 1945 there have been some partly successful attempts to reduce the autonomy of divisions and increase political control over policy-making, largely by introducing a unified and more democratic system for recruitment to the civil service. Efforts to introduce a civil service level between directors and ministers were not successful and were disliked by ministers and directors alike. In the few ministries which still have such a coordinating mechanism in place, the directors-general or secretaries of state normally coordinate the work of only two or three divisions. See, for example, Frederick Ridley and Jean Blondel, *Public Administration in France* (London: Routledge and Kegan Paul, 1964), especially pp. 28–34, on which much of this discussion is based. See also Ezra N. Suleiman, *Politics, Power, and Bureaucracy in France* (Princeton: Princeton University Press, 1974).

[94]By far the best analysis of the relationship between ministers (and ministerial cabinets) and directors is that of Suleiman. In his in-depth study of directors and members of ministerial cabinets, he found that while the ability of ministers to introduce their own or the government's preferred policies has increased with the greater governmental stability under the Fifth Republic, the autonomy of directors and divisions is still considerable. This is particularly the case in those divisions that have established close links with one of the prestigious "*grand corps.*" While the fragmentation has lessened with the success of the new recruitment and training processes, the "*grand corps*" have retained much of their ability to influence policy. See also Ezra N. Suleiman, *Elites in French Society: The Politics of Survival* (Princeton: Princeton University Press, 1978).

president of the republic. In special areas where this is deemed necessary, coordination of the government's work may be undertaken within the prime minister's office, either by the designation of a coordinating minister or by means of an inter-ministerial committee composed of several ministers whose responsibilities bear closely on the issue at hand.[95] An interministerial committee on Population and the Family was established in 1945 and reaffirmed in 1964; nevertheless, it appears to have been inactive for years until revived by President Giscard d'Estaing in 1979.[96]

Against the background just outlined, it is possible to trace a progressive decline in the significance attached to pronatalist policy after 1945 and a concurrent weakening of the mechanisms for coordinating policy. In essence, the practical work of formulating and implementing population policy is dispersed among several divisions situated sometimes in one and sometimes in several ministries. In addition, assistance in formulating policy has been provided by the High Consultative Committee on Population and the Family. At the start, responsibility for population policy was concentrated in the office of a minister for population—normally the minister of health—who was given wide authority to direct and coordinate the work of the public authorities on all matters relating to the family, population distribution, and international migration.[97] In the judgment of some close observers, however, it is doubtful if the minister for population has ever possessed the necessary powers for carrying out his responsibilities. The minister has never been allocated independent resources for population policy, and his coordinating capacity has been diminished by the location of several key divisions in ministries other than his own. Even within family policy family benefits are taken care of by the Division of Social Security, which is often part of the Ministry of Labor, while

[95]Ridley and Blondel, pp. 17–21.

[96]See "Le haut comité de la population." My judgment about the inactivity of this committee is based on the fact that it is not mentioned in any of the literature I have consulted on either population or family policy in France. Neither was the committee mentioned by any of the officials with whom I discussed coordination in 1978.

[97]Doublet and Villedary, p. 73. This monograph is probably the best analysis available in English on French population policy between 1939 and 1972.

general family policy is the responsibility of the Division of Social Welfare, usually in the Ministry of Health.[98]

The declining importance attached to population policy was underscored in the mid–1960s when the ministries of health and labor were combined in one vast Ministry of Social Affairs. The post of minister of population was abolished, and its responsibilities were divided between two secretaries-general. A further reorganization in 1970 increased still further the distinction between "population policy" and "family policy." In this change the two portfolios were separated once again, and the position of minister of population was re-created. This time the designated minister was the minister of labor and employment, whose responsibility for population was much reduced, specifically excluding the family.[99] In addition to formulating and implementing policy, the ministry is responsible for the supervision of INED and the National Office of Immigration, as well as for providing the secretariat for the High Committee on Population. All these activities are concentrated, in practice, in the Division of Population and Migration.[100] Commenting on these changes, the Director of the Division in 1978, Fournier, said that the responsibility for coordinating population policy devolved on him. He added that it is difficult to coordinate interministerial policy from his position and that, since taking office in 1975, he had not attempted to do so.[101]

In 1945, as in 1939, the High Committee on Population and the Family appears to have been the key organ for promoting population policy. Enjoying consultative status only, the committee's influence derived from its proximity and access to the

[98]Doublet and Villedary, pp. 73–75. See also Questiaux and Fournier, pp. 131–33. The dispersal of the responsible divisions is, of course, the reason for the Interministerial Committee. As noted, however, this committee appears to have been inactive most of the time.

[99]The designated position of Minister for Population appears to have been abolished again within a year or two.

[100]I am indebted to Michel Debré, Pierre Fournier, and Jacques Doublet for much of the information on which this discussion is based. See also Doublet and Villedary, pp. 74–5, and "Le haut comité de la population."

[101]Asked about the coordination of family policy with other ministries, Bertrand Fragonard, adjoint director of the personal cabinet of the former minister of health, Simone Veil, replied simply, "We do not subordinate everything to pronatalism." Interview, June 9, 1979.

highest centers of government. From its central location first in the office of the Provisional Government and later (1946) in the prime minister's office, the committee was instrumental in shaping the strong population/family policy of the immediate postwar years. Concurrently with the lower institutional status accorded population in the ministerial reorganization of the mid–1960s, the High Committee also lost its influential position with the prime minister's department. At this time, the committee was placed within the new Ministry of Social Affairs. In 1970 the committee, renamed simply the High Committee for Population, was once again moved, this time to the Ministry of Labor and Employment, where it remained formally until the change of government in May 1981. During the early 1970s the terms of office of the members were allowed to lapse pending an eventual reform of the committee. Commenting on these changes, Fournier said that the move of the High Committee to the Ministry of Labor denoted a decline of interest in population policy—especially pronatalist policy.

The early 1970s thus witnessed the formal abandonment of pronatalist population policy as it had been defined since 1945. The second half of the decade, by contrast, has seen the gradual emergence, instigated primarily by President Giscard d'Estaing, of an intention to strengthen family policy for pronatalist reasons. In April 1978 additional visibility was given to family policy with the creation of a ministerial portfolio for the family, previously the responsibility of a secretary of state within the Ministry of Health, and the promotion of the minister, Mme. Veil, to the third-ranking position in government.[102] At the end of the year, a new High Committee on Population was appointed. In March 1979 the Central Planning Council, meeting under the chairmanship of the president, requested the ministers of health, labor, and the environment to prepare a program of measures capable of halting the decline in fertility.[103] These, if approved, would be included in the Eighth Plan (1981–85). Later, the priority accorded family policy under the Seventh Plan was reaffirmed by the National Assembly for the Eighth Plan

---

[102]Several respondents suggested that this promotion was a personal recognition of Veil's achievements rather than a boost for family policy. No additional budget funds were made available to the minister at the time of her promotion.

[103]*Le Monde*, March 27, 1979, p. 46. *Le Figaro*, April 27, 1979, p. 2.

also.[104] Finally, in July 1979 the Council of Ministers announced the institution of a new Interministerial Committee for the Family in order to provide for better coordination of policy across a number of ministries.[105]

This series of steps taken by President Giscard d'Estaing in a little over a year appeared to have set in place an institutional structure capable of effectively formulating and coordinating a pronatalist policy. Nevertheless, problems remained. The High Committee on Population, once the key organ for formulating policy proposals, failed to regain its former status and remains at a considerable distance from the real center of power. Equally important, the membership has doubled in size since the early days and now includes twenty members, exclusive of three ex officio members representing all shades of political opinion. Not surprisingly there are signs of disagreement among the members over the direction that policy should take.[106] The recommendations reaching the policy-making system are likely to lack both coherence and authority.

It is not yet clear how population will fare under the administrative structure established by President Mitterrand. The new government contains no designated minister for population nor for the family; instead, these functions are both subsumed within a new global Ministry of National Solidarity. The new minister of state, Mme. Nicole Questiaux, an expert on family policy, has responsibility for social affairs, social security, old age, and immigrants, each of which becomes a secretariat of state.[107] This is the first time that social security and social affairs have been organizationally linked and also the first time that health has been separated from social affairs. In principle this arrangement should ensure much greater coherence among the different aspects of social policy. At the same time, the

[104]*Le Monde*, June 16, 1979, p. 9. Although the plans of the Central Planning Council are not binding, an exception is made for a strictly limited number of programs for which priority is accorded. Funding for these priority programs is guaranteed.

[105]*Le Monde*, July 13, 1979, p. 7.

[106]See the introductory remarks of the minister of labor and participation in the High Committee's *Rapport de synthèse* and the minority opinions annexed to this report.

[107]*Le Monde*, May 15–24, 1981. See also Questiaux's discussion of the functions and purpose of the new ministry, *Le Monde*, June 2, 1981, pp. 1, 44.

strong tradition of departmental and divisional autonomy in the operation of the French bureaucracy suggests that the degree of coordination actually achieved may fall short of what is anticipated. The new structure underscores, however, the lower priority attached by the new president to the demographic question.

Constraints on governmental action

Despite their convictions that continued low fertility would have serious consequences for the society, policy-makers interviewed in 1978 were doubtful of the possibility of intervening successfully to reverse the demographic trend. Discussions with government officials and other influential people suggest that there are three main reasons for this lack of confidence in their ability to influence fertility. First, while policy-makers subscribe implicitly to what is seen as an obligation of the state to attempt to forestall societal harm, there is an acute awareness among them that a democratic government is limited in its authority to intervene in the reproductive decisions of individual couples. Second, government officials were pessimistic about obtaining political and financial support for a pronatalist policy in a time of economic recession accompanied by severe fiscal constraints and high unemployment. Finally, policy-makers are at a loss to identify pronatalist measures that are at the same time acceptable to the public and likely to encourage fertility.

The principle which underlies belief in the state's obligation to intervene in the sphere of reproduction was clearly enunciated by Veil at an international meeting of population specialists in 1977. Arguing that the state is in a better position than the individual to protect the interests of both present and future generations, she observed that:

> Avoiding a long-term weakening of a country brought about by a dangerously low birth rate and, inversely, avoiding excessive population growth when it becomes an obstacle to development and to the well-being of the population, must certainly be among the basic goals of government.[108]

[108]"Human Rights, Ideologies, and Population Policies." The significance, and the weakness, of the "general interest" as an orienting principle of the

While subscribing to this abstract principle, responsible officials interviewed in 1978 still felt their hands were tied. The radical spirit that had developed in France after 1968 would brook no
interference by the state in what a majority of citizens felt
strongly to be an area of private decision-making. The liberal
trend was expressed not only in the great battles over contraception and abortion—in both of which the government, taking its
cue from the wishes of the majority expressed in successive opinion polls, guided liberal legislation through the policy process—
but also in the more subtle issue of family policy. In this area,
changes in the structure of family allowances in the early years of
the Seventh Plan quietly eliminated the more coercive pronatalist
incentives that had become offensive to the majority of couples.
As the director of the Division of Population and Migration remarked, "The statism of previous governments has entirely gone,
and people will not tolerate any form of coercion or interventionist measures from the government." Or in Doublet's words, "It is
pointless to have a whole lot of laws you cannot enforce."

It is true that in the last two years of the Seventh Plan, 1979–
80, the government reintroduced a number of financial incentives that placed the emphasis on the third or later children in a
family. The explanation for this "regressive" move may be
found in the worsening of the economic situation and the consequent redefinition by the people of the reasons for low fertility.
While in the early 1970s majority opinion believed that the liberalization of social mores could best explain the reluctance of
couples to have more than one or two children, by the end of
the decade most people felt that the growing economic depriva-
tions experienced by large families played a major role.[109] Because of this shift in public opinion, the government felt free to
offer more financial help to large families—a course that was
also less costly to the taxpayer than increasing allowances to all
families equally.

It remains to be seen whether President Mitterrand will be
able, on a continuing basis, to raise the money he needs to
carry out his promise to increase family and housing allow-

French bureaucracy is discussed in Suleiman, *Politics, Power, and Bureaucracy*, pp. 24–29, 294–96, 348–51.

[109]Girard and Roussel, p. 581.

ances, pensions, and allowances for the handicapped, as well as to help employers pay for the increase in the minimum wage. The cost of the new program for 1981 alone will require an additional 5 billion francs for social security and 3–4 billion francs for the general budget.[110] Part of the revenue will be raised by a special tax on the 100,000 richest people in the country, to be calculated on the basis of the taxes they have already paid in 1981. This tax is expected to generate some 2.5 billion francs.[111] In addition, the government intends to un-block certain reserve funds, the Fonds d'action conjoncturel, to raise a further 6.5 billion francs.[112] As the new minister for housing explained in an interview with *Le Monde*, the state is willing to accept a budgetary deficit because the new allow-ances and higher wages are expected to stimulate demand and reactivate the economy.[113]

In addition to the philosophical issue concerning the role of the state in a democratic society and the financial question of where the money is to come from, there are practical difficulties that inhibit the development of a vigorous pronatalist policy. Important among them is the lack of a clear vision of what such a policy would embrace. Confidence in the effectiveness of tra-ditional family measures as an encouragement to fertility has now totally gone, while newer ideas of measures to reduce the incompatibility between motherhood and labor force participa-tion by women ran into political problems with women's groups and labor unions. This is an area in which the Mitterrand ap-proach is likely to have more political success. It should be borne in mind, however, that although reduced or more flexible working time appears one of the better suggestions that has appeared for reducing the barriers to childbearing, it has not yet been tested. In general, moreover, while Mitterrand's overall social policy seems to have potential for increasing the quality of life for the mass of French citizens and might possibly encourage them to have more children, it bears little resemblance to any-thing that might be called "population policy" as defined in this study.

[110]*Le Monde*, June 4, 1981, p. 1.
[111]Ibid.
[112]Ibid., May 28, 1981, p. 9.
[113]Ibid., June 4, 1981, pp. 1, 44 "Interview with M. Roger Quilliot."

Population and Family Policy, 1945–80

Throughout this chapter references have been made to the deterioration that took place in the pronatalist family policy adopted in 1945 and the resurgence of pronatalism in some quarters since around 1975. It has been asserted, on the one hand, that a new pronatalist policy started to emerge during the Seventh Plan and, on the other, that it had little hope of developing into a strong and comprehensive policy comparable with that of the immediate postwar years. There has also been some discussion of the new approach being taken by the socialist administration that took office in May 1981. In order to give some coherence to these scattered and somewhat contradictory remarks, this final section will undertake a brief analysis of changes in family policy since 1945 and attempt to assess their meaning for population policy today.

If the restrictive laws on contraception and abortion are set aside, family policy has been at the heart of population policy since the introduction of the Code de la Famille in 1939. Just as family policy has been an integral part of pronatalist policy, demographic objectives have always inspired the choice of some family policy instruments. The two aspects are inextricably mixed, and to this extent it is correct to say that French family policy has always been pronatalist in intent. Despite the difficulty of distinguishing welfare from pronatalist measures, policy-makers in France have developed rather clear understandings of which measures were intended to serve the end of social welfare and which had a more instrumental demographic objective. It is largely because the latter measures were abandoned or weakened that pronatalist policy declined so seriously during the 1960s and early 1970s.

On the basis of discussions with policy-makers, it seems safe to assert that the principle underlying pronatalist measures has always been social justice, that is, an attempt to compensate families for the additional expenses they incur in bearing, rearing, and educating children.[114] Translated into policy, the most important rule guiding the design of demographic measures is what might be termed "universal application." That is, measures

---

[114]See the extended discussion in Doublet and Villedary, pp. 1–4, 49–57.

that apply to all families or that extend benefits to new and broader categories of recipient are considered pronatalist.[115] By contrast, limiting the applicability of a benefit to special groups, or subjecting recipients to a means test, for example, normally denotes a redistributive measure devoid of demographic intent. In addition to this basic principle, benefits that increase in amount for later children in a family, or that apply only to large families, are also considered pronatalist measures.

Against this background it can be seen that family policy, especially the pronatalist elements, declined seriously in the postwar period. For example, the proportion of GNP allocated to family allowances declined from 21.8 percent in 1949 to 5.4 percent in 1976;[116] relative to expenditures on health and pensions, the proportion of GNP spent on family benefits fell from 35.3 percent in 1960 to 18.8 percent in 1975.[117] Furthermore, while in 1945 one of the objectives of family policy was the maintenance of the purchasing power of families, benefits have fallen far short of this ideal. Between 1950 and 1964 the purchasing power of single persons grew from a base of 100 to nearly 240, but that of families with three children oscillated between 100 and a maximum of 120, even when all allowances are calculated at the higher rates for older children.[118] The lowest point for pronatalist policies was during the early 1970s, when the principle of universal application was largely abandoned and many benefits were made subject to a means test.[119] It was at this time that the first signs of the immigration problem resulted in the shift of responsibility for population to the Ministry of Labor and the formal separation of family policy from population policy.

There appear to be four reasons why the degradation in the level of assistance to the family was permitted to continue. First, fertility rose after the war and for twenty years maintained a level that had not been achieved since the early years of the century. Second, France's economy was booming, its growing

[115]Information given the author by the chief, Office of the Family, Ministry of Health and Family. Interview, May 31, 1978.

[116]Sullerot, p. 163.

[117]Questiaux and Fournier, p. 162.

[118]Doublet, p. 58.

[119]Doublet and Villedary, p. 3; see also Hecht, p. 51–52.

labor needs were increasingly met by migrant workers, and there was a feeling that the high wages being earned reduced the need for family allowances. Third, competent observers have suggested that a more fundamental reason for the diminished attention to family allowances was the reluctance of successive governments to increase taxation for welfare measures that were already more generous than comparable measures in neighboring countries. Doublet and Villedary point out, for example, that within the Common Market, social expenditures introduce an element of competition that affects the net cost of manpower. In their opinion, legislation on family allowances "has been subjected to the pressure of a market economy and the needs of the various branches of social security to fit into the framework of the Common Market."[120] Finally, as social security funding ceased to grow at the level of expenditures, rising costs in one part of the social security system could only be met by diverting funds from another. Thus the rapid escalation of expenditures on health and pensions during the 1960s and 1970s resulted in a degradation of the social transfers effected through family allowances. *Within* family policy the financial pressures were inevitably accommodated by a decrease in the importance of measures that were universally applicable and a concurrent increase in the number of measures applicable only to special groups.[121]

The new family policy introduced by Mme. Veil in December 1975 indicated a return to the principle of universal application in family and supplementary allowances as well as a new search for measures to ease the conflict for women between motherhood and participation in the labor force. In making these changes, the government endeavored to tailor its approach to the preferences of the public as stated in the INED survey of 1975. As was suggested above, the government moved slowly on introducing legislation affecting women and the labor force to avoid precipitating opposition from the political left. The right to take two years postmaternity leave was extended only to government employees and to those in large industrial enter-

[120]Doublet and Villedary, pp. 3, 57.

[121]The danger to the family program inherent in financing family policy from a common fund was pointed out by the High Committee on Population in 1939. See Alfred Sauvy, "La nécessité d'une nation jeune," *Le Figaro*, April 27, 1979, p. 2.

prises.[122] Furthermore, the leave is uncompensated, although it does count toward the calculation of a retirement pension. Similarly, although paid maternity leave was lengthened in 1979, the entitlement prior to July 1980 was only sixteen weeks. After this date paid maternity leave was extended to six months.[123]

Somewhat stronger efforts are being made to relieve the economic situation of families with children. In 1977 the complicated system of supplementary family allowances, many of which were available only to special target groups, was simplified and extended by the incorporation into one *complément familial* of five different benefits. This global benefit is now paid to any person responsible for the care of one child under three years of age or three children.[124] In December 1978 the president announced a plan to improve the purchasing power of families. As a first step changes that came into effect on July 1, 1979, brought to a family of three children a minimum of 1,000 francs a month in basic and supplementary allowances. This sum was exclusive of housing, education, or special benefits to which an individual family may be entitled. A second increase in 1980 guaranteed a minimum monthly income of 3,500 francs for a three-child family.[125] Also in 1980, the rate of increase in the purchasing power of families with three or more children was doubled to 3 percent per annum, while the rate remained at 1.5 percent for smaller families.[126] At the same time, the "birth grant" for third or later children was doubled, from 5,000 to 10,000 francs; noncontributable pensions were provided for mothers of three or more children to cover the years they spend at home caring for young children. Finally, priority was given to large families in the allocation of more spacious housing.[127]

The announcement of these new measures met with dismay on both sides of the National Assembly and by commentators in

---

[122]Laws 76–716 of July 9, 1976, and 77–766 of July 12, 1977.

[123]*Le Monde*, September 23, 1978, p. 14; November 24, 1979, p. 12.

[124]Hecht, p. 52.

[125]*Le Monde*, December 15, 1978, pp. 1, 11; March 27, 1979, p. 46. In 1979 FF 1,000 = U.S. $230 and FF 3,500 = U. S. $800, approximately.

[126]*Le Monde*, November 24, 1979, pp. 1, 2. In 1979 FF 10,000 were worth approximately U.S. $2,300.

[127]Ibid.

the press.[128] The measures fell far short of the "global" family policy that had been repeatedly promised since 1975. The reversal to the policy of providing benefits only to special groups—in this case the large family—was protested by socialists and communists alike. Others pointed out that a 3 percent annual increase in the purchasing power of family allowances, while welcome, did little to compensate for the erosion that had taken place since the 1950s. Observers were quick to point out that funding for housing was already inadequate and that there were long waiting lists for apartments.[129] Most significantly, the new measures did nothing to ease the strain of combining motherhood with labor force participation, to which public opinion has accorded first priority in all of INED's surveys since 1968.[130] Asked what else she had in mind, the minister, Mme. Pelletier, was forced to speak of measures that, while they are an important component of President Mitterrand's social policy, are of doubtful significance for the birth rate—improving the urban and suburban environment and permitting children to play on the grass in public parks and gardens.[131]

Conclusions

This chapter has shown that despite the intense pronatalism that engulfed the nation in 1945 and the pronatalist policy introduced at that time, the French people and their leaders have displayed a remarkable tolerance of low fertility and low population growth. This should not be surprising in a nation that has been controlling its fertility since 1750. After 1945, no less than after 1870, strong pronatalist sentiment appears to have characterized only a relatively small, intensely nationalistic segment of the population closely associated with the Church. There are signs, which would bear further investigation, that powerful pronatalist sentiment now resides predominantly among those who experienced at firsthand the events of 1940–45. This said, it is evident that policy-makers and influential people in circles close to gov-

[128]Ibid.
[129]Ibid., p. 12.
[130]Girard and Roussel, p. 581.
[131]*Le Monde*, November 24, 1979, p. 12.

ernment now consider that the demographic trend of the past fifteen years poses practical problems of adjustment for the society and also holds a generalized threat to the nation's well-being and vitality. Thus there is in process of crystallization a desire to raise fertility to a "safer" level.

Ironically, the nation with the most extensive experience in managing pronatalist policy is at a loss to know how to implement its resolve. Denied the use of "repressive" measures because of the change in the role of the state vis-à-vis the citizen, and aware that "traditional" incentives to fertility are no longer thought to be effective, the government is taking its cue from the preferences of the public. In response to opinions expressed in the INED survey of 1975, the government of President Giscard d'Estaing promptly dismantled the frankly pronatalist measures left over from more interventionist days. The same government was less successful in responding to the demand for greater economic assistance to the family which appeared in the survey of 1978. Because of the serious economic situation confronting the country, and perhaps because of the lowered sense of nationalism, there was a reluctance on the part of the authorities to increase taxation to finance substantial incentives to fertility. Moreover, there was no effort to attempt the radical restructuring of the social security system that appears to be essential if family policy is to be placed on a secure footing. Even more significantly, the Giscard government was unable to respond effectively to demands for measures to ease the burden for women of combining motherhood with participation in the labor force. The center-right administration failed to find a formula that would make such discriminatory measures acceptable to feminist groups and labor unions in a period of high unemployment.

It is possible that the change of government in 1981 may facilitate the introduction of measures intended to stimulate fertility. The Mitterrand government is less likely than the former administration to be constrained by fear of rising taxes, while the promise of shorter working hours for all employees may provide a way around the ideological difficulties associated with special labor force legislation for mothers or parents. Very soon after taking office, moreover, the new government returned to the principle of universal eligibility with respect to family allowances, reversing the later Giscardian emphasis on the large family. In general, the social and economic policy outlined by President Mitterrand is attuned to the needs and demands of a majority of French men and women as expressed in many opinion polls on the causes of low fertility. At the same time, the breadth of the program and the burying of the recognizably "pronatalist" measures in a global program of social transfers to all lower-income workers cast doubt on whether the Mitterrand program can be considered a strong population policy in the sense in which that term has been defined in this study. As several respondents observed in 1978, however, the family is always a "a good political issue" in France. The birth rate is likely to be used by groups on both the left and the right as a reason for requesting more assistance for the family. Thus, even with the new government's less focused policy, there should be occasion for trying out a number of measures that might appear to be helpful in encouraging higher fertility.

V

SWEDEN: IN PURSUIT OF SEXUAL EQUALITY

If ideas of nation and family form the context within which population trends are customarily perceived in France, the people of Sweden tend rather to apprehend the development of population against a background of individual and community. The distinction encapsulates a number of differences which influence the orientation of the two societies to low population growth. While French nationalism leads to a perception of population trends as the instigator of change in national attributes, the Swedish emphasis on society and social change engenders a view of demographic movements that emphasizes their dependent status. Most significantly, from the perspective of population policy, the former orientation implies a strain toward conservatism that is at variance with the overall trend of development in social mores; the Swedish approach, by contrast, provides an impetus to change that draws behind it the more traditional elements of the society. Thus in the mid–1930s Sweden was able to introduce public support for birth control thirty years before such a radical step became possible elsewhere in Europe. Today it has gone further than any other Western European country to make it possible for the parents of young children to work shorter hours with minimal loss of income.

A more immediate difference between France and Sweden is the latter's lack of research information relating to population trends and their attitudinal, social, and economic determinants and correlates. Paradoxically, the country with the oldest and one of the most complete systems of population registration is seriously deficient in demographic research and analysis. The appearance of low fertility on the political agenda in 1977 found policy-makers egregiously uninformed and precipitated a flurry of efforts at self-education among political elites. Political activity in 1977–78 was centered in the Riksdag and was directed as much to finding ways of filling the gap in the nation's research capacity as to the search for an appropriate response to the demographic trend itself. During 1976 and 1977 six motions were introduced by representatives of all five parties in the Riksdag[1] requesting that the government investigate the fertility trend and/or propose measures to assist families with children. In November 1977 the Social Affairs Committee decided to deal with these motions and took the almost unprecedented step of scheduling hearings, on the American pattern, for January 1978.[2]

The Demographic Situation

In Sweden, as in other Western European countries, fertility increased in the 1940s and 1950s and started to fall again after 1964. From an average level of 1.8 between 1930 and 1934, the period Total Fertility Rate increased to an average of 2.5 between 1946 and 1949, fluctuated around a somewhat lower level during the 1950s, and in 1964 started a regular and rapid decline. By 1978 the period TFR had fallen to 1.6, its lowest point, before rising slightly to 1.67 and 1.7 in 1979 and 1980.[3] In 1966, for the first time, deaths exceeded births in the Swedish population, although the population continued to grow as a consequence of higher birth rates among immigrants (see Table 6). As in other Western countries, the fertility decline has been particularly marked among older women, and childbearing is now heavily concentrated in the age-group 20–29. As Table 7 shows, however, since the mid–1970s there has been a slight rise in

[1]The Moderate Party (conservative); the Center Party (formerly the Farmer's Party); the Liberal Party; the Social Democratic Party; and the Communist Party.

[2]Gabriel Romanus, vice-chairman of the Social Affairs Committee, told me that the members of the committee recognized that the issue was complex and that they knew very little about it. They scheduled hearings in order to expose themselves to academic and government opinion. Interview, May 8, 1978.

[3]Bourgeois-Pichat "Recent Demographic Change," p. 24, table 1.

Table 6

Natural Increase in the Swedish and Foreign Populations in Sweden, 1971–78

	Excess of births* over deaths		
Year	Swedish	foreign	together
1971	22,116	9,651	31,767
1972	19,194	9,023	28,217
1973	15,779	8,244	24,023
1974	15,365	8,193	23,558
1975	7,266	8,158	15,424
1976	−600	8,268	7,668
1977	−232	8,087	7,855
1978	−4,602	8,169	3,567
1979	−3,235	8,416	5,181
1980	−3,321	8,585	5,264

Source: Murray Gendell, "Sweden Faces Zero Population Growth," *Population Bulletin* 35, 2 (Washington, D.C.: Population Reference Bureau, June 1980), p. 34, table 11. Figures for 1979 and 1980 kindly provided by Dr. Gendell.
*Births according to citizenship of the mother.

Table 7

Distribution of Births by Age of Mother

Age of mother	1955	1960	1965	1970	1975	1978
Under 20	7.8	9.5	12.1	8.3	7.2	5.4
20–29	55.7	57.9	62.1	69.9	69.2	65.6
30 and over	36.5	32.7	25.8	21.8	23.5	29.0

Source: UN *Demographic Yearbook:* 1956, 1962, 1966, 1971, 1976 (various tables). 1978 figures from Sweden, NCBS, *Population Changes,* 1978, part 3, table 3.3.

fertility among women over 30—perhaps because of the increase in cohabitation prior to marriage and a consequent delay in the timing of first births.

The fertility trends outlined here should be seen against the background of the remarkably stable completed family size that

Table 8

Cohort Fertility of Swedish Women

Year of birth	GRR	NRR	TFR*
1870/71	1.795	1.239	3.71
75/76	1.708	1.132	3.53
80/81	1.574	1.091	3.25
90/91	1.222	.900	2.52
95/96	1.043	.794	2.15
1900/01	.915	.714	1.89
05/06	.886	.722	1.83
10/11	.910	.762	1.88
11/12	.936	.789	1.93
12/13	.934	.797	1.93
13/14	.958	.810	1.98
14/15	.971	.823	2.01
15/16	.969	.830	2.00
16/17	.974	.843	2.01
17/18	.982	.852	2.03
18/19	.968	.848	2.00
19/20	1.043	.922	2.15
20/21	.976	.868	2.02
21/22	1.007	.899	2.08
22/23	.983	.882	2.03
23/24	1.002	.903	2.07
24/25	.993	.899	2.05

Source: Adapted from Bernhardt, *Trends and Variations in Swedish Fertility*, table 2.1, pp. 12–13.
*Dr. Bernhardt's GRRs were converted to TFRs by me using the sex ratios computed by Pravin Vasaria, "Sex Ratio at Birth in Territories with a Relatively Complete Registration," *Eugenics Quarterly* 14 (1967), pp. 134–35, as follows: GRR × (1.0 + Sex Ratio) = TFR.

has characterized Sweden throughout this century. While the period indices of fertility show wide fluctuations over the years, the average completed family size has varied little around a mean of approximately two. The stability of Swedish fertility is depicted in Table 8, which shows cohort TFRs that provide a measure of lifetime fertility of "real" rather than "synthetic" cohorts of

Swedish women from the end of the nineteenth century. The TFRs were computed by me from cohort GRRs calculated by Eva Bernhardt using the longitudinal method (see Appendix A). Dr. Bernhardt's cohort NRRs, included in the table, also show that when mortality is taken into account, no cohort of Swedish women since those born in the 1880s has succeeded in replacing itself. As can be seen in Figure 4, the sharp rise in the period index in the 1940s was occasioned by changes in the timing of births and did not signal a significant change in lifetime fertility.

Changes in population size and
age structure

Notwithstanding the recent slight rise in the birth rate, it is probable that fertility will remain below replacement level and that the population will start to decline before the end of the century. Of a set of projections made by the National Central Bureau of Statistics (NCBS) in 1978, based on the 1975 census figures, the one considered most likely by the bureau assumes that fertility will continue to rise until 1985 and will remain constant thereafter, with a TFR of 1.8. The main migration assumption presumes there will be a net gain of 10,000 a year between 1978 and 1984 and a net balance of zero thereafter. Finally, the expectation of life at birth is expected to increase slightly for men, from 72.1 in 1978 to 72.2 in 1986, and rather more for women, from 77.9 to 78.6 in the same period, both figures stabilizing from then on. On the basis of these assumptions, the 1975 population of 8.21 million is expected to increase for some years before declining to 8.12 million by the year 2000 and to 7.66 million by 2025.[4]

Table 9 shows the changing age structure of the population under these assumptions. The decrease in numbers starts in the lowest age-group, 0 to 19 years, prior to the year 2000. During the second half of the projection period, the decline will spread to the active population in the age-groups 20–64. At the upper

---

[4]The projection is presented here in the form in which it was set out in Carl Johan Åberg and Allan Nordin, *Befolkning och Ekonomi* (Stockholm: Trygg Hansa, 1977), pp. 53–54.

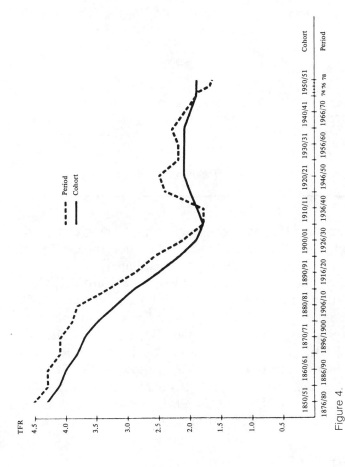

Figure 4.

Cohort total fertility rates, 1850–51 to 1950–51, and period rates, 1876–80 to 1971–75 (1974–78 estimated).

Source: Sweden, National Central Statistical Bureau, *Barn—Behov ella börda?*, URVAL, 1979, no. 11, p. 34.

Table 9

Swedish Population Projection, 1975–2025, Medium Alternative
(TFR = 1.8)

Age	Population ('000s)			Difference ('000s)		
	1975	2000	2025	1975–2000	2000–2025	1975–2025
0–19	2,231	1,963	1,734	−268	−229	−497
20–64	4,727	4,832	4,403	+105	−428	−323
65+	1,251	1,358	1,527	−108	+169	+276
Total	8,208	8,153	7,664	−56	−488	−544

Source: Åberg and Nordin, *Befolkning och Ekonomi*, p. 53, table 6.2.

---

end of the age spectrum, the age-group 65 and over will increase rapidly throughout the entire period, but not sufficiently to counterbalance the decline at younger ages. Finally, some calculations made by the Economic Commission for Europe (ECE)[5] show rather dramatically not only the increase in the elderly population but also the disproportionate increase in the most dependent age-group, those over age 75 (see Table 10). Although the ECE's projections were made in the early 1970s using slightly different assumptions than those of the Swedish NCBS, the statistics shown in Table 10 concern only people who are already living, and they are therefore consonant with those of the Swedish Central Bureau of Statistics.

Changing patterns of family formation

Despite the stability of lifetime fertility among Swedish women who completed their childbearing period prior to 1970, there are signs that future fertility might be considerably lower. Since the mid–1960s a number of changes have taken place in the structure of the family and its way of life that on the face of it could exert a downward influence on fertility. The pattern of cohabita-

---

[5]United Nations, Economic Commission for Europe, *Economic Survey in Europe in 1974*, Part 2 (New York: United Nations, 1975), ch. 7.

Table 10

Changes in the Structure of Population Aged 60 and Over and 75 and
Over, 1970–2000
index number, 1970 = 100

	Age 60 and over		Age 75 and over	
	men	women	men	women
1970	100	100	100	100
1980	113	124	116	135
1990	114	147	122	165
2000	108	149	116	174
Population numbers 1970 ('000s)	772	853	166	231

Source: Adapted from ECE, *Economic Survey of Europe in 1974,* part II, tables
VII.15, VII.16, A.VII.1.

tion that has extended to France, the United States, and other
Western industrialized nations appeared first in Sweden and
spread rapidly throughout the society before it was taken up in
other countries. At the time of the population census in 1975, 11
percent of the total population claimed to be living together without formal marriage. Among women the custom is most common
in the 20–25 age-group, of whom 22 percent were married in
1975, while 29 percent were cohabiting without marriage. At the
1965 census, by contrast, 43 percent of this age-group was
married.[6] According to a Swedish demographer, Erland Hofsten,

the number of contracted marriages, which in the peak year 1966
amounted to 61,000, had six years later declined to 38,000. In the
following years the number has varied somewhat, but no upward
tendency can be observed (1978: 37,000 marriages).[7]

[6]Klas Wallberg, director, Forecasting Institute, National Central Bureau of
Statistics, testimony before the Hearings held by the Social Affairs Committee
of the Riksdag, January 19, 1978. See Sweden, Sveriges Officiella Utredningar
(SOU), 1977/1978: 32, Socialutskottets betänkande, *Befolkningsutvecklingen*,
p. B54. This report is hereinafter referred to as "Hearings."
[7]Erland Hofsten, "Non-Marital Cohabitation: How to Explain its Rapid
Increase, Especially in Scandinavia," in *Economic and Demographic Change:*

However, the number of couples in consensual unions prior to the 1975 census is unknown.

It is not yet clear to what extent the institution of marriage is permanently changing and how the change will affect fertility in the long run. In the short term the 1975 census suggests that fertility among couples in consensual unions may be substantially lower than the fertility of couples in legal unions at the time of the census; the average number of children born to women in and out of wedlock were as follows:[8]

Age-group	20-24	25-29	30-34
Married	1.0	1.6	2.0
Cohabiting	0.5	0.8	0.9

Cohabitation without marriage appears to have greater legitimacy in Sweden than in other Western nations with the possible exception of Denmark. Annika Baude, formerly head of the Department of Social Care for Children and Youth in the National Board of Health and Welfare, has recently observed that the formal ties of marriage have come to be regarded as less and less significant. In Baude's words:

> Many unmarried couples expecting a child choose to remain unmarried. In 1965, 14% of all babies were born "out of wedlock." The figure climbed to 18% in 1970 and to 32% in 1975. In the majority of these cases, the parents continue to live together without marrying, so the child grows up with both parents present.[9]

By 1977, according to Hofsten, the percentage of children born out of wedlock had risen to 35 percent.[10] In neighboring Denmark, moreover, where by 1977, 13 percent of cohabiting couples were living in consensual unions, a survey carried out in October 1977 suggested that "a considerable proportion of the consensual unions . . . may be considered to be of permanent

---

Issues for the 1980s, vol. 3, Proceedings of the IUSSP Conference, Helsinki, 1978 (Liège: IUSSP, 1979), p. 306.

[8]Sweden, NCBS, *Barn—behov eller börda?*, URVAL, no. 11, 1979, p. 43.

[9]Annika Baude, "Public Policy and Changing Family Patterns in Sweden, 1930–1977," trans. Jeanne Rosen, National Board of Health and Welfare, n.d. (mimeo), p. 12. The term "out of wedlock" is placed in quotation marks as the distinction between "legitimate" and "illegitimate" children has been abolished in Sweden.

[10]Hofsten, p. 306.

character. The same data showed that there were children in almost one-third of the consensual unions."[11]

In an interview Jan Trost, a family sociologist, spoke of the the historical basis for this "new" pattern of cohabitation in Sweden and Denmark.[12] In his view cohabitation is a modern recrudescence of the institution of betrothal, a pre-Christian ritual that remained an accepted part of the marriage process in certain social classes until recent times. It was still observed by some in the post-World War II period. According to Dr. Trost, betrothal, which followed courtship, was an institutionalized status in which the young couple were permitted to live together and have sexual relations for some time prior to marriage. Betrothal was most commonly followed by marriage, but the institution itself was clearly distinguished from marriage. In Trost's view the rapid spread of cohabitation in Sweden and Denmark is related to the greater legitimacy of this status in these two societies compared with the rest of the industrialized world and has to do with the timing and rate of penetration by Christianity. Because fertility appears to be lower among cohabiting couples, the very legitimacy of this custom could have a permanently lowering effect on the Swedish birth rate.

Another factor that may have an inhibiting effect on reproduction is the high rate of labor force participation among women in Sweden, one of the highest in the Western world. In 1976, for example, 60 percent of all married women worked at least part time, and 57 percent of married women with small children did so.[13] These high levels of participation in the labor force have appeared quite recently, particularly among women who have children under 7 years of age and who are themselves between the ages of 20 and 45. Between 1963 and 1977 the

[11]Ibid. In this passage Hofsten is citing data presented at the Helsinki conference by Per Vejrup Hansen in an unpublished paper entitled "Consensual Unions in Denmark. Numbers, causes and consequences."

[12]Jan Trost, University of Uppsala. Interview, May 16, 1978. Professor Trost's ideas are elaborated in "A Renewed Social Institution: Non-Marital Cohabitation," *Acta Sociologica* 21, 4 (1978), pp. 303–15.

[13]"Women in Swedish Society," *Fact Sheets on Sweden*, May 1979 (Stockholm: The Swedish Institute). Lena Jonsson provides a detailed breakdown by number and age of children as of 1972. See, "Law and Fertility in Sweden," in *Law and Fertility in Europe*, Kirk et al., p. 559.

participation rate of women aged 35–44 with responsibility for preschool children increased from 40 percent to 60 percent; among women aged 20–24 with preschool children the rate almost doubled, from 35 percent to nearly 70 percent, in the same period.[14] Although the direction of the relationship between labor force participation and low fertility cannot be determined from these statistics, one respondent told the author that the Social Democratic government introduced in 1970 a very strong incentive to women to join the work force. At that time the system for the assessment of income tax was changed, the incomes of husband and wife no longer being combined and assessed as one. Given the extremely high marginal tax rates in Sweden, the fact that the two incomes were to be treated independently made labor force participation by women a paying proposition for couples. The change precipitated a rush of women into the labor market far in excess of the government's expectations.[15]

A third factor that clearly influences the birth rate is the legality of abortion and its incidence in the population. Abortion has been available free of cost and on demand in Sweden since January 1975, but for several years before that the existing legislation had been interpreted more and more liberally. After 1960 the number of abortions increased rapidly, reaching a peak in 1975, the year the legislation was adopted. Since 1975, however, the number of women seeking abortions has stabilized, and even declined somewhat, as is shown in the table.[16]

1960	3,000
1965	5,000
1970	16,000
1974	30,000
1975	32,000
1976	32,000
1978	31,000

[14]Wallberg, "Hearings," p. B54.

[15]Carl-Johan Åberg, formerly director, Economic Division, Department (Ministry) of Finance, in the Social Democratic administration. Interview, May 18, 1978.

[16]Source: "Swedish Legislation on Birth Control: Contraception, Sterilization and Abortion," *Fact Sheets on Sweden* (Stockholm: The Swedish Institute, July 1977). Figures for 1978 from "Legislation on Family Planning." *Fact Sheets on Sweden*, March 1980.

Swedish observers judge that there have been no illegal abortions in Sweden since the late 1960s. Prior to that, illegal abortions are estimated to have numbered between 3,000 and 4,000 a year, while an additional 1,000 annually are thought to have obtained legal abortions in Poland. The latter practice has also ceased.[17] Happily, moreover, since 1976 there has been a disproportionate decrease in the number of teenagers seeking to terminate pregnancies.[18] Nevertheless, while the period TFR for 1977 indicated a family size of 1.65 children per woman on the average, the lifetime abortion rate, calculated by an analogous method, attained a level of 0.6 abortions per woman in the same year.[19] Without the abortions, therefore, fertility would have been comfortably above replacement.

Swedish Perceptions of Low Fertility

At the start of this chapter it was observed that Swedish policy-makers were taken by surprise in 1977 at the appearance on the political agenda of low fertility. Policy-makers were disquieted, moreover, to find the society ill provided with information and research about both the causes of the low birth rate and its likely consequences for the country. In large measure both the unpreparedness of political elites for the fertility crisis and their ignorance of its dynamics had their origins in a set of circumstances that had engendered an almost universal lack of interest and concern about domestic population issues. For one thing, there had been a rapid decline in the pronatalist sentiment of the 1930s and early 1940s as fertility attained a satisfactory level throughout the late 1940s and 1950s. For another, lessened anxiety over the birth rate had been reinforced by the country's commitment to the control of rapid population growth in the Third World. Both of these factors require some elaboration if Swedish attitudes toward low fertility are to be understood.

It will be recalled from Chapter 3 that the pronatalist policy of the 1940s was introduced by a Social Democratic government

[17]Karl-Gösta Nygren, Professor of Gynecology, Uppsala, testimony at the Hearings, January 19, 1978. See "Hearings," p. B29.

[18]"Legislation on Family Planning."

[19]Nygren, "Hearings," p. B29.

that had little or no commitment to population growth but which used the population issue as a lever for obtaining conservative support for social policy. As birth rates rose at home, any lingering traces of pronatalist sentiment evaporated, and the attention of the nation turned to the "population explosion" of the Third World. In 1958 Sweden became the first developed nation to provide assistance to a family planning program in a developing country, Ceylon, as part of its official foreign aid program.[20] Although the level of assistance was low, it was followed in 1961 by a larger involvement in Pakistan; since that time Sweden has become one of the major donors of family planning program assistance in the Third World. Toward the end of the 1950s, Sweden joined the small group of countries that was exerting pressure on the United Nations to encourage that organization to involve itself in the problem of rapid population growth, a very sensitive issue at the time.[21] In order to increase Sweden's credibility with developing country governments, Sweden's Social Democratic minister for social affairs stated publicly that Sweden did not have a domestic (pronatalist) population policy.[22] Throughout the late 1950s and 1960s, the population debate in Sweden focused on what was defined as the imperative need to achieve a stable population at home as well as abroad. This goal seemed the more necessary in the light of the social and economic problems Sweden was encountering as the large birth cohorts of the late 1930s and 1940s reached the schools, universities, and labor market.[23] During this period there was little or no overt pronatalism, even among conservatives; the population was growing, the economy was booming, and immigrants were appearing in large numbers to satisfy the demand for workers.

As a consequence of the predominance of antinatalist feelings during the 1950s and 1960s there was little understanding in Sweden of the long-term consequences of subreplacement fertility. The warnings of one demographer, Erland Hofsten, that the growing proportion of old people in the population would cause

[20]D. S. Greenberg, "Birth Control: Swedish Help to Underdeveloped Nations," *Science* 137 (September 1962), pp. 1038–39.

[21]A good account of this campaign is contained in Symonds and Carder. The relevant passage is on pp. 97–98.

[22]Erland Hofsten, Interview May 2, 1978.

[23]Carl-Johan Åberg, Interview.

problems for the labor force and the economy went unheeded by political elites and public alike.[24] More significantly, several respondents explained to me that there had arisen a strong feeling that it was somehow illegitimate and shameful even to think that a rich country like Sweden should encourage fertility when much of the world was overcrowded and starving. As one academic bluntly put it, one of the main causes of the dearth of informed opinion was "the conflict with the global population problem and Sweden's feeling of superiority." Despite the earlier neglect of the issue there was, in May 1978, a growing recognition that continued subreplacement fertility could pose serious difficulties for the country. In particular, attention was turning to the consequence of age-structural imbalance for the social security system and the effect of continued immigration on racial harmony. As in the 1930s and 1940s, however, the most pervasive public reaction was a feeling that something is wrong with a society in which couples hesitate to have the number of children they want. This, most people felt, was the problem that had to be dealt with.

Age structure and social security

The deleterious consequences of low fertility for the social security system—and, by implication, for the nation's social plan—were mentioned by almost all of the persons interviewed in 1978, and particularly by those who participated in the hearings. Among the most significant influences on these people, and especially on members of the Social Affairs Committee, was the publication in late 1977 of a book by Carl Johan Åberg and Allan Nordin on the economic and welfare implications of continued low fertility.[25] Started when Åberg was director of the Economic Division of the Department of Finance under the Social Democratic administration, the study was the first of its kind in Sweden. In brief, it was an attempt to assess the long-term effects of population trends on con-

---

[24]Almost every person interviewed in 1978 mentioned Hofsten's warnings and how they were laughed off year after year.

[25]Åberg and Nordin. See also the summary presented by Åberg in "Hearings," pp. B31–36.

sumption patterns and standards under three different fertility assumptions: TFR = 1.5, 1.8, and 2.1. Based on the Central Bureau of Statistics' projections, and assuming the continued implementation of the government's social plans for children and youth and the retired population, the authors found that there will be an increasing convergence of the consumption of the two dependent groups toward the standard of the active population. That is, under the medium alternative the consumption of the elderly will equal that of the active population by the year 2025. By this time the consumption of the young will have increased to 50 percent of the standard of the active population, compared with only 40 percent in 1975. The study also found that because the economy will be growing more slowly owing to the decreased, or even negative, rate of growth of the labor force, the increase in the consumption standards of the two dependent groups will be at the expense of the active population. The consumption of the productive population will grow more slowly than that of the other two groups, particularly under the lower fertility assumptions.

The authors interpret these results as posing the need for a choice between continued low fertility and the implementing of the social plan. In Åberg's words, "It will mean a big program of reeducation for both the public and the party. The Social Democratic Party will have to make a choice; if they prefer to live with low fertility, they will have to give up some of their social programs. There is no other way."[26] According to respondents, Åberg's presence in the Riksdag, where his party office is located, was a powerful influence on the opinions of members of parliament during 1977. The impact of the study may also be seen in the fact that soon after it was published, the government established a commission to undertake another study along similar lines. The commission arrived at broadly similar conclusions to those of Åberg and Nordin but, in addition, pointed out that even with more children and fewer elderly people, the goals of the social plan will be hard to attain.[27]

Although members of the Social Affairs Committee and the government have been influenced by Åberg and Nordin's analy-

[26]Interview.
[27]Sweden, SOU, 1978:1979, *Langtidsutredning, 1978.*

sis, the pessimistic views of these scholars about the coming short-age of workers are not shared by all participants in the debate. Arne Arvidsson, of the Central Bureau of Statistics, has gone on record as saying that "if low fertility is compared with the effects of introducing a 30-hour week, it is almost negligible."[28] Arvidsson is more concerned about the fluctuations in the age structure that would be engendered by a sudden and marked in-crease in the birth rate. Such oscillations cause great difficulties for economic and social planners, who have to cope with fluctua-tions in the demand for schools, jobs, hospitals, and other social infrastructure. Arvidsson's opinion was shared by an official re-sponsible for the regional development program of the Depart-ment of Industry. This official was confident that there are still significant reserves of untapped female labor in various pockets of the society that could be mobilized by what he called "mop-ping-up operations." Moreover, in his view, "it would be a very bad government that could not cope with a diminishing popula-tion. It would be simply inefficient."[29] However, another official in the same department expressed a different opinion. This offi-cial felt that there was an imperative need to "do something" about the birth rate "before the crunch comes in 1990–2000, mainly because it takes so long to influence demographic trends, and we will not be able to rely on immigrants any longer."[30] How-ever, he was not confident that attempts to stimulate the birth rate would be successful in Sweden's "materialistic climate."

While the respondents just cited were speaking in very gen-eral terms, others have more substantial reservations about the Åberg and Nordin analysis. Economists at the Confederation of Swedish Trade Unions are convinced, admittedly on the basis of "relatively superficial" studies, that there are no grounds for Åberg and Nordin's position.[31] Their opinions are shared by two scholars at the University of Stockholm who are engaged in an analysis of the labor force. These scholars are critical of the

---

[28]Cited in Ingvar Holmberg, "The Population Debate in Sweden in Recent Years," *Current Sweden*, 169 (August 1977) (Stockholm: The Swedish Insti-tute), p. 4.

[29]Interview, May 19, 1978.

[30]Ibid.

[31]Ingemar Lindberg, Confederation of Swedish Trade Unions, Interview, May 11, 1978.

macroeconomic methodology employed by Åberg and Nordin. In their view more realistic forecasts of the labor force can be made through the use of microeconomic techniques which take more account of alterations in the composition of the labor force, especially those that are occurring through changes in the division of labor between the sexes.[32] While these scholars agree that the coming changes in the age composition of the population will call for a restructuring of the labor market to provide a better balance between the public and private sectors of the economy, Gosta Rehn and Lena Gonäs are not convinced that the needs of the economy as a whole cannot be met with available human resources.[33] One of these scholars, Lena Gonäs, told the author that she had undertaken a small study of the labor force for the Secretariat for Future Studies, a governmental organization that sponsors policy-oriented research. She added that the study did not arouse much interest within the government because, in her judgment, "the government is not much interested in this kind of statistics."[34]

National power, cultural integrity, and
the immigration question

In marked contrast to the situation in France, where discussions of low fertility inevitably included remarks about its consequences for national power and international influence, national

---

[32]Gösta Rehn, Institute for Social Planning, and Lena Gonäs, Center for Studies of Working Life. Information obtained in an interview with Gonäs, May 11, 1978.

[33]The loss of jobs in industry in recent years is attributable not only to the economic recession but also to major structural changes in some of Sweden's basic industries—for example, steel, shipbuilding, and textiles. It is expected that many of these jobs will be permanently lost. Partly balancing the jobs lost in industry has been a large increase in the number of jobs in the public (service) sector, which now employs one in every four Swedish workers, or more than are employed in industry. It is expected that this changeover from industrial to public service occupations will continue in the future. See, for example, Bo A. Ericsson, "The Employment Situation in Sweden: Some Main Issues Looking Ahead to the 1980s," *Election Year '79* 2 (New York: Swedish Information Service, June 1979).

[34]Interview, May 12, 1978.

power in any conventional sense seemed far removed from the thinking of Swedish policy-makers and influentials. Respondent after respondent was at pains to explain, as did Gunnar Myrdal in the 1930s, that Sweden has long since given up crudely nationalistic ambitions. Only one academic tentatively expressed his suspicion that although nothing is said openly, nationalistic sentiments are present at a deep level in many people. While it would be surprising to find a society whose members were totally unconcerned about its security, integrity, and international "image," there is no doubt that compared with people of many other nations, the Swedes seem free of a desire for national aggrandizement and world power.

If it is true that Sweden has long come to terms with her small nation status, there is nevertheless a strong sense of pride in the nation's cultural identity and homogeneity. A desire to preserve this cultural integrity, and the security that is seen to derive from it, has surfaced as one of the most fundamental determinants of support for a pronatalist policy. Despite a suggestion that Sweden might demonstrate her sense of environmental responsibility and "solidarity" with the Third World by accepting more immigrants to compensate for her deficient natural increase, the policy-makers and influential people interviewed were unanimous that increased immigration is out of the question.[35] Reasons for the rejection of increased immigration as a response to low population growth are frequently expressed in technical terms—deteriorating relations with traditional sending countries in Europe, the high cost of Sweden's generous programs to facilitate the integration of immigrants, and the impossibility of compensating for age-structural imbalances through immigration. Nevertheless, the underlying reason seems to be a desire to maintain the cultural integrity of the nation, or at least to slow down the rate of transition to a more pluralistic society.[36] Thus an academic expressed his "terror" at the pros-

[35]Among respondents, only Ingred Sundberg, a leading Conservative and a member of the Social Affairs Committee, explicitly rejected this view. At the committee hearings, while all the experts were asked by members of the committee to comment on the feasibility of increasing immigration rather than the birth rate, expert opinion invariably ruled out the possibility of accepting more immigrants.

[36]In an interview with me, Jonas Widgren, director, Expert Group for Immigration Research in the Department of Labor, expressed the view that

pect of the racial tensions that would follow in the wake of new flows of immigrants, and a government demographer believed that Sweden will remain closed to non-Nordic migration for ever because "with the traditional European sending countries trying to reduce their out-migration, that leaves only India, Asia, and Africa as possible sources, and they are too different."[37] Respondents of all political persuasions insisted that their opinions were based on practical rather than racial or ideological considerations; nevertheless, the views of Ulla Tillander of the Center Party, expressed during the Riksdag debate on the committee's report, probably capture the feelings of most Swedes about immigration. Speaking of the "human problems" involved in importing labor, Tillander stressed the necessity for the Swedish population to continue to have a future in the country.

> This is not a question of being nationalistic or of wanting a continued population increase. But, as we unhesitatingly grant all other peoples the same right, I believe it is essential that we Swedes should also have a right to the hope that we do not belong to a declining branch of the human tree.[38]

Social policy and low fertility

Since low fertility made its appearance on the political agenda, a distinctive characteristic of the Swedish debate has been a continued emphasis on the deeper causes of the low birth rate. So

---

the deteriorating relations with sending countries in Europe, including Finland, which enjoys the right to unrestricted immigration into all Nordic countries, is the most serious and far-reaching issue in immigration at the present time. A brief account of Sweden's immigration policy is given in "Immigrants in Sweden," *Fact Sheets on Sweden*, April 1978. As an example of the high cost of integration programs, the "home language" program, under which instruction in the home language is made available for several hours each week to all foreign preschool and schoolchildren, already costs 210 million kroner (U.S. $43.3 million) a year. In 1978 over fifty languages were taught to some 30,000 children. On the point about compensating for age-structural imbalance, see Kjell Oberg, director general, National Immigration and Naturalization Board, "Hearings," p. B51.

[37]Interviews.

[38]Sweden, *Snabbprotokoll från Riksdebatterna*, 1977/78, no. 149, Thursday, May 18, 1978.

marked was this tendency in 1978 that with some exceptions, it was difficult to get respondents to focus on the likely consequences of the fertility trend; inevitably, after a few moments, the discussion would circle back to the more absorbing question of causation. As a result of this societal introspection, the discussion of low fertility has been shaped by a conception of Sweden as a society that is "hostile to children." The argument goes that because of the strains caused by the separation of work and home, modern industrial society has lost its sense of community. Swedes are seen as driven by material desires—a house in the country, a boat, holidays abroad—which absorb their time and energies and turn the family in on itself. In this process children become something of a burden to their parents and, in response, are increasingly excluded from the world of adults. Children are encouraged to involve themselves in different activities from adults; they are provided with segregated facilities and have little opportunity to develop a sense of community or society. Many Swedes believe that while parents feel the need to restrict the number of their children, those they do have are incompletely socialized because of the way children are segregated. Even the profusion of specialized entertainment, educational, and sporting facilities provided for children is coming to be viewed as means of assuaging the guilt feelings of adults over their psychological neglect of children. While opinions differ about how child care can be made less of a drain on the physical and financial resources of parents, there is a large measure of agreement that the low birth rate is a danger signal that must be attended to.[39]

[39]A strong intellectual basis for these views has been developed in recent years in the context of the government's policy on equality between the sexes. Much of this work has emanated from the pen of Dr. Rita Liljeström, professor of sociology at the University of Gothenberg, in connection with her work for the Delegation for Equality between Men and Women and for the Secretariat for Future Studies. Condensed versions of her work have been prepared in English by Liljeström for various publications of the Swedish Institute. See, for example, "Children - Parents - Jobs: 'Rearranging' the Swedish Society," *Social Change in Sweden* Introductory Issue (May 1977); "Are Children Better Off in the 'Post-Industrial' Society?" ibid., 2 (November 1977); "Integration of Family Policy and Labor Market Policy, Paper prepared for the Conference on Equal Pay and Equal Opportunity Policy for Women: Europe, Canada and the United States," Wellesley College Center for Research on Women, Wellesley College, Wellesley, Mass., 1978 (mimeo.). This article has

Population Policy Formulation in Sweden

One of the main questions addressed by the Social Affairs Committee at the hearings of January 1978 was the desirability of requesting the government to establish a population commission to examine aspects of the birth rate and recommend policy. The committee's report fell short of recommending that a commission be appointed but did ask the government to investigate the issue. Explaining this more limited focus to the author, the vice-chairman of the committee, Gabriel Romanus, said that the committee did not wish to ask for a commission, an act that normally signals an intention to introduce legislative proposals, before the results of a fertility survey were available in the summer of 1979.[40] In addition, it would be considered bad form to try to take the initiative away from the minister for social affairs who had commissioned the survey. Romanus also explained that the establishment of a commission at a later date was implicit in the wording of the committee's report. Another indication that the government was considering the introduction of a pronatalist policy is its reply to the Fourth United Nations Population Inquiry of June 1978. In an interview with me, an official of the Department of Social Affairs who drafted part of the reply said that for the first time, the government had acknowledged that a population policy was under consideration. "So," he concluded, "the issue is coming to the fore."[41] Yet a year later, in the spring of 1979, the Riksdag approved the establishment of a commission to study the economic conditions of families, a much narrower concept than the population commission earlier envisaged.[42] What were

---

been abstracted by Liljeström in *Social Change in Sweden* 9 (December 1978). See also "Sweden" in Sheila B. Kamerman and Alfred J. Kahn, eds., *Family Policy: Government and Families in Fourteen Countries* (New York: Columbia University Press, 1978), pp. 19–48.

[40]In October 1978 Gabriel Romanus became minister for social affairs in the minority Liberal government that took office after the unexpected collapse of the "bourgeois coalition" over the issue of nuclear power. After the general elections of September 1979, the Department of Social Affairs reverted to the Center Party.

[41]Department of Social Affairs, Interview, May 17, 1979.

[42]See Lillemor Melsted, "Swedish Family Policy," *Election Year '79*, no. 6 (New York: Swedish Information Service, July 1979), p. 12.

the reasons behind this more limited focus? Did the appointment of this commission signal the abandonment of interest in a more broadly based pronatalist policy? The present section will attempt to provide some answers to this question.

The information gap:
demographic research in Sweden

An important factor contributing to the country's lack of awareness of the implications of the fertility trend is the dearth of demographic research information available and accessible to government. This gap in the nation's research armory is the more surprising in a country that almost alone in Europe was able to base its population policy during the 1930s on sophisticated analysis of the demographic trend. The research gap is associated, moreover, with what may be a more lasting impediment, a serious deficiency in demographic training. It is hard to escape the conclusion that the shortage of demographers is related to the general lack of interest in national population trends on the part of government leaders during forty years of Social Democratic government.[43]

On the basis of remarks made at the hearings by a leading demographer, Dr. Hannes Hyrenius,[44] and from information obtained in interviews, it would appear that demographic training in Sweden was originally organized as part of the teaching of statistics. As the discipline of statistics became more complex and more methodologically oriented, the time devoted to demographic concepts and methods was gradually reduced until, by the late 1970s, there remained only a two- or three-week course

[43]Although Sweden became very much involved in population policy in the Third World, the country's activities did not depend on sophisticated demographic study. Sweden's population assistance to developing countries has been concentrated on assisting Third World governments to deliver integrated family planning and public health services. It should also be pointed out that the administration of universities in Sweden is a responsibility of government. There is a special department for this purpose, known as the Office of the University Chancellor.

[44]"Hearings," pp. B5–8. Hyrenius was professor of statistics at Gothenburg University.

taught in three undergraduate departments of statistics. One may assume, perhaps, that as fewer and fewer graduates were produced with solid demographic skills and knowledge, awareness of the need and interest in maintaining support for demographic training and research deteriorated.[45] The point has now been reached at which Sweden is being passed over in the competition for chairmanships of international demographic committees and activities.[46]

In 1969 an unsuccessful attempt was made to revitalize the discipline. At the instigation of Hyrenius, a demographic institute was established at the University of Gothenburg to undertake demographic research and to offer training to the doctoral level as an option for students in the Department of Statistics. From the start the project ran into trouble. Difficulties were experienced in finding qualified faculty and attracting students to a discipline that still did not have independent recognition. No doctorates were awarded, and only a handful of licentiates graduated. Based on Hyrenius's remarks, it is hard to escape the conclusion that the program did not receive adequate support from the authorities. The entire program was due to terminate in 1981 on Professor Hyrenius's retirement, and much of the attention of members of the Social Affairs Committee, the Humanistic Social Science Research Council, and other organizations has been devoted to developing plans to continue and expand the work of the Gothenburg Institute.[47]

Notwithstanding the lack of formally qualified demographers, Sweden is not entirely without population research. The country's population statistics are excellent and there is an active forecasting unit in the Central Bureau of Statistics that prepares projections for various departments. In addition to this basic

---

[45]This is my judgment based on the above information.

[46]Hyrenius, "Hearings," p. B6.

[47]The unexpected death of Professor Hyrenius in 1979 will presumably bring these activities to a halt before 1981. I understand that a decision has been made to establish two chairs of demography, one in a department of sociology and one in a department of history (in order to develop the discipline of historical demography using Sweden's unparalleled historical data). The intention is to break away from the purely statistical approach to demographic training. Information provided me by Ann-Sofie Kälvemark in a conversation, Ann Arbor, October 23, 1979.

work in statistical demography there are a number of university departments of medicine, history, sociology, anthropology, and geography that are engaged in research projects related to population. However, while much of this work is relevant to an understanding of current fertility trends and could provide information of value for the formulation of population policy, it does not reach policy-makers in a systematic way. Several of the expert witnesses at the hearings referred to the need for the creation or designation of a government agency to collect and evaluate the research output of these disparate groups.

From the perspective of policy-making the most critical gap may be the lack of surveys similar to those that in France and the United States have documented changes in reproductive behavior and in attitudes toward family formation, reproduction, and contraception since the 1940s.[48] The significance of this lacuna is attested to by the interest aroused by a small survey carried out as part of a course requirement by sociology students at Uppsala University.[49] Although the professor who supervised the study acknowledges that the survey had many scientific

[48]The French studies have been conducted by INED on a regular basis ever since 1946. They are reported in the journal *Population*, also in the series *Travaux et Documents*, published for INED by the Presses Universitaires de France. In America the period from around 1940 to the present has been covered by a series of major studies as follows: (a) the Indianapolis Study by Pascal K. Whelpton and Clyde V. Kiser: *Social and Psychological Factors Affecting Fertility*, 5 vols. (New York: Milbank Memorial Fund, 1946–58); (b) the Princeton Studies: Charles F. Westoff, Robert G. Potter, Jr., Philip C. Sagi, and Eliot G. Mishler, *Family Growth in Metropolitan America* (Princeton: Princeton University Press, 1961); C. F. Westoff, R. G. Potter, and P. C. Sagi, *The Third Child* (Princeton: Princeton University Press, 1963); Larry Bumpass and C. F. Westoff, *The Later Years* (Princeton: Princeton University Press, 1970); (c) the Growth of American Families Studies, I and II: Ronald Freedman, P. K. Whelpton, and Arthur A. Campbell, *Family Planning, Sterility and Population Growth* (New York: McGraw-Hill, Inc., 1959); P. C. Whelpton, A. A. Campbell, and J. E. Patterson, *Fertility and Family Planning in the United States* (Princeton: Princeton University Press, 1966); and (d) the National Fertility Studies: Norman B. Ryder and C. F. Westoff, *Reproduction in the United States, 1965* (Princeton: Princeton University Press, 1971), and C. F. Westoff and N. B. Ryder, *The Contraceptive Revolution* (Princeton: Princeton University Press, 1977).

[49]The study was conducted under the supervision of Jan Trost. Its significance as an indication of the sort of information that would be helpful was cited by a number of the persons interviewed by me.

weaknesses, it nevertheless indicated clearly that couples in Uppsala "desired" more children than they were having. The reasons given by the persons interviewed for limiting their families to this extent formed a fairly standard list of economic and social impediments to fertility—lack of time, lack of space, lack of childcare facilities, and inadequate financial resources. Widely publicized in the press, the study played a role far in excess of its intrinsic merit in bringing this aspect of the population question to the attention of the public and political elites. Specifically, the survey provided empirical support for the idea circulating that correctable deficiencies in the society were preventing women from having the number of children they wanted.

The lack of national fertility surveys may be seen as another consequence of governmental disinterest in domestic population development. For years successive directors of the Forecasting Institute of the Central Bureau of Statistics annually requested funds for a fertility survey, but the requests were always refused.[50] Thus there is little information available to the government on the reproductive aspirations of the population or the factors that condition them. When the fertility question was first taken up by the Social Affairs Committee at the end of 1977, the minister for social affairs, a member of the Center Party, hastily requested the bureau to carry out such a survey for the department. For political reasons the bureau was instructed to have the results available by the summer of 1979, in time for the general elections scheduled for September. The time constraint posed difficulties for the bureau, which lacks experience and expertise in this type of research. In the end the bureau did not undertake an interview survey of Swedish couples but confined itself to making a thorough review of the literature on fertility decline in the industrialized nations.[51] In particular the study examined what is known or thought about the social, economic, and demographic factors that determine the reproductive behavior of couples in contemporary advanced societies. Although an interview survey was not carried out at that time, the bureau recommended that such a study should be mounted in the future.

[50]Both Erland Hofsten, former director of the Forecasting Institute, and Klas Wallberg, who succeeded him, told me that their requests for funding for a fertility survey were repeatedly turned down.

[51]Sweden, NCBS, *Barn—behov eller börda?*

Political ideology

Members of the Social Affairs Committee, interviewed just as their report was issued in May 1978, were proud that they had been able to reach agreement on the concerns expressed in the motions of all five political parties. In the Riksdag debate that followed, the report and its recommendations were endorsed without reservation.[52] The background to the feeling of satisfaction expressed by members of the committee in reaching agreement was explained to me by Carl Johan Åberg as follows:

> One has to go back to the 1930s to understand the population question in its political aspects in Sweden. In the 1930s it was the Social Democrats who responded so strongly to Myrdal and used his argument as a lever to push family and social policy. At the same time, the right wing also picked up the policy issue but was stressing the defense and nationalistic aspects of it. It is important to remember the distinction because the same split in perspective has appeared again.

Although there is once again an ideological split over the population question, the basis for the division has changed since the 1930s. Without the fear of war that set the tone of the 1930s, the spirit of nationalism has declined; and while some conservatives seem more ready than many liberals and socialists to believe that a declining population spells problems for the society, the distinction may be simply a function of age. It was noticeable in Sweden, as in France, that respondents of all political hues who had lived through World War II were more perturbed about the fertility trend than those who had not. In 1978 conservatives seemed as much concerned to preserve or restore the structure of the traditional family as to raise the birth rate for economic or other reasons. For their part, Liberals, Social Democrats, and Communists were more concerned about the social causes of the low birth rate. Nevertheless, even on the left there was a growing appreciation—especially among members of parliament—that the economic consequences of declining population could threaten the social plan. Outside of the Riksdag many Social Democrats were not yet convinced of the need to raise fertility, but there were signs that as in the 1930s, the issue

[52]See the official record of the debate, *Snabbprotokoll från riksdagsdebatten.*

might be used as a lever for pushing social policy. As a spokes-man for the massive and powerful Confederation of Swedish Trade Unions (LO) told me, "If taking a pronatalist position will result in higher priority being given to the family, then LO will join the bandwagon—but only for reasons of expediency. There would be no real pronatalist intention."[53]

In 1978, therefore, the parties were agreed that something should be done to encourage fertility by easing the burdens of childrearing, but opinions differed over the means that should be employed. Behind the debate over means lay signifcant dif-ferences over the nature of the society that should be developed and the place of the family within it. Throughout the last decade Social Democratic policy, always concerned with individual wel-fare and development, has been consciously geared toward the creation of equal educational and occupational opportunities for women. Taxation, labor market, and education policy have been modified to remove impediments to the full and equal participa-tion of women in the labor force. Simultaneously, the main thrust of family policy has been toward a more adequate provi-sion of day care facilities for preschool and school children. As already indicated, these policies have facilitated very high levels of education and labor force participation among Swedish women.

Conservatives of both the Moderate Union (formerly the Conservative Party) and the Center Party (formerly the Agrar-ian Party) have become disturbed at what they see as the disin-tegrative effect on the family of the women's movement and the economic pressures they perceive as pushing women willy-nilly into the labor market. Members of both parties regard the poli-cies of the left as providing a forced choice for women between continuing in the labor force after childbearing, with all the strains involved in managing two jobs, or suffering economic deprivation by giving up the family's second income. There are differences in detail between the two parties, but both would like to see a less one-sided emphasis on day care. Both parties agree that child care at home must be recognized as socially useful work; they consider it unfair that women who elect to care for their young children themselves, or who cannot find a place in a municiple day care center, get no share of the govern-

[53]Ingemar Lindberg, Interview, May 10, 1978.

ment subsidies that go into the provision of child care centers.[54] Agreeing with the left that more day care facilities are needed, conservatives would like to see the introduction of a "child care benefit" with which families could purchase the type of day care they preferred, including that provided by themselves. In answer to the Social Democratic goal of "equality between the sexes," conservatives offer a movement toward "greater freedom of choice."

Paradoxically, while the social policies introduced by the left have done much to ensure that Swedish women have educational levels and occupational rates as high or higher than women in any other Western European country—with attendant downward pressures on the birth rate—the same policies also go far beyond the efforts of other Western European countries to make it easier for Swedes to combine parenthood with employment outside the home. In the opinion of one respondent, the women's movement has achieved so much in Sweden because early in the 1960s Swedish women realized that the concept of "feminism" was too narrow. If real changes were to be made in women's roles and status, parallel changes would also be needed in the roles and status of men. "Women's liberation" was therefore abandoned in favor of a broader objective, "equality between the sexes."[55]

[54]Currently running at about 35,000 kroner (U.S. $8,000) per child place per year. Places are allocated by income; it is rarely that a two-income family can secure a place in a municipal (government) day care center. Extending this argument to the low fertility issue, Ingred Sundberg, a prominent Moderate member of parliament, member of the Social Affairs Committee, and mother of four, observed to me that the state provides a great deal of help for smaller families but does little for larger ones. Based on her own experience, she remarked, "the state will pay for places in day care centers, but *physically* how does a woman manage who has to scurry around and get four children off to school and nursery center before she gets herself off to work? It is the same at the other end of the day. Therefore, the choice is not free; people are forced to have smaller families." Interview, May 12, 1978.

[55]Annika Baude, Director, Department of Social Care for Children and Youth, National Board of Health and Welfare, Interview, May 12, 1978. Even prior to the 1960s there were glimmerings of what was to become the Swedish concept of sexual equality. See, for example, Alva Myrdal and Viola Klein, *Women's Two Roles* (London: Routledge and Kegan Paul, 1956). Much of the intellectual background of the movement for sexual equality in Sweden is summarized in a volume edited by Edmund Dahlström entitled *Kvinnors liv och Arbete* (The Life and Work of Women). The book was published in

Equality between the sexes, originally promoted and still most vigorously pursued by the Liberal Party, was taken up by the Social Democrats and became government policy in 1972 with the appointment of an Advisory Council on Equality between Men and Women, responsible directly to the prime minister. The council was charged with the task of devising measures to "give women increased opportunities for gainful employment and to give men increased responsibility for care of the children."[56] In 1974 the Social Democratic government started to implement a "parental insurance scheme" intended to encourage men to relieve women of some of the burden of child care and enable women to make a more equal showing in the labor market. Under the scheme either parent became eligible to receive a benefit equivalent to approximately 90 percent of full pay for a period of seven months, later extended to nine months, after the birth of a baby. The leave may be shared by the parents in a variety of ways. The last three months, for instance, may be taken at one stretch, piece by piece, or in the form of six-hour working days or four-day working weeks, at any time up to the child's eighth birthday. Parents who were not previously in paid employment are entitled to an allowance of 32 kroner a day, approximately $7.00, for an equivalent period. In addition, the same benefit is payable to either parent who has to stay at home to care for a sick child. Originally available for only a few days a year, entitlement to this benefit has now been extended to sixty days per child per year.[57]

As a means of furthering sexual equality, the parental insurance scheme has had only limited success. Five years after the program was introduced, only about 12 percent of fathers availed themselves of the opportunity to take the leave or elected to be the one to remain at home with a sick child.[58] It

---

English in 1967 under the title *The Changing Roles of Men and Women* (London: Gerald Duckworth and Co., Ltd.).

[56]Annika Baude, p. 6.

[57]Melsted, pp. 1–2, 4–5. The allowance is taxable and counts toward the calculation of the supplementary income-related pension.

[58]Although the number of men electing to take some of the parental insurance leave is increasing slowly they are drawn predominantly from among the more highly educated and those in occupations where brain is of greater importance than brawn. Several of the younger men interviewed for this study

can also be argued, however, that under the rubric of "equality between the sexes," Sweden has been able to help women combine motherhood with participation in the labor force, without arousing the opposition of militant feminists.[59] In the judgment of the present writer, however, there was not, in May of 1978, a clear appreciation among policy-makers of how far the country had already gone in enacting potentially "pronatalist" legislation—albeit under a different guise. The establishment in 1979 of the more limited commission to study the economic circumstances of the family argues that there may have developed a more precise recognition of the areas in which there was still scope for governmental action.

Coordination of Policy

Students of Swedish policy have commented on the unusual capacity of the policy-making system to formulate and implement

---

told me that they had taken of intended to take "papa leave." Not only can academics and professionals in bureaucratic positions carry their work home with them, their superiors are more receptive of the new behavior pattern than are, for example, executives and managers in industry. For an insight into the reactions of factory workers and managers, see the remarks cited by Rita Liljeström, Gunilla Furst Melstrom, and Gillan Liljeström Svensson, *Roles in Transition* (Stockholm, 1978), especially pp. 110–11.

[59]Even in Sweden, Social Democrats are not entirely happy about the entitlement for parents to take parental leave in the form of shorter working hours. It is felt that allowing certain categories of employees to work shorter hours reduces the chances of attaining the Social Democrat's long-term goal of a 30–hour working week for all. Although this objective has been shelved in very recent years because of the economic recession, it is generally anticipated that a 30–hour week will be introduced by one means or another, probably before the end of the century. In addition to the Social Democrat's general distrust of the effect of shorter hours for parents, the Women's Organization of the party feared that the measure would encourage further discrimination against women in the labor market, since it is mainly women who take the parental leave. In order to exert pressure on working-class men, who are resisting the transformation of sex roles, the Social Democrats proposed that the entitlement to the additional two months leave that was introduced in 1977 be made contingent on the equal sharing of the additional period between both parents. This proposal was adopted in principle, but its effect was undermined by the inclusion of a provision that permits one parent, by filling in a simple application form, to transfer his or her share of the leave to the other.

broadly based, innovative policies that often involve radical restructuring of existing arrangements.[60] A distinctive characteristic of the Swedish policy-making system that helps to explain its exceptional capacity to introduce sweeping policy change is the physical and functional separation of the processes of formulating and implementing policy. Responsibility for policy formulation is concentrated within the fourteen departments of state, each under the control of a cabinet minister; responsibility for implementing policy is assigned to some seventy or eighty autonomous agencies and boards grouped under appropriate departments but responsible directly to the cabinet as a whole and not to individual ministers.[61] Scholars who have studied Swedish policy-making point to the freedom of the departments from the constraints of existing policy and day-to-day administrative responsibilities as important reasons for Sweden's ability to formulate radical policy changes.[62] Equally important, in the opinion of most observers, are the "absence of haste," the emphasis on "rationality," "expertise," "cooperation and consensus," and the small physical size of the system.[63]

[60]Thomas Anton, for example, cites a period during the late 1960s when at one and the same time the country was engaged in: a complete revision of the education system; a major reorganization of local government that involved a reduction in the number of local governments by a factor of ten; a restructuring of the Riksdag from a bicameral to a unicameral institution; the creation of a new metropolitan government for Stockholm; and the introduction of a massive new program of government investment for the northern half of the country. See "Policy-Making and Political Culture in Sweden," *Scandinavian Political Studies*, ed. Olof Ruin, vol. 4, 1969, p. 93.

[61]Pierre Vinde and Gunnar Petrie, *Swedish Government Administration*, 2nd rev. ed., trans. Patrick Hort (Stockholm: Bokförlaget Prisma/The Swedish Institute, 1978), p. 36. There are also twenty-four county administrations under the Department of Local Government which have the same status as agencies and boards.

[62]See, for example, Jack Brand, "Reforming Local Government: Sweden and England Compared," in *The Dynamics of Public Policy: A Comparative Analysis*, ed. Richard Rose (Beverly Hills: Sage Publications, 1976), pp. 35–56.

[63]A comprehensive discussion in English of Swedish government and the legislative process that takes account of constitutional changes introduced throughout the 1960s is contained in Neil Elder, *Government in Sweden* (Oxford-New York: Pergamon Press, 1970), esp. pp. 41–57, 119–37. Vinde and Petrie provide an up-to-date discussion of the formal structure and functions of government. Although all modern policy-making systems and processes are characterized by the qualities cited—except perhaps "absence of haste" and "small size"—virtually all students of Swedish government and

The division of labor between departments and boards has given rise to a distinctive pattern of policy-making which provides several opportunities for formal and informal coordination of policy. Because of their limited functions, the departments of state have remained very small and are unable to provide the manpower needed to carry out the in-depth investigations that in Sweden are considered an essential prelude to the drafting of legislative proposals. Moreover, this work cannot be undertaken by the Riksdag as the secretariats of the standing committtees are also small. On all issues of consequence, therefore, it is customary to make use of ad hoc commissions to carry out the necessary research, explore the acceptability of various proposals to a wide range of interested parties inside and outside of government, and present a report making recommendations for policy.[64] The significance of study commissions in Swedish policy-making can be judged from the fact that at any one time in recent years, some 300 commissions have been at work, employing approximately 300 full-time and over 3,000 part-time staff in addition to the commissioners themselves.[65]

Although the extensive use of ad hoc commissions would seem to pose considerable problems for coordinating policy, formal arrangements for coordination are not strongly developed. In the view of two experts on policy formulation in Sweden, there are two points in the process at which the overall coordination of government policy can be considered.[66] First, there is a constitutional requirement that prior to finalizing a commission's terms of reference (directives), the documents must be circulated for comment to all ministers and interested civil servants. Second, at the drafting stage, the Ministry of Justice is required

---

policy-making comment on the exceptional degree to which Sweden's policy-making institutions display these qualities.

[64]Hans Meijer, "Bureaucracy and Policy Formulation in Sweden," *Scandinavian Political Studies*, vol. 4, 1969, pp. 103–16, remains the most comprehensive account of the functions and process of study commissions. Thomas Anton, *Administered Politics: Elite Political Culture in Sweden* (Hingham, Mass.: Martinus Nijhoff, 1980), ch. 8, provides an interesting discussion of the *remiss* process. Christopher Wheeler discusses the role of interest groups in the work of commissions. See, *White Collar Power* (Urbana, Ill.: University of Illinois Press, 1975), pp. 38–43.

[65]Vinde and Petrie, p. 24.

[66]Ibid., pp. 33–35.

to coordinate the legislative work that takes place in the various ministries, and the Ministry of Budget is responsible for ensuring budgetary consistency. When, as at present, there is a coalition government, political coordination among the parties is managed through special offices attached to the party leaders concerned.[67]

Despite these formal arrangements, the Commission on the Constitution that reported in 1963 was critical of the large amount of discretion accorded individual ministers concerning consultation with their colleagues over directives and other government business. The commission's report pointed out that the existing procedures could easily lead to little more than a rubber-stamping of individual departmental proposals at a busy Cabinet meeting.[68] As part of the subsequent reorganization of the administrative system, a Cabinet Office was established within the Prime Minister's Office to "watch over the coherence of legislation and of administrative regulations."[69] The (currently) six Ministers without Portfolio were also given special responsibility for coordination, both in specialized areas and overall.[70] Nevertheless, as these new institutional arrangements are expected to oversee all government business, formal mechanisms for achieving coherence and coordination in the development of new policy still seem weak.

It is usually thought by students of Swedish policy-making that the success of the system, and the relatively high level of coordination that is achieved, must be attributed more to informal consultation than to formal arrangements for coordination. Meijer, in particular, emphasizes the large part played by informal discussions in the conduct of Swedish government. He lays stress on the fact that long before draft directives are circulated or formal approval sought, responsible ministers will have secured the implicit or explicit support of their colleagues. Although special cabinet meetings may be held on matters of exceptional importance for the society, most of this consultation and discussion occurs at the informal daily cabinet luncheons

[67]Ibid., pp. 34–35.
[68]Cited in Elder, *Government in Sweden*, pp. 51–52.
[69]Ibid., p. 56.
[70]Vinde and Petrie, p. 17.

which all ministers are expected to attend if possible, and at which the most critical decisions in Swedish government are actually made.[71] This opportunity for informal discussion continues throughout the life of a commission and provides an opportunity for amending directives, increasing the membership of a commission, or taking other steps that appear to be necessary.

The success of the informal process of coordination can be attributed in large measure to the small size of the policy-making system. Daily meetings of only twenty ministers over lunch would seem to foster collegial relations in a way that would be much harder, if not impossible, to achieve in a larger system.[72] At the level of the civil service, where a parallel series of discussions is held over the drafting of directives, the small size and physical proximity of the departments—all of which are located in one building close to the Ridsdag—also facilitates informal cooperation and coordination. There seems little doubt that these physical arrangements, together with the freedom from administrative demands, go far to ensure that policy-making is reasonably well coordinated at the civil service level.[73]

In sum, the Swedish policy-making process combines a number of formal and informal mechanisms for the overall coordination of government policy. Although the success of almost any policy-making system is ultimately dependent on the judgment of those responsible for initiating the process of consultation and

[71]Meijer, p. 105; Elder, p. 52; Vinde and Petrie, p. 33.

[72]The spirit of cooperation that appears to suffuse the whole process of policy formulation and administration is also crucial. Anton's *Administered Politics* is an in-depth attempt to identify the bases for the extraordinary valuation of cooperation and consensus in the Swedish policy system.

[73]James L. Sundquist has commented on the greater policy-making capacity of Western European governments compared with the United States. He attributes this in large measure to the informal ties that develop among civil servants who have worked together on many projects over the years. In the United States these close relationships are less likely to develop because of the large number of political appointments in the higher levels of the bureaucracy. See "A Comparison of Policy-Making Capacity in the United States and Five European Countries: The Case of Population Distribution," *Policy Studies Journal* 6, 2 (Winter 1977), pp. 194–200. I had an opportunity to observe at first hand the amount of interaction among civil servants from different departments over lunch in the Chancery cafeteria in Stockholm. Compared with other European governments, the Swedish system seems to foster exceptionally strong informal relationships among civil servants.

discussion, there seems to be agreement among observers that the Swedish system is one of the more effective in producing coherent and coordinated policy.

Constraints on government action

Unlike their opposite numbers in France and Germany, the policy-makers and influential people interviewed in Sweden gave little indication that serious constraints existed on the government's ability to introduce a pronatalist policy if it wished to do so. Particularly striking was the apparent lack of awareness and concern that the introduction of pronatalist measures might infringe the liberty of the individual in a private and personal area of decision-making. Only one politician in replied response to a direct replied, "Well, one would not call it pronatalist policy; people would not like that. But they would probably guess it was meant to be pronatalist because there has been so much discussion of the birth rate." Other policy-makers doubted that Swedish women would respond to marginal financial incentives, and the secretary of a small government research unit suggested that the birth rate would not survive long as an issue as the people were not very interested in it. In his view the current concern over low fertility had been stimulated by the earlier discussion about demographic training and research and would soon subside. None of the people interviewed appeared to question the state's right to attempt to intervene in this area.

Several explanations may be suggested for this difference between the perceptions of the Swedes and those of the French and West Germans. Because of the lack of fertility-related survey research, there is no systematic information on how the fertility decline is perceived by the general population and subgroups within it. The apparently widespread acceptance of the "theory" that deficiencies in the society prevent couples from having the number of children they desire can be interpreted to imply that it is the duty of the state to attempt to ease the burdens of childrearing. In addition, given the societal commitment to furthering equality between the sexes, it must seem inconceivable to Swedes that there could be a serious effort to restrict educational and occupational opportunities for women.

Similarly, after nearly fifty years of contraceptive liberalism, an attempt to restrict access to contraceptives or even legal abortion appears to be out of the question.[74] Thus the context within which the issue is being discussed in Sweden is entirely different from those of France and West Germany, where traditional elements are stronger. It is possible, moreover, that Swedes are more tolerant than are other Western peoples of mildly coercive efforts by the state to structure society in ways about which there is a broad consensus. A proposal by the Social Democrats to make it mandatory for both parents to share part of the parental leave is only one example of the sort of mild coercion that might be attempted.[75]

Like other Western nations, Sweden is encountering financial constraints on its ability to introduce expensive pronatalist measures. The economic recession that hit Sweden later than it did other countries has put many people out of work and aggravated fundamental structural economic problems. Many of Sweden's basic industries are now outdated, and it is felt by many people that the government's efforts to shore them up in order to protect employment have only delayed the development of new industries.[76] Many observers are pessimistic about the ability of industry to create enough new jobs even after the recession passes. Because of the government's policy of subsidizing indus-

[74]One respondent commented, "There had to be such an intense educational effort to get the abortion law through a few years ago, it is quite inconceivable that it could be changed now."

[75]Asked if this measure would not have constituted an intolerable intrusion in a purely private and personal area of decision-making, a university professor responded, "Yes, it would. But the official answer to your question would be that it is not coercive as no one is made to do anything. They are just told that if they want something they have to pay a price." Roland Huntford's book *The New Totalitarians* (New York: Stein and Day Publishers, 1972) is a well documented attempt to depict Sweden under Social Democratic government as an authoritarian society closely reminiscent of Huxley's *Brave New World*. In his concluding chapter Huntford says,

The price of contentment in Sweden is conformity. Personal desires must be tailored to the desires of the group. Mostly this is forthcoming. Where it is not, society imposes uniformity. Methods are civilized, rational and humane, but remorseless . . . (p. 345).

[76]See, for example, individuals and organizations cited by John Vinocur, "Sweden's Economic Success Sours," *New York Times*, March 24, 1978, pp. A1, D3.

try to retrain redundant workers as a means of reducing open unemployment, most firms already have more employees on their payrolls than they can readily absorb into productive positions.[77] In addition, Sweden's taxation is one of the highest in the world. The average worker now pays around 50 percent of his wages in taxation, and marginal tax rates are so high that many people in higher income brackets have started working only part time.[78] The need to restructure the taxation system was the topic of increasing debate and discussion throughout the 1970s; it became one of the main issues in the general elections of 1979, in which the "bourgeois coalition" of Moderates, Center Party, and Liberals was returned to power for the second time since the fall of the Social Democrats in 1976.[79]

Interparty differences over the way to handle the worsening economic situation caused the collapse of the government coalition in April 1981, halfway through its term of office.[80] During 1980 the budget deficit had increased sharply, as had the deficit on current account. By the end of the year the weakness of the economy had given rise to a steadily growing outflow of currency, which was succesfully halted in January 1981 by a 2 percent increase in interest rates, but at the cost of increasing government expenditure and reducing the rate of industrial investment. By this time the media were strongly critical of what they considered to be the government's failure to do anything about the economic crisis; but in fact, the government had little room to maneuver. In

---

[77]Ericsson.

[78]One respondent, a middle management professional, told me that he works only four days a week because it gives him more time with his family for almost no cost. In 1978 this respondent was paying approximately 77 percent of his salary in taxes. By working only four days his gross income was reduced by 1,400 kroner a month, but his loss after tax was only 360 kroner. Most of this loss was offset because he was spared the cost of day care for his small daughter on the fifth day of the week. Bo Sundian of the Swedish Employers Federation told me that between 25 and 35 percent of employees work part-time. Interview, May 17, 1978.

[79]Pia Brandelius, "Taxes: One of the Main Issues in the 1979 Election," *Election Year, '79*, no. 6, July 1979.

[80]This was the second time the "bourgeois coalition" had collapsed since 1976. The previous occasion, in the fall of 1978, the split was over nuclear energy policy. From that time until the general election in fall 1979, the country was run by a minority Liberal government.

the first instance, because 75–80 percent of government expenditure had been inflation proofed, it was difficult to restrain government spending. Second, no one was prepared to accept a tax increase; indeed, for years while in opposition, the Moderates and Liberals had both protested Sweden's high taxes, and the three-party coalition was pledged to hold the line on taxation or, preferably, to reduce it.

In February 1981, after negotiations among the government parties, the prime minister announced the introduction of an "economic program of action" as an emergency measure. Included in the program was a further 5 billion kroner spending cut that would reduce food subsidies and travel deductions on personal income tax returns. In addition, the program called for a 50 percent decrease in marginal income tax, to take effect over three years. The cut would affect a large majority of wage and salary earners and was to be paid for by increases in other taxes.[81] In an effort to secure widely based support for the economic action program, the government then entered into negotiations with the opposition parties; and in April 1981 the Liberal minister for the budget announced that he had come to an agreement with the Social Democrats. Included in the agreement were limitations on the extent of tax deductions which would have the effect of offsetting part of the tax cut. Most importantly, the starting date was postponed until after the next general elections due to be held in the fall of 1982. The agreement was seen by the Moderates as tantamount to a rejection of the entire program, and the eight Moderate ministers resigned, leaving the country once again in the hands of a minority government, this time composed of the Center and Liberal parties. Under these circumstances it seems unlikely that any government will undertake to introduce further expensive extensions to the social programs in the near future.

Recent Changes in Family Policy

During its year in office following the first collapse of the "bourgeois coalition" government in 1978, the Liberal Party intro-

[81]For a brief discussion of the background to the government collapse, see "The Swedish Government in Crisis, Spring 1981," *Political Life in Sweden*, no. 10, July 1981 (New York: Swedish Information Service).

duced a number of changes in family policy. Since the minister for social affairs, Gabriel Romanus, had served as vice-chairman of the Social Affairs Committee of the Riksdag at the time of its hearings on low fertility and had been worried about the impending population decline, it is reasonable to assume that the new measures were motivated, at least in part, by pronatalist concerns. Starting in January 1979, the basic child allowance, payable for all children up to the age of 16, was increased to 2,500 kroner per child per year.[82] Later the payment was increased to 3,000 kroner. Since the same date parents have had the legal right to nine months' uncompensated leave in addition to the nine months covered by parental insurance. Like the last three months of parental leave, the second period may be taken flexibly either as one bloc of full-time leave, as six-hour days, or four-day weeks at any time until the child's eighth birthday. As might have been anticipated, the introduction of this additional benefit was strongly opposed by the Social Democrats, who argued that the unpaid leave would increase discrimination against women in the labor market and, in any case, gave an unfair advantage to the richer families who could afford to live on one income for a longer period. Liberals, who are sympathetic to this argument, nevertheless contend that the possibility of working shorter hours provides women with a more realistic chance of entering the labor market, even if it does lessen their chances of promotion to responsible positions.[83]

Also in 1979, two extensions of parental insurance benefits were introduced. The first, an increase in the entitlement to parental leave for the purpose of caring for a sick child under ten years of age, has already been mentioned: the entitlement now stands at sixty days per child per year.[84] The second new benefit permits all prospective parents to attend child care classes in paid working time, both before and after the birth of a baby. Under this scheme new fathers are also invited to spend a day at the maternity hospital to learn how to handle the baby.

[82]A good account of current family policy measures and political party opinions about them can be found in Melsted.
[83]Ibid., pp. 11–12.
[85]Ibid., p. 5.

These last two benefits are clearly intended to foster equality between the sexes in the long run. However, they could exert a mildly pronatalist effect by giving fathers more confidence to handle young children and easing the burden on mothers. In addition to these new programs, efforts are continuing to complete the program instituted in 1976 by the Social Democrats to create 100,000 new places in day care centers and a further 50,000 places in "free time centers" for school children. Although this program is running one year behind schedule, it is expected that some 90,000 additional day care places will have been created by 1982.[84]

Finally, as part of the economic program of action proposed by the three-party government in February 1981, family allowances are to be raised for children of higher birth orders. Behind the rather surprising willingness of the government to increase government expenditure at this time of economic stringency lie the findings of the Commission on the Economic Condition of Families, which completed its work early in 1981.[86] The committee had found that while the number of families with three or more children is declining, they still account for approximately 25 percent of all children under 18 years of age. Moreover, larger families are concentrated in the poorer and least skilled strata of the society, among industrial and agricultural workers.[87] The committee also found that it is difficult for large families in these strata to rise above the "minimal existence" level of income because income tax deductions do not take account of the number of children in a family, because more larger than smaller families have only one income, and because wage increases are counterbalanced by concomitant increases in marginal income tax. In addition, the income ceiling on eligibility for the housing allowance, one of the more effective income support measures for large families, is set too low, so that wage increases tend to disqualify families that would most benefit by the allowance. The government therefore proposed that family allowances be increased by 750 kroner per year for the

[85]"Child Care Programs in Sweden," *Fact Sheets on Sweden* (Stockholm: The Swedish Institute, February 1980).

[86]Sweden, Department of Social Affairs, *Flerbarnsfamiljerna—kartläggning och analys* (Stockholm: Departementens Offsetcentral, 1981).

[87]Ibid., pp. 3–4.

third child in a family and by 1,500 kroner for fourth and fifth children. Not surprisingly, given the interest of the left-wing parties in increasing income and social equality, this proposal survived the changes made in the agreement with the Social Democrats and is to be implemented in January 1982—even before the rest of the program.[88] It is noteworthy that differentiated family allowances have now been accepted in Sweden for the first time.

Conclusions

In the course of its modern history, Sweden has never suffered a traumatic experience with population decline. On the contrary, the rapid growth of population during the nineteenth century and the widespread poverty that ensued may have played a part in shaping both the nation's lack of concern over low population growth and its consuming interest in social welfare. There is a distinct parallel to be drawn between the attitudes of Swedish political elites in the 1930s and those of policy-makers and influential people in the late 1970s. At both times a tempered anxiety over possible consequences of low fertility has been overshadowed by a stronger tendency to view the population trend as a consequence of unsatisfactory social conditions rather than as a possible cause of social ills. Although there is some polarization between the perceptions of conservatives and socialists, the differences are less dramatic than in France and West Germany. The views of the left tend to predominate, but there is a basic consensus on fundamental objectives. From the characteristic Swedish perspective the population trend is eminently susceptible to social policy; or, more precisely, if social conditions can be improved, the population trend is inconsequential.

Sweden's orientation to fertility issues has resulted in a neglect of demographic research that leaves the country with a large task of fact-finding if policy measures are to accord with the preferences of the electorate as well as demographic and social exigencies. However, the importance attached to in-depth research as a preliminary to policy formulation provides a mechanism whereby the immediate handicap of inadequate research information can

[88]*Svenska Dagbladet*, July 12, 1981.

be overcome while more permanent arrangements are established. The process will take time, but policy-making in Sweden is never hasty. More significantly, the generally shared view of fertility as a dependent rather than an independent variable not only applies a pressure toward remedial action but legitimizes acts that might otherwise be perceived as an intrusion on personal liberty. The fundamental consensus over social goals and the elaborate process of consensus-building that characterizes Swedish policy-making go far to ensure the continuation of the broad thrust of social policy even if the preferred means differ among political parties.

In summary, it would seem that Sweden is unlikely to enact a large package of legislation that could be labeled "pronatalist policy." More likely, there will be a gradual but broadly coordinated shaping of policy in a variety of sectors—taxation, housing, urban development, family, labor market—in an effort to create a society that can bend to accommodate to the changing needs of its members. In doing this, Sweden's social policy in the 1970s and 1980s, as in the 1930s and 1940s, may well become a model for the rest of the Western world.

VI

WEST GERMANY: PRISONER OF THE PAST

Of the three countries selected for study in this research, West Germany provides the most striking evidence for the basic proposition that demographic variables alone do not determine population policy. Clearly concerned about the absolute population decrease which started in 1972, the present government is still far from adopting a corrective policy. At a fundamental level the reasons for this hesitance may be sought in the emotional and other legacies of the Third Reich. It is only in recent years that it has become possible in West Germany even to speak of population policy. Today the question of an interventionist response to population decline still arouses highly charged and painful emotional reactions among those Germans who vividly recall the period of Nazi rule. In addition, the fragmented governmental structure established by the Basic Law (Constitution) of the Federal Republic raises questions about the capacity of the Federal government to implement a coherent population policy even if it wished to do so.

The sensitive nature of population policy in the Federal Republic placed severe restrictions on my ability to discuss the issue with policy-makers in West Germany. Some older respondents found the subject so disturbing that they avoided answering questions that called for expressions of opinion about the consequences of low fertility. In an atmosphere markedly at variance with the openness of France and Sweden, my contacts with governments officials and other informants were carefully screened, and more junior respondents had been told to restrict their remarks to certain "safe" topics. In large measure this extreme sensitivity was a consequence of the timing of my visit to the Federal Republic. For six months prior to the visit, a project had been underway in the Ministry of the Interior with the objective of synthesizing the range of scientific and bureaucratic opinion on low fertility and preparing a report for the Cabinet. Delicate and difficult negotiations were in progress between the Ministry of the Interior and other ministries in an effort to resolve marked differences in perspective and opinion, and it was considered desirable that all my questions concerning governmental views should be referred to the official responsible for preparing the report, Dr. Gerd-Dieter Schoen.[1] Dr. Schoen himself was open and candid but obviously unable to express the personal views of other policy-makers. Officials of Land (state) governments which have started to implement pronatalist policies were far less inhibited in discussing the population issue and commenting on the position adopted by the Federal government.

The Demographic Situation

The trend of fertility in the Federal Republic is similar to that of France and Sweden but has gone further. From the point of view of reversing the trend, therefore, the situation is more difficult than in either of the other two countries. Throughout the 1970s the period NRR in West Germany has been the lowest in the world, falling to 0.627 in 1978 for the population of German extraction.[2] In the same year the TFR for the total population, including immigrants, was 1.39.[3] The annual number of births in the total population declined by 45 percent between 1964 and 1977, the decline being even greater in the indigenous German population. For this group the number of births fell by 50 percent in the same period, from 1.06 million to 576,468.[4] As

[1]In addition, several officials were overextended drafting a reply to a searching parliamentary question.

[2]This is the statistic used by the Federal Statistical Office for a recent population projection. See Federal Republic of Germany (FRG), Ministry of the Interior, *Bericht über die Bevölkerungsentwicklung in der Bundesrepublik Deutschland* (Bonn: Deutsche Bundestag, 8 Wahlperiode, Drucksache 8/4437, August 1980), p. 45.

[3]Bourgeois-Pichat, "Demographic Change," pp. 24–25, table 1.

[4]FRG, *Bericht über die Bevölkerungsentwicklung*, p. 17, table 11.

Table 11

Balance between Births and Deaths in the German and Foreign
Populations

	Together	German	Foreign
1960	+325,667	+318,119	+7,548
1965	+366,700	+334,377	+32,323
1970	+75,954	+20,963	+55,002
1971	+47,856	−23,793	+71,649
1972	−30,050	−111,900	+81,850
1973	−95,395	−184,846	+89,451
1974	−101,138	−200,131	+98,993
1975	−148,748	−235,630	+86,882
1976	−130,289	−208,679	+78,390
1977	−122,578	−192,812	+70,234
1978	−146,750	−213,691	+66,941

Source: FRG, *Bericht über die Bevölkerungsentwicklung,* p. 17, table 11.

Table 11 indicates, deaths have exceeded births in every year since 1972 in spite of the excess of births over deaths in the sizable immigrant population. The table underscores the important contribution of the immigrant population to population growth, even during the period of restricted immigration after 1973.

For the most part, the pattern of family formation accompanying the decline of fertility in the Federal Republic follows that already observed in France and Sweden. For example, there is the same development of the one- or two-child family, and there are few couples desiring three or more children. Behaviorally, while there was an overall fertility decline of 44 percent between 1966 and 1976 in the German population, the number of infants born to families where there were already three or more children decreased by 67 percent, and the number of third children born declined by 58 percent. By contrast, the numbers of second and first births declined only by 40 and 33 percent.[5] In terms of

[5]Schwarz, "La baisse de la natalité," p. 1003.

Table 12

Labor Force Participation by Women of Reproductive Age

	total ('000s)	<20 %	20–30 %	30–40 %	40–50 %
			Age-group		
All women					
June 1961	9,932	20.0	62.4	45.5	43.7
May 1965	9,559	60.3	58.4	44.0	47.5
April 1970	9,683	47.3	60.2	45.8	48.7
May 1975	10,002	50.6	62.7	51.3	43.8
April 1978	10,159	44.1	65.1	53.4	51.9
Married women					
June 1961	4,515	55.1	43.1	37.1	36.6
May 1965	3,779	54.2	44.0	36.3	39.8
April 1970	5,402	57.7	47.8	40.4	34.1
May 1975	6,088	57.9	55.6	46.4	37.1
April 1978	6,108	54.6	56.6	48.9	36.3

Source: FRG, *Bericht über die Bevölkerungsentwicklung*, p. 39, table 27.

reproductive intentions, a larger proportion of couples choose to remain childless than in France. An opinion survey carried out in 1977 showed that more than half (51 percent) of young couples said they wanted two children, and 21 percent preferred only one. Ten percent said they wished to remain childless, and 11 percent that they wanted three or more.[6] In France at much the same time, only 3 percent of couples thought no children or only one to be most desirable "in general," while 6 percent opted for no or one child for themselves.[7]

Another area in which the three countries show similar developments is that of female labor force participation. As in France and Sweden there has been a large increase in the number of women in the childbearing years entering paid employment since fertility started to decline after 1964. As can be seen in Table 12, the increase has been particularly strong among mar-

[6]Ibid., p. 1005.
[7]Girard and Roussel, p. 570, table 1.

ried women. In addition to the overall increase in female labor force participation, moreover, there has been a marked movement of women out of the self-employed and family-employed categories and into industrial occupations that are usually thought to be less compatible with motherhood.[8]

Although the patterns and correlates of fertility decline in the Federal Republic mirror the main trends observable in most European nations, there is a fundamental difference in the significance of subreplacement fertility in a declining as opposed to a stable or growing population. In the former case subreplacement fertility per woman is superimposed on a progressively smaller base population of women in the childbearing years. Under these circumstances the amount of fertility increase needed to bring the overall birth rate up to replacement level becomes greater each year. Population decrease is likely to continue, therefore, until fertility decline ceases and population stability is achieved at some smaller population size.

Table 13 shows the results of a small calculation made by Dr. Karl Schwarz to illustrate the magnitude of the behavioral change needed to bring the West German birth rate of 1975 up to replacement level. The first segment of the table shows the distribution of size of achieved family of 100 West German couples who by 1975 had completed at least nineteen years of marriage. The second part shows one possible distribution that would ensure the production by 100 couples of the 220 children needed for replacement[9] under the following assumptions: (1) 10 percent of couples will be childless because of the biological sterility of one or both partners, and an additional 5 percent of couples will be voluntarily childless; and (2) no couples will have five or more children, and only 10 percent will have four. As the third segment of the table indicates, the realization of the model distribution would require that more than 90 percent of couples with one child would also have a second, compared with 59

[8]Gerd-Rüdiger Rückert, "The Employment of Women as a Cause of a Declining Number of Births," in *Materialien zur Bevölkerungswissenschaft*, no. 5, pp. 197–221.

[9]Under the actual conditions obtaining in West Germany in 1975, 220 children were required to be born to 100 married couples in order to achieve the 211 needed for the replacement of 100 women on the average (i.e., including married women).

Table 13

Numbers and Distribution of Children per 100 Couples in 1975,
Actual* and in Replacement Model†

Distribution of family size for 100 couples			Number of children for 100 couples			Additional children for 100 children already born		
couples	1975*	model†	birth order	1975*	model†	for 100 children	1975*	model†
No children	24	15	—	—	—	—	—	—
1 child	31	5	1	76	85	1st child/marriage	76	85
2 children	33	35	2	45	80	2nd child/1st child	59	94
3 children	10	35	3	13	45	3rd child/2nd child	29	56
4 or more	2	10‡	4 or more	4	10‡	4th or more/3rd	31	22§
Total	100	100	Total	138	220	—	—	—

Source: Karl Schwarz, "La baisse de la natalité," p. 1015, table 9.
*Actual fertility rates for 100 couples in 1975.
†Model of reproductive behavior to produce replacement level fertility (220 children per 100 couples).
‡4 children only.
§4th children per 100 3rd children.

percent who did so in 1975. It would also require that almost 60 percent of couples with two children would go on to have a third, compared with only 30 percent in 1975. Although there has been a slight upturn in fertility between 1978 and 1980,[10] it seems unlikely that replacement level fertility can be achieved in the near future.

Table 14 shows the projected development of the German-born population between 1980 and 2030 under two fertility assumptions. The first assumes that fertility will remain constant at the 1978 level, NRR equals 0.627, throughout the projection period. The second projection assumes that the NRR will increase to 0.8 by 1990, remaining constant thereafter. In both cases it is assumed that the migration balance will be zero and

[10]In 1980 the crude birth rate for the total population (German-born and foreign) was 10 per 1,000, compared with 9.4 per 1,000 in 1978. This corresponded to a TFR of 1.45 in 1980, up from 1.39 in 1978. See Bourgeois-Pichat, "Demographic Change," pp. 24–25, table 1.

Table 14

Projected Changes in Age Distribution of the German-Born
Population, 1980–2030, under Two Fertility Assumptions

	Together			Age-Group								
				0–19			20–59			60+		
	population 1979 ('000s) =100		%	population 1979 ('000s) =100		%	population 1979 ('000s) =100		%	population 1979 ('000s) =100		%
NRR = 0.627												
1980	57,084	100	100	15,009	97	26	30,463	101	53	11,613	100	20
1990	54,893	96	100	10,990	71	20	32,010	106	58	11,894	102	22
2000	52,140	91	100	10,479	68	20	29,182	97	56	12,479	107	24
2010	47,929	84	100	8,610	56	18	27,070	90	56	12,250	105	26
2020	43,339	76	100	7,000	45	16	24,050	80	55	12,289	105	28
2030	38,275	67	100	6,233	40	16	18,590	61	49	13,452	115	35
NRR rises to 0.8 between 1980–1990												
1980	57,094	100	100	15,018	97	26	30,463	101	53	11,613	100	20
1990	55,613	97	100	11,709	76	21	32,010	106	58	11,894	102	21
2000	53,867	94	100	12,196	79	23	29,191	97	54	12,479	107	23
2010	50,538	88	100	10,508	68	21	27,780	92	55	12,250	105	24
2020	47,240	82	100	9,204	60	19	25,747	84	55	12,289	105	26
2030	43,405	76	100	8,813	57	20	21,139	70	49	13,452	115	31

Source: Adapted from FRG, *Bericht über die Bevölkerungsentwicklung*, pp. 46–47,
table 29.

that there will be only minor decreases in mortality[11] The most
striking feature of both projections is the rapid decline in total
population size from 57 million in 1980 to 43.4 million under the
higher fertility assumption and to 38.3 million under the lower
one. Even by the year 2000, when the effect of errors in the
assumptions will be less marked, there will be declines of 5 and
3 million respectively. More significant, from a planning perspective, are the changes that will appear in the age structure of
the population. Under both assumptions there will be a steady
increase in both the size and the proportion of the population in
the oldest age-group, those aged 60 and over. This is accompa-

[11]FRG, *Bericht über die Bevölkerungsentwicklung*, pp. 44–45, 49.

nied by a steady decrease in the size and proportion of the youngest age-groups, those under 20 years of age. The active population, aged 20–59, shows an increase between 1980 and 1990 but thereafter declines rapidly in numbers and more erratically in proportions.

Not visible in Table 14, which shows only the broadest age-grouping of the population, is the rapid aging of the population within the active categories, those aged 20–59, that will accompany continued low fertility. Already the age-group 40–60 is increasing relative to that aged 20–40, and by the end of the century it will be bigger than the latter group.[12] Since it is usually believed that younger workers adapt more readily to new technologies and are more mobile geographically, the aging of the working population may affect productivity even before the active population starts to decline in absolute numbers.[13] In addition, the growth of the older dependent population will place enormous strains on the social security system, despite the lightening of the burden from the younger dependent population. It is interesting to note, however, that while it is commonly found that the cost to the *state* of maintaining an elderly dependent exceeds the cost of educating a young person to adulthood, the cost to *society* may be greater for the young person. Hilde Wander has shown for Germany that when private and public expenditures are considered, it costs between one-fourth and one-third more to bring up an average child from birth to age 20 than to support an elderly person from age 60 to the end of his or her life.[14] Thus it is difficult to anticipate the impact of declining population on social expenditures.

Perceived Consequences of Fertility Decline in the Federal Republic

How is population decline perceived by government officials and influential people in West Germany? What are the chances that the government will decide to introduce a pronatalist policy?

[12]Hilde Wander, "The Working Population," in *Population Decline in Europe*, Council of Europe, ed. (New York: St. Martin's Press, 1978), p. 59.
[13]Ibid., p. 62.
[14]Idem, "Zero Population Growth Now: The Lessons from Europe," in Espenshade and Serow, p. 50.

While the number of officials interviewed in the Federal Republic was small, there was not one who did not seem anxious to see a greater effort to stop the fall of fertility. In the colorful words of one respondent

> The development of population in the Federal Republic is like an airplane in descent—getting faster and faster. Unless you can apply the brakes in some way and slow down the acceleration, there will be a crash.

Notwithstanding the dramatic metaphor employed by this official, it will be observed that his implied objective was not a reversal of the rate of growth, nor even a leveling out of the trajectory, but merely a slowing down of the rate of decline. In setting out this limited goal, this respondent was echoing the remarks of others who were keenly aware that a marked increase in fertility, sufficient to bring the birth rate up to replacement level, is unlikely to occur. While opinions vary about the optimal size at which the population should be encouraged to stabilize, ranging from the present size down to 40 million, as Dr. Schoen stated:

> The aim and objective of our group—insofar as we have such a unified aim—is to get a smooth curve of fertility and population growth. This means that there will never be growth, only decline.

As government officials saw the situation in 1978, the most that could be hoped for was stabilization of the population at approximately the existing level. Much of the discussion by technical personnel was over ways to lessen the "frictions" that will be experienced during the decline to a considerably smaller population size.[15]

Declining population and economic growth

Not surprisingly, much of the technical discussion and investigation of the consequences of low fertility in the Federal Republic

---

[15]An excellent analysis of the anticipated impact of population decline on school enrollment and the demand for teachers in the Federal Republic is presented in Jean-Claude Chesnais, "La baisse de la natalité et ses conséquences sur l'enseignement," *Problèmes Economiques* 1, 715 (March 18, 1981) (Paris: La Documentation Française), pp. 20–28.

centers on the question of whether economic growth can be maintained in a declining population. Few respondents were willing to offer opinions on this issue, recognizing that the variables involved are so many and so highly interrelated that personal opinions amount to little more than speculation. Only one policy-maker indicated that while he does not think that economic growth depends on a growing population, he is doubtful it can occur in a declining population.

The Federal Ministry for the Economy is also hesitant to form an opinion on this question and, in June 1978, had "no official view."[16] According to Schoen, the ministry pointed out that because population deficiencies in the past were overcome by means of labor immigration and by moving production to more populous parts of the world, insufficient scholarly attention had been paid to the interrelationships between population and economic growth. The implication was that much more research was needed before an informed judgment could be made. Schoen expressed his personal view that the Federal government is unlikely to be greatly concerned about the effect of the birth rate on economic development because economists in the Ministry for the Economy believe that population size is a relatively minor factor in the generation of economic growth. Much more serious, they argue, is the fact that the Federal Republic lacks energy-producing and other essential natural resources. Against this lack they set what they believe to be probably the decisive factor—the productivity of the individual worker. This has been high in the past, and in the ministry's opinion there are good prospects for further improvement.[17] According to Schoen, officials in the Ministry for the Economy also point out that much will depend on evolving trends in worldwide political and economic development that will affect the growth of demand for German products from overseas. But while West German analysts profess their confidence in continued technological progress and world demand, some outside observers fear that the real problem is that labor shortages and rising costs will price Ger-

---

[16]Information provided by Dr. Schoen, Interview, June 4, 1978.
[17]See, for example, FRG, Ministry of the Economy, *Wirtschaftspolitische Implikationen eines Bevölkerungsrückgangs. Gutachten des Wissenschaftlichen Beirats beim Bundesministerium für Wirtschaft* (Bonn, 1980).

man—and European—goods out of the market. In this view newly industrialized countries in Asia and elsewhere, endowed with plentiful supplies of labor, will be better able to meet the growing world demand for industrial products.[18]

Age structure and social security

Like their counterparts in France and Sweden, officials interviewed in the Federal Republic seemed most concerned over the anticipated effects of age-structural change on the social security system. Despite Wander's demonstration that the overall cost of maintaining a young person is greater than the cost of an elderly person, discussion seems to focus on the growing number of elderly dependents in the society. The director of the Planning Department of the Bavarian State Ministry of Labor and Social Affairs, for example, remarked that while there are at present four workers to every elderly dependent in the Federal Republic, the ratio will fall to three to one within twenty-five years if fertility remains at approximately the present level. By then, 24 percent of personal income, shared equally between employer and employee, will be needed for the financial support of the elderly, compared with 18 percent in 1978. In the opinion of this official and other respondents, any government will encounter difficulty raising social security taxes to this extent. For several years past the government tried unsuccessfully to increase the tax and finally managed to raise it to 18.5 percent in 1980. There has been discussion, therefore, of the difference between biological and social aging and the possibility of reducing pressures on the social security system by allowing more flexibility in the age of retirement.

West German officials and scholars were anxious to see an immediate improvement in the birth rate in order to minimize age-structural imbalance. They doubted, however, that politicians would sufficiently appreciate the effect of demographic inertia to take the necessary steps in time. For approximately

---

[18]Jean-Claude Chesnais, "Le modèle économique de l'Allemagne Fédérale, est-il compatible avec son modèle démographique?" *Revue d'Economie Politique* 91, 2 (1981), pp. 163–77.

the next decade demographic indicators will assume a favorable cast, at least in the short-term view. As Table 14 showed, the size of the active population will increase during the present decade irrespective of what happens to fertility. Dr. Karl Schwarz, at that time director of the population division of the Federal Statistical Office, and Dr. Schoen both observed that the ratio of elderly dependents to active population will be satisfactory until around 1990, when the first real decrease in the active population will become evident. Both men stressed that there will be no serious difficulties until the end of the century. In addition, regardless of the level of individual fertility, there will be an increase in the crude birth rate during the 1980s because of the larger number of young women entering their reproductive period during that time. Demographers and officials concerned with population fear that both politicians and public will be lulled into a sense of false security by the rising birth rate, especially as there will also be difficulty creating jobs for the increase in the number of new entrants to the labor force during the 1980s. After 1990, however, the drop in the number of young women will be dramatic. It is important, therefore, to take the tide on the flood and attempt to increase individual fertility at a time when policy can exert the greatest effect at the societal level. In light of this discussion it is interesting to note that the increase in the birth rate observed in 1980 was, at least in part, the result of a real increase in individual fertility. The TFR rose from 1.39 in 1978 to 1.45 in 1980.[19]

Declining population and regional development

Unlike France and Sweden, whose populations have not yet shown an absolute decrease in numbers, the Federal Republic finds itself in a dilemma over the question of population distribution. For some years the Federal government has implemented a regional development program under which special assistance has been made available to some of the more backward agricultural regions situated on the periphery of the country to the east, west, and northwest. The program provides

[19]See Note 4.

incentives for people to remain in the countryside and was introduced with the objective of reducing the rate of population increase in the already overburdened cities and industrial areas. More recently this objective has changed, and the program is now intended to prevent further weakening of the already severely depleted rural areas, from which out-migration had already reached the level of 20 per 1,000 by 1971.[20]

Since the Federal Republic closed its borders to immigration in 1974, a new problem has made its appearance which, in the opinion of regional planners at the Institute for Population Research, will soon require the government to make a clear choice between the cities and the backward rural areas. Without the inflow of a large number of migrants from abroad, the industrial cities have also been losing population. Fertility is extremely low, not only in the cities proper but also in suburban areas and in the interconnecting rural areas surrounding the large centers of population. The situation is complicated by the fact that the rural areas that form the target for regional policy are the sole remaining parts of the Federal Republic where fertility is still at replacement level or slightly higher. The population of these areas, numbering only three million, thus constitutes something in the nature of a reserve. Population experts feel that there is a need for government to decide whether it should continue to provide incentives to young people to settle in the rural areas where their fertility may be higher than in the cities. Should the government feel it necessary to maintain the concentration of industrial productivity in urban areas where the existing infrastructure is located, it will be necessary to permit migration to the cities even at the expense of further decline in the rural areas. In the minds of planners interviewed at the Institute for Population Research, "The government's present stance on population policy is too vague to be useful as a guide for planning."

---

[20]Much of the information in this section was given me by two geographers at the Federal Institute for Population Research in an interview on June 13, 1978. Several of the points made here are elaborated in Karl Schwarz, "Regional Differences in Natality and Consequences of the Decline of the Birth Rate for Problems of Regional Planning," Federal Institute for Population Research, *Materialien zur Bevölkerungswissenschaft*, no. 5, 1978, pp. 223–33.

Population decline and national power

A few lines from an article by the director of the research institute of the German Society for Foreign Affairs neatly capture the dilemmas which daily confront the Federal Republic as it emerges to take its place as a leading West European power. "In the European Community," writes Karl Kaiser,

> a renationalization of policy along the former Gaullist or present British line would unleash fears of German nationalism and be counterproductive for Bonn. But the opposite course, a pro-Community policy, immediately causes suspicions that West Germany wants to dominate the Community.

Turning to West Germany's relations with Eastern Europe, Kaiser states,

> On the one hand, a hawkish position in *Ostpolitik* is likely to threaten the achievements of détente with regard to West Berlin, East Germany and Eastern Europe; on the other hand, an active détente policy nurtures fears of a new Rapallo or reproaches of being too soft vis-à-vis the Soviet Union.[21]

It is difficult to determine to what extent, if at all, the reluctance of the Federal government to adopt a pronatalist policy is influenced by a perceived need for circumspection in the handling of a domestic matter with a potential for generating alarm in its neighbors to east or west. Nothing in the remarks of the small group of influential people who were interviewed in June 1978 suggested that the government might adopt a pronatalist policy out of fear of its neighbors. A spokesman for the CDU/CSU Fraktion (party) in the Bundestag remarked to me that "some people and politicians see the problem of recruiting enough soldiers when there is a declining population, but this is an aspect few people think of."[22] The contribution of the Ministry of Defense to Schoen's report, a bare half-page in length, merely noted that the base population of draftable age would be insufficient after about 1992 to provide, under present recruitment practices, for the needs of the armed forces.[23] Neverthe-

[21]Karl Kaiser, "Schmidt's Foreign Policy," *New York Times*, January 21, 1979, p. E21.

[22]Interview, June 14, 1978.

[23]The current contribution of the Federal Republic to NATO is 300,000 men. One respondent commented that after 1990, it may become necessary to

less, in a country on the boundary between East and West it would be surprising if some attention were not paid to empty territory along the border. Two respondents told me that special efforts to develop industrial centers on the eastern border had been unsuccessful in preventing more depopulation in that area than in any of the "remote and backward" agricultural regions on the western periphery, notwithstanding the poorer quality of the land in the west.

Immigration and cultural integrity

No less than in France and Sweden, policy-makers in West Germany see the questions of fertility decline and immigration as intimately linked. Like other Western European nations, the Federal Republic came to rely heavily on "guest workers" to meet the demand for labor during the 1960s and early 1970s. Though always rejecting the imputation that it had become a "country of immigration," the Federal Republic had a resident foreign population of over 4 million by 1974 when it closed its recruitment bureaus overseas. Five years later, in 1979, after dropping slightly between 1975 and 1978, the foreign population attained its highest level ever, 4.14 million, or 6.8 percent of the total population.[24] Positive migration balances were registered in both 1978 and 1979, and the rising trend accelerated in 1980.[25] However, the most important reason for the rise was an unprecedented increase in the number of applications for political asylum, a phenomenon the government is attempting to control. Under German law persons granted political asylum are automatically given work permits.

Although the economic contribution of Germany's "guest workers" is undisputed, and their higher fertility a welcome addition to the ailing birth rate, the people I interviewed were

---

restrict the alternative forms of national service from among which draftees are currently permitted to choose. "If so," he added, "this will cause a big social problem—one of many." The pacifism of German youth that has made international headlines throughout 1981 bears witness to the validity of this respondent's remarks.

[24]*SOPEMI, 1980* (Paris: OECD, 1980), p. 42.

[25]Ibid., p. 20.

unanimous that further large-scale immigration would be totally unacceptable as a solution to the problem of population decline. Several policy-makers cited as one of their main concerns the fact that "there cannot be a vacuum in the center of Europe; the spaces will fill up with people who are culturally very different from Germans." As in other countries, the reasons advanced for the rejection of further immigration were the difficulty and the great cost of integrating so many people of diverse origin and culture into German society. Racial tensions, especially those arising from competition over jobs in a period of high unemployment, were also mentioned. One official commented that the competition becomes more intense in the case of second-generation immigrants. Having been educated in German schools, the children of immigrants are more inclined, in his opinion, to compete for more socially desirable jobs than those that were acceptable to their fathers, and this is perceived as a threat to German youth.

Although the Federal Republic has attempted to close its borders to migrant labor from countries outside of the European Community, it is interesting to note that West Germany has recently concluded a number of agreements with Poland, Romania, the Soviet Union, and other Eastern European countries for the repatriation of ethnic Germans. According to a recent report, 70,000 ethnic Germans arrived in the Federal Republic in 1978.[26] There is no suggestion that these repatriations are intended to compensate for deficient natural increase; nevertheless, the report commented on the favorable age structure of the ethnic Germans from Eastern Europe, noting that "nearly a third of them were children and young people." By contrast, the report noted that most of the 12,000 who arrived from the Democratic Republic and East Berlin were elderly.

Population Policy Formulation in the Federal Republic

In recent years the Federal government has evinced signs of marked ambivalence in its attitude toward the birth rate and the

---

[26]*The Week in Germany*, January 5, 1979, p. 2. *The Week in Germany* is a weekly newsletter published by the German Information Center, New York.

need for a corrective population policy. In its reply to the UN Third Population Inquiry in 1976, for example, the government clearly stated its view that the birth rate was "too low." This view was repeated in the government's reply to the Fourth Inquiry in June 1978, and in addition the government stated that in its view, "the current rate of population growth both contributes to and constrains the achievement of various objectives; however, the constraints are more important."[27] At the start of 1978 a special section was established in the Ministry of the Interior, the ministry with "competence" for population, to bring together inter-ministerial views on the long-term consequences of low fertility and to assess the need for intervention to halt or reverse the trend. Although not an uncommon procedure in the case of issues which are highly politicized or which are deemed to be of special significance for the society, the creation of such a unit is not routine.[28] These signs of concern notwithstanding, in public statements the Federal government has consistently asserted that the situation, although suboptimal, is not serious; that reproductive behavior cannot be influenced by traditional pronatalist measures; that the quality of citizens is more important than the quantity; and that it is not the place of government to set numerical population targets or to interfere in the reproductive decisions of couples.[29] After discussing Schoen's report at the end of 1978, moreover, the Cabinet was still hesitant about taking corrective

[27]Response of the Federal Republic of Germany to the United Nations Fourth Population Inquiry Among Governments, document in the possession of the United Nations Population Division, New York.

[28]This information was given me by Schoen. For a discussion of the role of "sections" in the policy-making process, see Renate Mayntz and Fritz W. Sharpf, *Policy Making in the German Federal Bureaucracy* (Amsterdam-London-New York: Elsevier, 1975), pp. 67–76.

[29]See, for example, the replies of the Federal government to questions asked in the Bundestag by members of the CDU/CSU opposition, FRG, "Langfristige Bevölkerungsentwicklung" (Deutscher Bundestag, 8, Wahlperiode, Drucksache 8/680, June 24, 1977); and FRG, "Langfristige Sicherung des Generationenvertrages in der Alterssicherung im Zusammenhang mit der Geburtenentwicklung" (Deutscher Bundestag, 8. Wahlperiode, Drucksache 8/1982, June 10, 1978). See also the remarks of Katharine Focke, minister for youth, family, and health, during the debate on the Second Family Report, FRG, *Verhandlungen des Deutschen Bundestages, 7. Wahlperiode, 1972* (Stenographische Berichte, vol. 93, Bonn, 1977), pp. 12092–99.

measures. Instead, it set up two working groups to further investigate the demographic trend and to study ways to create a social
environment that is "friendly to children" (*kinderfreundlichen
Umwelt*).[30]

In West Germany, as in France and Sweden, the primary
determinants of population policy can be subsumed under the
rubrics of information, political ideology, coordination, and constraints. Specifically, the slowness of the Federal Government to
interest itself seriously in population issues, and its reluctance to
commit the country to a concerted effort to regulate the fertility
trend, can be traced primarily to four interrelated factors: (1)
the country's weak base in demographic and population research; (2) the political ideology of the government coalition,
which favors the individual over the family or the state; (3) the
decentralization of the policy-making and policy-implementing
structures; and (4) constitutional and budgetary constraints on
the government's ability to act. In the presence of these obstacles to the formulation of a pronatalist policy, the anticipated
consequences of continued low fertility outlined above have not
yet convinced government leaders of the need to restructure
their priorities.

*The information gap: demographic research
in the Federal Republic*

The slowly growing interest in demographic trends displayed by
the Federal government during the 1970s is largely attributable
to the efforts of a small group of social scientists within and
outside the federal bureaucracy. Toward the end of the 1960s,
members of the German Association for Population Science
started to alert the government to the need for thorough analysis
of the falling birth rate. At that time the nation's population
research capacity was severely limited, and there was little systematic research on the causes and dynamics of the fertility decline. An important reason for this gap in the nations's information is the disrepute into which the discipline of demography had
fallen as a consequence of National Socialist population policy.

[30]Information contained in a letter from Dr. Max Wingen, December 13,
1978.

For many years after the war, demographic research and population policy were identified with the Third Reich, and even mention of these topics prompted strong negative reactions. Demographic training was in eclipse; and as late as 1974, Hermann Schubnell could write that there were only two university professors of demography in the entire Federal Republic, and no university-based population research institutes existed.[31] Throughout the entire postwar period almost the only demographic analysis carried out in the Federal Republic was undertaken by the Federal Statistical Office, the West German equivalent of the U.S. Bureau of the Census, under the leadership of Schubnell.

In response to the pressures brought to bear by the Association for Population Science, the newly elected Social Democratic/Liberal coalition government undertook in the early 1970s to establish a population research institute within the Ministry of the Interior. The Federal Institute for Population Research, located within a few yards of the Federal Statistical Office at Wiesbaden, was opened in 1973 with a small research staff led by Schubnell. During its short life the institute has failed to grow satisfactorily, and its research capacity remains small.[32] Part of the reason for this failure to thrive may be lack of suitably qualified social scientists for senior positions at the institute. When Schubnell retired in 1976, the direction of the Institute fell to Dr. Hans Jürgens, who also retained his position as director of a new population research institute at the University of Kiel. Jürgens had to divide his time between the two positions, and as one respondent commented to me, "He spends most of his time on the train." In 1979 Dr. Karl Schwarz replaced Jürgens as director.

The lack of vigor shown by the Population Research Institute may also reflect a weak commitment on the part of Federal government leaders to population research or a failure to understand what such research would comprise. As one acute observer outside the country remarked to me, ministries of the interior in any country are likely to be unsuitable locations for

---

[31]Hermann Schubnell, "West Germany," in Berelson, *Population Policy in Developed Countries*, p. 702.

[32]This is Schwarz's view conveyed to me in an interview.

demographic research institutes. The multiple and pressing problems for which interior ministries are responsible militate against proper attention being paid to relatively invisible research units buried in their midst. Even under the most favorable circumstances, such a location is far from the centers of power in a government. Dr. Max Wingen, director of the Office of Family Affairs in the Ministry for Youth, Family, and Health, told me that the Association for Population Science had hoped to get an agency for research on population and the family established in the Ministry for Youth, Family, and Health. The Federal government rejected this proposal on the grounds that family-centered research is too complex for one institution to handle. The government felt that the ministry would do better to make use of academic research. At this stage the Ministry of the Interior made a successful bid for the proposed research institute, arguing that it made sense as the ministry already "owned" the Federal Statistical Office. The Ministry of Youth, Family, and Health did manage to get a small research unit for the family established within an existing organization at Munich. However, the work of this institute was concentrated on problems of socialization, an issue that is far from central for understanding the behavior of the birth rate.[33] It should be pointed out, perhaps, that a research institution within the Family Ministry would still be distant from the center of governmental power, although its research might be closely directed to issues underlying reproductive behavior. Moreover, as this volume has tried to make clear, the decline of fertility raises questions that go far beyond problems in the family.

In conjunction with the paucity of university-based population research referred to by Schubnell, the failure of the Population Research Institute to grow leaves the government without a solid foundation of empirical information on which to base a pronatalist policy.[34] To date there has been no large-scale na-

---

[33]Interview, June 14, 1978.

[34]The lack of university-based research may not be restricted to the field of population studies. Two West German students of policy-making in the Federal Republic draw attention to the overall shortage of "policy-oriented, large-scale and interdisciplinary research" emanating from universities. They remark that the social sciences in particular suffer from inadequate support in time and other resources. In their words, "With the exception of law and economics,

tional survey of attitudes and opinions about reproduction and the birth decline. There is little information on measures that women themselves think would encourage fertility. One member of the Population Research Institute told me that the institute is engaged in a small fertility survey carried out on a longitudinal basis. This psychologist explained, however, that both Jürgens and he attached little significance to survey data on attitudes to fertility since "reasons for childbearing are largely unconscious."[35] The institute was experimenting with questions which would tap motivations to fertility at a deeper level but which would also be suitable for use in large-scale surveys.

Political ideology: the family
and the individual

A second source of governmental inhibitions over the adoption of a pronatalist policy is the political ideology of the present Social Democratic/Liberal (SPD/FPD) government coalition as it relates to the individual and the family. An important objective of Social/Liberal policy is the creation of a better legal and social status for the traditionally weaker members of the family—women and children. The Basic Law (Constitution) of the Federal Republic accords equal status to men and women, and the various bodies of law pertaining to the family, labor, and education protect the rights of women and children comparably with law in other European countries.[36] In practice it is possible that realization of social equality may have lagged a little behind the achievements of other European nations. Vladimir Trebici shows, for example, that the proportion of West German women

---

most social science departments are quite small and most research is limited to the scale of one- or two-man projects, often favoring library research over empirical work." See Mayntz and Scharpf, p. 13.

[35] Interview, June 19, 1978.

[36] Aspects of West German law relating to the family, women, and children are set out in Hermann Schubnell and Sabine Rupp, "Law and Fertility in the Federal Republic of Germany," in Kirk et al., pp. 298–334. The first four chapters of this volume, which summarize conditions in most European countries, indicate that the legal status of women and children in West Germany is at least as good as in other countries.

in higher education in the early 1970s was smaller than in other Western European nations, and it is reasonable to assume that this may have adversely affected the status of women in employment.[37] As far as children are concerned, a government researcher told me that it is not only the inadequate numerical provision of day care centers, nurseries, and kindergartens that worries the government, but also the philosophy of education they embrace. In the Social Democrat/Liberal government's view a change is needed in the quality of these facilities in order to lessen the emphasis on academic achievement and increase the attention given to the social development of the child. The present government believes there is a need to provide more facilities for the enrichment of the lives of women and children outside the home. The government's intentions can be better understood by first considering both the concept of the family and governmental policy toward the family as they evolved during the life of the Federal Republic.

During the period of reconstruction after the war, exceptional significance was attached to the family—one of the few social institutions that remained intact—as a vehicle through which the legacy of Nazi indoctrination might be overcome and the pressures of daily life relieved.[38] The new government, formed by the broadly based, center-right Christian Democratic Union (CDU) together with the Christian Socialist Union (CSU) of Bavaria, saw its role vis-à-vis the family as one of minimal intervention. In the government's view the central task was to dismantle state controls over the family and to maintain a watch for forces that might threaten its integrity. Economic assistance was provided in the form of child allowances and tax exemptions aimed at equalizing the economic situation of families in the same socioeconomic bracket with and without children. A large housing program was developed to replace homes destroyed in

[37]See, "Law and the Social Status of Women," in Kirk et al., p. 104, table 5. Until the late 1970s economic activity rates for women under 25 years of age were higher in West Germany than in other highly industrialized Western nations, also indicating that there was less emphasis on higher education for women. See I.L.O., *Yearbook of Labor Statistics* (Geneva: I.L.O.), various years, table I.

[38]Friedhelm Neidhardt, "The Federal Republic of Germany," in Kamerman and Kahn, pp. 217–18.

the war and to accommodate the growing population of young families. There was no intention to use family support as a means of effecting a redistribution of income.

Efforts on behalf of the family were upgraded in 1957 by the creation of a Ministry for the Family, but even after this government policy remained narrowly defined; beyond the basic measures just mentioned the government intervened as little as possible. It was assumed that young children should be cared for by their mothers, and the provision of day care facilities and other social services for families was delegated to voluntary agencies, frequently religious organizations, supported by state subsidies.[39] One consequence of this policy is that the number of places in day care centers is inadequate for present-day needs, especially for children under three. Neidhardt cites a study published in 1975 which showed that 20 percent of women at home at that time would have preferred to work outside the home if they had been free to do so.[40] He also points out, however, that by the late 1970s there were sufficient day care places for about 70 percent of children between the ages of three and five. This is mainly because the low birth rate during the 1970s has reduced the number of children in the preschool years.

Family planning services, like other health and medical services, were also left in the hands of private providers. The spread of family planning clinics and the availability of contraceptives through private practitioners was handicapped, however, by a carry-over from the strict anticontraceptive laws of the Third Reich. Nazi restrictions on the distribution of contraceptives and contraceptive advice remained in force until well into the postwar period, though they gradually fell into disuse.[41] A more serious consequence of Nazi policy was that a whole generation of medical doctors had qualified without any training in family planning techniques or family planning counseling methods.[42] During twenty years of Nazi rule, moreover, many doctors had come to absorb the pronatalist values of the Na-

---

[39]Ibid., p. 219.
[40]Ibid., p. 233.
[41]Schubnell and Rupp, p. 307.
[42]Ibid., p. 308.

tional Socialist state.[43] In sum, as Schubnell and Rupp have commented, "Only the most recently qualified doctors today treat the whole matter completely without prejudice and accept family planning as a normal part of their professional practice."[44]

In contrast to the traditional, unitary concept of the family fostered by the policies of the CDU/CSU government throughout its twenty years of office, the Social/Liberal coalition tends rather to view the family in terms of its individual members. It is argued that the integrity of the family as a unit is sometimes obtained at the cost of the individual development of its weaker members—women and children. There is also an appreciation that some of these inequalities may also have clear public costs. For example, the fact that in the Federal Republic only one-third of all women trained as physicians actually practice their profession, primarily because of family responsibilities, is viewed as a waste of time and educational resources. Since taking office the Social/Liberal government has attempted a number of reforms aimed at raising the legal and social status of women and children. From the perspective of population policy, some of the most significant changes have been a modification of the divorce law to make it easier and less stigmatizing for couples to obtain a divorce; the allocation of state subsidies for primary family planning associations; and, in the face of strong CDU/CSU opposition, the liberalization of abortion.[45] In addi-

---

[43]Howard M. Leichter, *A Comparative Approach to Policy Analysis* (Cambridge: Cambridge University Press, 1979), p. 136.

[44]Schubnell and Rupp, p. 308.

[45]The day after a bill was passed that legalized abortion on demand during the first twelve weeks of pregnancy, 193 members of the Bundestag, together with the conservative governments of five Länder, sent the bill to the Constitutional Court which declared it unconstitutional. The court declared that it violated the "protection of life" clause of the Basic Law. Two years later, in May 1976, the Bundestag adopted legislation that legalized abortion during the first twelve weeks of pregnancy on judicial (rape) and social grounds. Any abortion is now legal on medical and eugenic grounds. See U.S. Library of Congress, Law Library, "The Abortion Decision of February 25, 1975 of the Federal Constitutional Court, Federal Republic of Germany," trans. and intro. by Edmund C. Jann (European Law Division, 75–5 LL, November 1975). The number of legal abortions has started to rise since the new legislation was introduced. A recent report states that there were 54,300 in 1977 and 73,500 in

tion, in order to effect a greater redistribution of income, tax exemptions for dependent children, a measure that favored higher-income families, were abolished a few years ago when family allowances were increased.

Most importantly, the Social/Liberal government has argued that social and economic developments in the Federal Republic since the war have resulted in the creation of a society that is hostile to children. In response to opposition accusations that the government's legislation has hastened the decline of the birth rate, the Federal government takes the position that the decrease in the number of births is a consequence of neither its family policy nor its support of contraception and abortion. Rather, the government takes a position similar to that of the Social Democrats in Sweden, arguing that the birth decline is a result of inadequate social and community support for families and their individual members. This position is based in part on the "Family Reports" prepared for the Ministry of Youth, Family, and Health by academic social scientists and other experts outside the ministry.[46] The reports have drawn attention to the small size and inconvenience of the apartments hurriedly built during the early postwar years, to the "sterile" suburban environment, with its lack of transport and cultural facilities, and to the pollution of residential areas by noise and traffic. Moreover, the reports have laid much of the blame for the problems of children and youth on the role conflict increasingly experienced by women and the tensions it creates within the

---

1978. See *The Week in Germany*, June 14, 1979, p. 6. The article notes that there may have been some underreporting in 1977.

[46]FRG, *Erster Familienbericht: Bericht über die Lage der Familien in der Bundesrepublik Deutschland* (Bonn: Bundesministerium für Jugend, Familie and Gesundheit, 1968); FRG, *Zweiter Familienbericht: Familie und Sozialisation-Leistungen und Leistungsgrenzen der Familie hinsichtlich des Erziehungs und Bildungsprozesses der jungen Generation* (Bonn-Bad Godesberg: Bundesministerium für Jugend, Familie und Gesundheit, 1975). The preparation of these independent reports every four years is a statutory requirement laid on the ministry by the Bundestag in 1968. A report was prepared in 1972 but was not submitted to parliament nor published. A third family report was debated in the Bundestag during 1979. See FRG, Sachverstandigen kommission der Bundesregierung, "Die Lage der Familien in der Bundesrepublik Deutschland," Dritter Familienbericht (Deutscher Bericht, Drucksache 8/3120, August 20, 1979).

family. The government contends that these and similar factors combine to create a societywide emotional and psychological climate unfavorable to children which will not be overcome through simple material incentives. What is called for, in the government's view, are radical changes that will produce a more "child-oriented society."[47]

During the past several years the CDU/CSU opposition has attempted to gain political mileage out of what it terms the government's "neglect" of the serious birth deficit. On a number of occasions the opposition has asked pointed questions in the Bundestag which have elicited defensive replies denying that the fertility decline is a result of governmental policy and outlining the steps taken by the government to stimulate research on the issues involved.[48] A member of the CDU/CSU's research staff in the Bundestag told me that the party had made the fertility question one of its first priorities in recent years. He indicated that the population question would be one of the main issues raised by the CDU/CSU in the federal elections of 1980.[49] Although the campaign discussions of population issues were largely ignored by the international press, the issue was indeed hotly debated throughout the entire period.

Beyond the specifically political aspects of the population debate lie deeply held value differences over the nature of the society that is emerging in the Federal Republic. Although the CDU/CSU party contains many "progressives" and is not a Catholic party *per se*, it nevertheless counts many older people, conservatives, and Catholics among its members and adherents. The party expresses the concern felt by these individuals over what they see as the weakening of the family encouraged, if not inspired, by the government's policies toward women and children. Explicitly, the party is anxious to see a repeal or considerable modification of the new laws on divorce and abortion.[50]

---

[47]What is comprehended in this rather vague term is illustrated in the new family policy being introduced in West Berlin in order to encourage an increase in population and fertility. This policy is discussed below.

[48]See the examples cited in Note 26.

[49]Interview, June 14, 1978.

[50]In practice the new divorce law, which sought to abolish the concept of "guilty party" and provided for the equal division of all property owned by the couple, including pension rights accrued during the duration of the marriage,

In addition, the CDU/CSU supports the provision of more material assistance to the family, including a maternal salary for mothers who elect to stay at home to care for children in the first three years of life. The party acknowledges privately that the fiscal base is weak and that there is little that can be done until the economic situation improves. But as a party spokesman summed up the situation in an interview,

> A policy to strengthen the family is complicated by the old Nazi legacy. Therefore, in recent years politicians have hesitated to do anything. Now the hesitations have gone, and we face the problems. Now it is a fiscal problem.

Within the area of population policy, the divorce and abortion issues were the primary focus of the election campaign mounted by the CDU/CSU in 1980. For the first time the Catholic Church came out openly in support of the CDU/CSU. A Pastoral Letter published by the leader of the Conference of German Bishops a few days before the election vehemently attacking the Social/Liberal coalition was tantamount to an instruction to the faithful to vote for the CDU/CSU.[51] The instruction was largely ignored, and the SPD/FPD alliance was once again returned to power, albeit somewhat weakened by a shift of the electorate toward the right.

Coordination of policy

Much more than in either France or Sweden, the structure of the policy-making institutions of the Federal Republic casts seri-

---

has been difficult to interpret. At least four rulings by the Constitutional Court in 1980 and 1981 have given a conservative interpretation to the law. These judgments imply a partial return to the principle of the "guilty party" and bear on questions of child custody, alimony, and division of property. See *The German Tribune*, August 9, 1981, p. 5 (article reprinted from *Die Zeit*, July 24, 1981). As far as abortion is concerned, it is not quite as easy to have a pregnancy terminated as the intent of the law would suggest. The conscience clause, which permits hospitals and clinics as well as individual physicians to refuse to perform terminations, makes it more difficult in some areas than others to find a facility willing to perform the operation.

[51]See *Der Speigel*, "Das ist geistliche Nötigung?" September 1980, p. 19. This article provides an interesting account of the role of the Church in the 1980 election.

ous doubts on the capacity of the Federal government to formulate and implement a comprehensive pronatalist policy. Like West Germany's weak base in population research, the highly decentralized policy-making system is ultimately a consequence of the Nazi era. But while the discipline of demography fell into disrepute from an emotional reaction to Nazi policy, the policy-making institutions of the Federal Republic were deliberately designed to prevent "an excessive or dangerous centralization of authority in the new German political system."[52] In the words of an official historian of the West German federal government structure, the system was "founded upon a clear-cut division of authority between the central and state governments." The writer continued that

> The essence of this system was that the powers of the Federal government were limited to those prescribed in the constitutive act, whereas member states—vis-à-vis the Federal government—were to enjoy all remaining governmental authority. Federal powers therefore are of a *delegated* nature, whereas the Länder possess all *reserved* authority.[53]

Despite some strengthening of the position of the Federal government vis-à-vis the Länder since 1949, there are three features of the policy-making system that pose problems for a broadly based pronatalist policy at the federal level. They are: (a) weak mechanisms for coordinating the development of policy among ministries; (b) the division of responsibility for policy formulation and implementation between the Federal and Land administrations; and (c) the veto power of the Bundesrat, or Federal Council. These three obstacles to the implementation of a federal pronatalist policy deserve some discussion.

a) *Coordination among ministries*: Although the Chancellor and Cabinet of the Federal Republic have broad formal powers to initiate and coordinate the formulation of federal policy, students of policy-making in the Federal Republic have commented on the *de facto* weakness of the Cabinet and Chancellor in exercising this function. Heidenheimer and Kommers, for example have stated:

[52]Elmer Plischke, with the assistance of H. J. Hille, *The West German Federal Government*, Office of the U.S. High Commissioner for Germany, Historical Division, 1952, p. 18.
[53]Ibid.

The ministries are the real power units within the federal bureaucracy, and views of their prime missions are shaped by their higher civil servants. Many ministers absorb their bureaucrats' views of their ministries' interests, and often function more as their ministries' ambassadors to the cabinet rather than as representatives of the cabinet to their ministries.[54]

The apparent weakness of the Cabinet and Chancellor to direct and shape policy would seem to be a real obstacle to the formulation of a coherent pronatalist policy. At the very least, a modern population policy requires the participation of the ministries responsible for the family, labor, education, health, social welfare, housing, budget, and finance, and it presupposes an effective high-level mechanism for coordination. Recent efforts to introduce centralized planning in the Federal Republic have met with failure, in large measure because of resentment among senior civil servants and some ministers at what is seen by them as a usurpation of their functions.[55] It would appear that a comprehensive and coordinated pronatalist policy is unlikely to emerge from the routine activities of the Federal bureaucracy; rather, it will call for the exceptional creation of a high level institutional structure capable of orchestrating the efforts of several ministries in this special area.

b) *Functions of Federal and Land governments*: A more fundamental obstruction to the introduction of a Federal pronatalist policy is the division of responsibility for policy formulation and policy implementation between the Federal and Land administrations. With the exception of the ministries of Foreign Affairs, Finance, Post and Telegraph, and Transport, which possess their own administrative structures, the Federal ministries tend to be small organizations specialized for policy formulation. For the implementation of their policies, these ministries rely on a variety of arrangements with the Land governments. In addition, some policy areas, including education and the police, fall entirely within the competence of the Länder for both policy development and implementation. Thus Heidenheimer and Kommers distinguish four

[54]Arnold J. Heidenheimer and Donald P. Kommers, *The Governments of Germany*, 4th. ed. (New York: Thomas Y. Crowell Company, 1975), p. 185.
[55]Mayntz and Scharpf, pp. 116–18.

different methods of administration: (1) execution of Federal laws by Federal administration; (2) execution of Land laws by Land administration; (3) execution of Federal laws by Land administrations as a matter of right, as is the case of labor law and social welfare; and (4) execution of Federal laws by Land administrations at the request of the Federal government, as in the case of administration of autobahns and waterways.[56]

The record shows that throughout most of the history of the Federal Republic, these complicated arrangements have worked more smoothly than might have been expected. Heidenheimer and Kommers observe, for example, that Länder officials have commonly followed Federal regulations even when this was not obligatory: that is, in the case of their own Land laws.[57] Nevertheless, on a highly politicized and divisive issue like population policy, respondents expressed reservations about the ability of the Federal government to ensure the implementation of its policy in Länder controlled by the political opposition.[58]

c) *The role of the Bundesrat*: The most critical point at which the present government is likely to have its legislative proposals blocked is in the second chamber of the Federal parliament. The Bundesrat, or Federal Council, is a unique institution in that its members are ministers of Land governments who are *appointed* by their governments and vote in accordance with governmental instructions. According to the Basic Law, each Land delegation must vote as a bloc, and voting in the Bundesrat therefore usually reflects the position of the majority party in each Land.[59] Because seats are allocated by an arrangement that takes some account of population, the Bundesrat has been controlled by the CDU/CSU coalition continually since the creation of the Federal Republic. In the Land elections of 1978, the CDU/CSU ob-

---

[56]Heidenheimer and Kommers, p. 216.

[57]Ibid., p. 218. See also Robert G. Neumann, *The Government of the German Federal Republic* (New York-London: Harper and Row, 1966), p. 114.

[58]This point was made particularly by Schoen and by V. Schmidt, director, Political Division, and director, Planning Division, Office of the Regierender Bürgermeister, West Berlin, Interview, June 16, 1978.

[59]Good brief discussions of the Bundesrat appear in Heidenheimer and Kommers, pp. 104–8; Neumann, pp. 118–22; and Mayntz and Scharpf, pp. 36–38.

tained a clear voting majority of 26 out of 41 seats.

The formal and actual powers of the Bundesrat to control the passage of legislation are considerable. The Council possesses *absolute* veto power on all legislation affecting the taxation, administration, and territorial interests of the Länder. This means that the consent of the Bundesrat must be obtained for all federal legislation that would be administered by the Länder. Experience has shown that about half of all legislative proposals fall in these categories. On all other legislation, if a conference committee fails to iron out differences between the two chambers, the Bundesrat has the right to exercise a *suspensive* veto that can only be overridden by an equal majority in the Bundestag. Mayntz and Scharpf have noted, however, that

> The limited categories of 'consent legislation' have been so expanded by interpretation and a series of constitutional amendments that in actual practice the Bundesrat possesses an effective veto over most domestic legislation.[60]

In addition, Heidenheimer and Kommers draw attention to the relative advantage enjoyed by the Bundesrat on matters that are dealt with in conference committee. Because the time of Bundesrat members is so valuable, their place is usually taken in conference committee by their alternates, high-level civil servants of Land governments. These officials have much greater experience and knowledge of the substantive issues in the legislation than do most of the Bundestag members with whom they are conferring and tend, therefore, to exercise more influence over the proceedings.[61]

Students of policy-making in the Federal Republic have observed that the Bundesrat has done much to improve the quality of federal legislation, using its veto power mainly in defense of Land interests and to improve the technical quality of bills. However, Mayntz and Scharpf have noted that since the Social/ Liberal coalition took office at the Federal level, the character of much of the work done by the Bundesrat, now controlled by the opposition parties, has changed. They cite several studies that indicate that the CDU/CSU majority in the Bundesrat has focused its opposition on the political substance of the legislative

[60]Mayntz and Scharpf, p. 36.
[61]Heidenheimer and Kommers, p. 250.

program passed by the Social/Liberal government in the Bundestag; moreover, they state that the resulting compromises are clearly determined by party political bargaining.[62] On this point also, officials interviewed for this study in 1978 doubted that the present federal government would be able to get its favored "population policy" measures through the Bundesrat. They pointed out that the only measures likely to succeed would be tax exemptions and family allowances, which fall entirely within the competence of the Federal government and which are also supported by the CDU/CSU opposition.

Constraints on governmental action:
the constitution and the budget

A reason advanced by the Federal government for its hesitation over the adoption of a pronatalist policy is that such a policy might constitute—or be seen to constitute—an infringement of civil liberties. Unlike the French Constitution of 1958, which merely reaffirms the "attachment" of the French people to the civil liberties set out in the preamble of the Constitution of 1946, Article 1 of the Basic Law of the Federal Republic stipulates that the basic rights elaborated in the main text of the Law "shall be binding as directly valid law on legislation, administration and judiciary."[63] As Mayntz and Scharpf observe, "the list of specific constitutional limitations on governmental authority is quite comprehensive and it is vigorously enforced . . . through an elaborate system of judicial review of legislative and administrative action."[64] Several respondents in West Germany called attention to the sensitivity of the German press to possible infringements of civil liberties. They commented on the necessity for extreme delicacy on the part of government in handling issues that might be interpreted as manipulative of the private decisions of individuals.

[62]Mayntz and Scharpf, p. 37.

[63]*Basic Law of the Federal Republic of Germany*, adopted at Bonn by the Parliamentary Council, September 1948–May 1949, agreed Anglo-American translation, n.p., article 1 (3). My attention was drawn to the greater emphasis on civil liberties in the West German as compared with the French Constitution by Neumann, p. 13.

[64]Mayntz and Scharpf, p. 15.

The Basic Law of the Federal Republic places marriage and the family under the special protection of the state. Soon after its election to office in 1969, however, the Social/Liberal coalition government formulated population policy guidelines that clearly placed the liberty of the individual over the need of the state for any particular size or kind of family. As elaborated by the minister of the interior in 1972, the government's policy on population is based on three principles that invoke both the Basic Law and the Declaration of Teheran.[65] The three principles state that:

1. The freedom of couples to decide on the number of children they want to have and the time they want to have them must be guaranteed;
2. The state has to guarantee to all its citizens the right to a life that maintains the dignity of man;
3. The protection of marriage and family does not oblige the state to aim at the family with many children as a population policy objective.[66]

In formulating these population policy principles, the government was in all likelihood responding in part to the environmental as well as the feminist lobby. Schubnell notes that a group of scientists in 1972 formed an association, called "Ecology," dedicated to study of the relationships between population and the environment.[67] Some of Ecology's members advocated a reduction in population size. Ironically, 1972 was the first year in

[65]The Declaration of Teheran, which emerged from the UN International Conference on Human Rights held at Teheran in May 1968, affirms that couples have a basic right not only to decide freely and responsibly the number and spacing of their children, but also to have adequate education and information on how to do it. See UN Resolution XVIII of the International Conference on Human Rights, Teheran, April-May 1968 (UN Doc. A/CONF.32/41), ch. 3.

[66]Schubnell, "West Germany," p. 703. See also, Schubnell and Rupp, "Law and Fertility in the Federal Republic," p. 301. Schubnell notes that the Minister of the Interior made a statement along the lines cited in a television broadcast soon after the Social/Liberal government took office in 1969. The relevant passages of the Basic Law read: Article 1 (1), "The dignity of man shall be inviolable. To respect and protect it shall be the duty of all state authority." Article 6 (1), "Marriage and family shall be under the special protection of the state." See, *Basic Law of the Federal Republic of Germany*.

[67]Schubnell, p. 699.

which the total population of the Federal Republic showed a decrease.

Budgetary constraints: In common with other industrialized nations, the Federal Republic has experienced financial problems in recent years as a consequence of slow economic growth. Like other governments, the Federal government has been faced with greatly increased costs for pensions and social and health services for the elderly. Simultaneously, the government has been under pressure to ease the heavy tax burden on citizens. In 1978 personal income tax in the Federal Republic ranged from a low of 22 percent of income to high of 56 percent.[68] Currently 18.5 percent of the income of each German worker goes to the pension fund and a further 12 percent toward health insurance, contributions being shared equally between employer and employee. In July 1978 the Federal government announced a two-year tax cut that was expected to reduce the tax burden by $3 billion annually during 1979 and 1980. In making this cut, it has been suggested that the government was responding both to domestic political pressure and to international demands that West Germany stimulate its economy in order to help the West recover from the recession.[69]

Under these circumstances the Federal government is especially unwilling to commit itself to costly financial incentives that it believes would have little influence on the birth rate—despite the overwhelming number of women who say that it is financial constraints in the family that deter them from having additional children.[70] As long ago as 1974, Schubnell wrote that a large increase in financial assistance to the family would require a

[68]OECD figures cited in an article in the *New York Times*, July 30, 1978, p. E3.

[69]Ibid.

[70]Unpublished figures from a national sample survey conducted by the Institute for Population Research show that women in the Federal Republic give the following reasons for not having another child (in %):

Financial constraints	53%
Inadequate housing	12%
Children are a burden	12%
Mother is working	4%
Problems with education	3%
Other	16%

major change in income distribution that would be politically unacceptable.[71] The government has pointed out, furthermore, that larger personal incomes are no guarantee that family size would increase. They note that the birth rate has continued to fall in France despite the very substantial financial help given the family in that country. However, in 1978 one respondent expressed the opinion that the government's insistence on the ineffectiveness of money benefits was an effort to buy time. He argued that the budget was already allocated and that increased taxation was, for the present, "out of the question."[72] Essentially the same point was made by the director of the Planning and Political Departments in the office of the Regierender Bürgermeister in West Berlin, who listed the priorities of the Federal government in the following order: (1) the economy; (2) social security; (3) internal security; (4) the price of housing; (5) the "pupil mountain" (high unemployment among school leavers); and (6) urban reconstruction and renewal.[73]

Despite the financial difficulties of the Federal government, rather large increases in family allowances came into effect on July 1, 1979. The changes raised the amount of the allowance for the second child by 20 DM a month, from 80 to 100 DM, and for the third child by 45 DM, from 150 to 195 DM per month. The allowance for the first child remained constant at 50 DM.[74] From January 1979 postmaternity leave was extended from eight weeks to six months. The first eight weeks of this term are taken on full pay, and a benefit of 750 DM a month is payable during the additional four months.[75]

Expected increases in the number of elderly dependents, together with the slower economic growth of recent years, has prompted a recognition that the social security system requires modification to bring it into line with future demands and re-

[71]Schubnell, p. 692.

[72]Information provided by an official in the Planning Department, Bavarian State Ministry of Labor and Social Affairs, Interview, June 21, 1978.

[73]Interview, June 16, 1978.

[74]*The Week in Germany*, November 21, 1978, p. 1. As of July 1, 1979, 100DM = $54 approximately; 195DM = $105.

[75]*The German Tribune* (Hamburg), October 15, 1978, p. 4 (reprinted from the *Kölner Stadt-Anzeiger*, September 29, 1978). In 1978, 750DM was approximately $400.

sources. It has become obvious that the economy can no longer support a social security system in which pensions are indexed to gross wages and virtually tax-free, and an overhaul of the system is scheduled for 1984. In the meantime, however, the worsening economic situation and large federal budgetary deficits in 1980 and 1981 have brought the issue to a head sooner than expected. The social security problem has been compounded by a large increase in the number of workers taking early retirement under a scheme that permits workers to take their pensions at any time after age 60 (instead of 65), provided they have been unemployed for 12 months. Thus, in the face of productivity declines, employers have been laying off workers as they turn 59, bringing about a depletion of both unemployment insurance and pension funds. By July 1981 some 800,000 persons aged between 59 and 65 were no longer employed, an increase of 27 percent from the previous years.[76]

In September 1981, after protracted debate that threatened the continued existence of the SPD/FPD coalition, the cabinet approved the budget proposals for 1982. Intended to reduce the size of the federal deficit, the proposals contained a mixture of increased taxes on consumer items and government spending cuts. To deal with the social security issues, it is proposed that the equivalent of 0.5 percent of wages be shifted from the pension funds to the unemployment insurance funds, where the need is even greater. From a demographic perspective the most significant item is a proposal to cut the family allowance budget by 1.5 billion DM, thus undermining its pronatalist potential.[77] No announcement has yet been made about how the cut will be effected, but it is likely that an income ceiling on eligibility for the allowances will be introduced.

On the basis of the interviews conducted in 1978, it appeared that the Federal government lacked convincing evidence that population decline constitutes a serious threat to economic growth. The government was also aware that expert opinion is doubtful of the lasting effect of traditional pronatalist incentives.

[76] *The German Tribune*, July 19, 1981, p. 4, (reprinted from the *Rheinische Post*, July 8, 1981).

[77] *The German Tribune*, August 16, 1981, p. 3, (reprinted from the *Rheinischer Merkur/Christ and Welt*, August 7, 1981). See also *Le Monde*, August 16–17, 1981, p. 1.

Under these circumstances the Federal government was reluctant to embark on a costly program of incentives to childbearing, the more so since such a program violates the ruling parties' ideological beliefs about the family and the individual and might be interpreted as an infringement of civil liberties. It is too soon to judge whether the major difficulties currently being experienced by the social security system will encourage the Social/Liberal government to attach more importance to stimulating the birth rate. Over and above the technical and ideological impediments to the introduction of a pronatalist policy by the present government, the decentralized structure of policy-making in the Federal Republic casts doubt on the capacity of any Federal government to coordinate the formulation and implementation of a comprehensive pronatalist policy for the nation as a whole. If stronger pronatalist measures are considered necessary, it seems more likely that there will be an extension of pronatalist policies within the Länder rather than one full-fledged Federal policy. To give some idea of the shape such policies might take in the future, the final section of this chapter will outline the measures recently introduced by the CSU government in Bavaria and the Social/Liberal coalition in West Berlin.

Population Policies in the Länder

In recent years pronatalist policies have been introduced in four of the six CDU- or CSU-controlled Länder—Saarland, Bavaria, Baden-Württemberg, and Rhineland-Palatinate—and in the city of West Berlin. Together these territories include a population of more than 26 million, some 35 percent of the total population of the Federal Republic.[78] The policies selected for study in these final pages are illustrative of the two fundamentally different orientations to pronatalist policy in West Germany. The policy of Bavaria, a large southern state with a high proportion

[78]The populations of these territories in 1979 were as follows:

Bavaria	10,849,000
Baden-Württemberg	9,160,000
Rhineland-Palatinate	3,632,000
Saarland	1,081,000
West Berlin	1,905,000

of Catholics and a history of thirty years of continuous conservative government, is typical of the traditional approach favored by the Christian Democrats and Christian Socialists in all four pronatalist Länder. The policy of West Berlin, by contrast, although in many ways unique because of the special status and location of the city and the special problems to which they give rise, is the only available example of a pronatalist policy introduced by a Social Democratic/Liberal government. In addition, West Berlin affords an illustration of the types of problems that will be increasingly experienced by the other large industrial cities as population decline gains momentum.

Bavaria

The movement for the adoption of a pronatalist policy in Bavaria was initiated in the early 1970s by the Planning Department of the State Ministry of Labor and Social Affairs. Studies undertaken by the department had shown that rapid changes were taking place in the population structure, and it was recognized that they would create difficulties for the state in the years ahead. Despite the presence of a large immigrant population with relatively high fertility, the number of children in Bavaria has declined by 40 percent since 1966.[79] Moreover, although Bavaria is also an area of in-migration for German nationals from the northern Länder, projections showed that the number of young women in the reproductive age bracket will decrease rapidly after 1990. From a high of 955,000 in 1988, the number of young women aged 20–30 will have fallen to 481,000 by 2020.[80] In the words of the director of the planning unit in the Bavarian State Ministry of Labor and Social Affairs, "if completed family size remains as it is, the fertility situation will be catastrophic, and it will be too late to do anything."[81]

---

[79]Information given me by the director, Planning Department, Bavarian State Ministry of Labor and Social Affairs.

[80]Bavarian State Ministry of Labor and Social Affairs, "Situationsanalyse und Projektionen der Bevölkerungsentwicklung," First Action Report of the Interministerial Working Group on Population Trends and Family Policy (Munich, n.d., mimeo), p. 7.

[81]Interview.

Despite the pronaltalist stance adopted by the CDU/CSU Fraktion in the Bundestag, this official said that it was not easy to convince Bavarian politicians of the need to act, and to act quickly, to stimulate the birth rate. Even greater opposition was encountered from civil servants in other ministries who saw their own new policies threatened by expensive incentives to fertility. The difficulties were overcome, however; an interministerial working group was formed to study the demographic trend and its implications for different sectors of the economy and society,[82] and funds were obtained for a study of the causes of the birth decline in Bavaria. The latter study, carried out by Professor Walter Toman at the University of Erlanger-Nürnberg, found that the principal reasons given by couples for having or desiring very small families were financial; families with children have lower standards of living than families in the same educational and occupational strata with no children or with fewer children. Also important were the high cost of housing for larger families, the desire of women to continue working after marriage, and the desire of couples to take regular vacations and to travel.[83]

The principal pronatalist measure employed in Bavaria is clearly modeled on the marriage loans of the 1930s. As of July 1978, low-interest loans of up to 5,000 DM are to be offered to young couples on the occasion of their marriage and at the birth of a first baby.[84] Repayment of each loan must be completed within seven years of the granting of the loan, with the proviso that a portion will be canceled at the birth of each child born within seven years of receiving the loan or loans. The table shows the scale of cancellations in effect.

[82]See, Bavarian State Ministry of Labor and Social Affairs, "Bisherige and Künftige Bevölkerungsentwicklung und ihre Auswirkungen in Sozialbereich" (Munich: Ministry of Labor and Social Affairs, Planungsgruppe 407/56/77, 1977).

[83]Walter Toman, Siglinde Hölzel, and Volker Koreny, "Factoren der Bevölkerungsentwicklung - Ursachen und Beweggrunde für den Kinderwunsch" (Munich: State Ministry of Labor and Social Affairs, 1977). Officials at the Federal Institute for Population Research were critical of this study. They felt the sample was too small to permit generalizations to be made. They also believe the survey method tapped only superficial motivations.

[84]Information given me by officials of the Bavarian State Ministry of Labor and Social Affairs.

At the birth of a first child	1,500 DM
For the second child	2,000 DM
Third and subsequent children	2,500 DM

The cost of this program will be considerable. In 1978, for six months only, the cost was expected to amount to approximately 10 million DM. It is anticipated that after about seven or eight years, the cost will have increased to between 120–130 million DM. Thereafter the number of marriages will decrease as smaller cohorts of young women will be reaching adulthood, and the cost of the program is expected to remain stationary.[85]

It is evident that this basic measure is intended to work in several ways. It is hoped that the loans will encourage young couples to marry earlier, delay less before having their first baby, and shorten the interval between children. These changes will extend the time available for childbearing, thus making a larger family more likely, but they may also increase overall fertility by shortening the length of a generation. Although these "family foundation credits" fall within the "frankly pronatalist" category of measures that the French government of Giscard d'Estaing was at pains to eliminate from its program, the Bavarian government is also discussing the possibility of introducing some more "modern" instrumentalities of population policy. They include the possibility of giving mothers of young children an opportunity to work shorter hours and to take extended post-maternity leave of up to two or three years. It is suggested that this leave should be compensated by a benefit of at least 300 DM a month and that the time should count toward the calculation of a pension.[86] Officials in Bavaria pointed out, however, that these measures fall within the competence of the Federal government and that they are too costly to be seriously entertained in the present economic situation.

West Berlin

In common with other cities in the Federal Republic, West Berlin experienced population decline throughout the 1970s. The

---

[85]It should be noted that since this is a loan program, much of the cost will be recovered.

[86]Approximately $160 in 1979.

decrease of the population of Berlin is more advanced and the outlook less hopeful than in other cities because of the exceptionally elderly age composition of the population. At one level the unusual age structure of the city may be seen as a consequence of earlier out-migration of young people; at a deeper level the out-migration may be viewed as a response to the isolation of the city in the heart of the Democratic Republic and the desire of young people to be nearer the centers of activity in the Federal Republic. The population of just under 2 million at the present time is expected to decline to 1.5 million by the end of the century.[87] Because there is a particularly severe shortage of young people in the city, population decline in West Berlin will outstrip that in other cities unless an effort is made to attract individuals and couples in the childbearing years into the city.

During the past decade or more, West Berlin has lost as many as 100,000 skilled jobs. Some of them have gone as a consequence of a program of industrial modernization and rationalization which, according to Dr. Schmidt, director of Planning in the Office of the Regierender Bürgermeister, has raised per capita output in the city to the highest level in West Germany. After the oil crisis of 1973, the loss of work was greatly accelerated; and West Berlin, in competition with the other great industrialized cities in West Germany, started to develop a program of economic assistance to attract industry and immigrants into the city. The objective is the creation of 100,000 new jobs which, it is hoped, will attract young people from other parts of the Federal Republic.[88] Because of the great political and symbolic importance of the city, the Federal government has taken the unusual step of assisting West Berlin in this program by contributing 50 percent of the budget.

In 1975 a Presidential Commission was appointed to draw up a comprehensive development plan for West Berlin. According

[87]Figures cited by V. Schmidt, Interview, June 16, 1978.

[88]It was Schmidt's opinion that greater interregional migration could reduce unemployment in the Federal Republic by 50 percent. However, unemployment benefits are so good and home ownership so widespread that polls show many workers prefer to ride out hard times in their own homes rather than take the risk of moving. See *The German Tribune*, October 15, 1978, p. 4: "Survey Shows Why Jobless are Staying on the Dole" (reprinted in translation from *Die Welt*, October 4, 1978).

to Schmidt there was some controversy among the members over population policy. While members of the government parties viewed economic stabilization—regional economic policy, labor market policy, and better conditions for the working population—as the main instrument of population policy, Christian Democrats on the commission insisted that there must also be financial incentives for the family. There was also dissensus over the population target for 1990. Christian Democrats do not wish to see the city's population remain below the two million mark, which is an important psychological threshold for West Berlin, but Social/Liberal members believe that the city's age structure makes inevitable some decline below this level. Nevertheless, the city's new family policy contains financial incentives to encourage fertility and adoption of children among residents and immigrants to West Berlin. Both policies together form part of a broad effort to halt the decline of the city's population.[89] However, Schmidt told me that only the economic policy is actually called a population policy; the other is known simply as "family policy."

On the economic front firms electing to relocate in West Berlin from the Federal Republic are given substantial assistance in getting established. The site for the new plant is donated free of charge by the local government, and in addition, 25 percent of the investment costs incurred by the firm are reimbursed. Should the investment made by the firm include research, an additional 10 percent of the cost is chargeable to the city. Over and above this assistance toward the cost of physical plant, firms can obtain a subsidy for each worker they employ. The city also pays a subsidy to each person employed in the city which amounts to 8 percent of salary. Employees in the private sector are given a further 25 DM per month on top of the 8 percent subsidy. Under discussion in the Commission in June 1978 were proposals to reduce air fares between Berlin and the Federal

---

[89]Details of the overall plan and the proposals of the Commission are set out in documents published by the Congress (parliament) of West Berlin and by the Regierender Bürgermeister. See, Abgeordnetenhaus von Berlin, 1 Enquete-Kommission, 7. Wahlperiode, *Schlussbericht*, Drucksache 7/1171 (Berlin: March 15, 1978); Der Regierender Bürgermeister von Berlin, *Bericht über Leitlinien für die Stadtenwicklung* (Berlin: Senatskanslei-Planungsleitstelle, n.d.) (circa 1978).

Republic and to introduce tax incentives to firms located in West Berlin. Both of these measures are considered important for businesses, but the latter is unconstitutional. Under the Basic Law all tax rates must be uniform throughout the Federal Republic.

Asked about the success of this program, Schmidt said that there were some signs of success but that he felt they were "more psychological than real." In his view the most significant change has been a marked rise in the morale of the business and industrial communities. There are a larger number of immigrants coming into the city, and the migration balance, though still negative, is improving. However, most of the newcomers are unemployed foreign immigrants who will ultimately add to the problems of integration already experienced by the city. At the present time nearly 10 percent of the population of West Berlin, and 25 percent of the city's schoolchildren, are of foreign origin.

Compared with the direct and highly specific approach used in the economic sphere, family policy in West Berlin follows the diffuse and generalized model favored by the Social/Liberal government in Bonn. Under the city's new proposals family policy is fully integrated into the overall development plan for West Berlin, which includes the rebuilding of some 60 percent of the city's dwellings and further upgrading of its already fine cultural facilities. Although there can be no doubt that the new family policy will greatly enhance the quality of life for young people and families in the long term, its direct effect on fertility appears likely to be low.

/One of the more significant new proposals falling under the rubric of family policy is the extension into a third phase of the city's plan for improving the school system. The proposed changes will take advantage of the smaller cohorts of schoolchildren to reduce the size of classes, improve curriculums, and reduce social class inequalities among the city's schools. Universities and technical colleges will also be improved in the hope of attracting students from other parts of the Federal Republic. Other projects intended to assist families with children include plans to increase cultural and sporting facilities and to allow children to use all the city's parks, museums, swimming pools, skating rinks, and other facilities free of charge. More "drop-in" neighborhood leisure-time centers for children and young people are to be built, as well as crèches, nurseries, and kindergartens for infants and preschool children. Educational counseling centers for young people, parents, battered wives, and other categories of adults are to be increased in number and upgraded in quality. There is even a plan to introduce a new type of social worker trained to coordinate the multiple services drawn on by families.

It is hoped that these ambitious plans for the city as a whole, and for the improvement of the environment, facilities, and services for families and the individuals in them, will help to hold young couples in West Berlin. In addition, the commission has proposed the introduction of a specific financial incentive to directly increase the number of children brought up in the city. Having undertaken an opinion poll which indicated that couples would be prepared to relocate in West Berlin if they were assured of a significant increase in income, the commissioners proposed that the city pay an additional allowance to couples who have or intend having two children and who agree to move into West Berlin. The allowance, 500 DM a month for the second child and 750 DM a month for the third and subsequent children, will also be awarded to couples resident in Berlin who adopt two or more children.[90] Benefits are payable for five years, and the scheme is expected to attract 4,500 new families each year. According to Schmidt, the commission was unable to agree on any further financial incentives for families.

Taken as a whole, West Berlin's population policy relies in the first instance on attracting migrants into the city in order to increase the base population of young people in the reproductive years. Since the major part of the plan will take many years to implement in full, any effect on individual fertility that ensues will probably not be felt before the medium and long terms. In the context of a declining population in the Federal Republic, the success of the scheme in the short term can only be at the expense of other cities that do not have the benefit of Federal assistance. The help given to West Berlin may thus be seen as a measure of the exceptional significance attributed to the survival and strength of the city by the Federal government.

[90]Approximately $270 and $400 a month at the exchange rate in effect in July 1978.

Conclusions

The Federal Republic of Germany has the lowest fertility in the world, so low that population experts within the country can see no prospect of achieving population stabilization at the present size. The case of the Federal Republic is of special interest as it underscores the qualitative difference in the impact of subreplacement fertility once a population starts to decline in absolute size. Although West Germany has the dubious distinction of being the first large country in the world to achieve this status, the Federal government has no real plans for attempting to halt the declining trend in fertility.

The reasons for German sang-froid in the face of population decline are complex and in large measure parallel those that have also deterred France and Sweden from making a deliberate and concerted attempt to stimulate the birth rate. The continuing economic recession, high unemployment, the refusal of citizens to pay more taxes, and a disinclination to interfere in private decision-making are only the most obvious of the similarities between the countries. In addition to these constraints, which are shared by France and Sweden, the emergence of a pronatalist policy in the Federal Republic is inhibited by special problems whose origins lie in the National Socialist experience.

By far the most concrete and durable impediment to the adoption of a federal pronatalist policy is the decentralization of the policy-making institutions of government. As competence in several substantive areas germane to pronatalist policy lies with the Länder, it is perhaps unreasonable to expect comprehensive and coherent policies intended to stimulate fertility to appear at the federal level. In the opinion of respondents interviewed in this study, the areas over which the Federal government has power both to formulate and implement legislation relevant to the birth rate are limited to fiscal policy, including child allowances. In other important areas like health, education, and labor market policy, authority either for implementation or for both formulation and implementation is vested in the Länder. The greater ability of the Länder to adopt broadly based policies in the population field is reinforced at the present time by the division along party lines of control over the Bundestag and the Bundesrat. So long as the CDU/CSU opposition maintains its majority in the Bundesrat and remains united in its determination to confront the SPD/FPD government on the population question, the Federal government is likely to have its legislative proposals blocked by the Federal Council. However, even if the Federal government is successful in securing the assent of the Bundesrat to its legislative proposals, their implementation by individual Länder is still problematic.

Constitutional protection of the right to individual freedom of choice in matters concerning the family, which is frequently invoked by the Federal government to explain its reluctance to deal with the fertility issue, is possibly a less fundamental and more psychological impediment to the introduction of pronatalist measures. It is noteworthy that constitutional objections have not been raised to the introduction of frankly pronatalist measures in the Länder with CDU/CSU governments. It is possible that the Federal government may be unduly sensitive to the likelihood of stirring up unpleasant memories of Nazi excesses among the people who would be the main targets of a pronatalist policy. While commenting on the extreme care needed to avoid awakening recollections of population policy under the Third Reich, respondents also observed that young people are no longer obsessed by the past. Young people were described as "practical," "pragmatic," and "concrete," and their thoughts and energies were said to be directed toward the future and the quality of their individual lives rather than to the failures of their parents. Because of the lack of research, however, little scientifically adequate information is available on a national scale about the opinions of young people relevant to population decline or their own fertility wishes and intentions.

Of greater significance for policy-making may be the inability of political elites in West Germany to formulate an ideological-theoretical position that as in Sweden, for example, would allow the government to present "pronatalist" measures as liberating rather than confining for women. With varying degrees of explicitness there seems to be an assumption among government leaders in the Federal Republic that pronatalist policy means sending women back to the kitchen as well as the cradle. As the example of Sweden shows, however, this assumption is no longer tenable. The emergence of an acceptable population policy that falls somewhere between the vague generalities of the Social/Liberal coalition and the more traditional pronatalism of the conservative parties may depend on the prior acceptance of a more rather than less liberal conception of the roles of men and women in modern society.

VII

POPULATION POLICY IN THE LIBERAL DEMOCRACIES: CONCLUSIONS

This study has attempted to provide an explanation for the differential response of governments to prolonged subreplacement fertility. I have argued that in formulating population policy, governments are seldom if ever responding to demographic trends *per se*. I suggested, rather, that the governmental attitudes toward population growth are shaped by considerations of national power, international influence, and economic well-being. I further hypothesized that the responses of governments to low fertility will ultimately depend on the role of the state in the society. In other words, the policy measures adopted are likely to be determined by the extent to which it is considered legitimate for the state to intervene in the reproductive decisions of couples for the benefit of the society as a whole. By itself this last hypothesis suggests that while there may be differences in detail and emphasis among the countries of Western Europe, there will be an underlying similarity of response, since all embrace a limited view of the legitimate role of the state. The real differences may lie between the liberal democracies and countries in which the state is expected to play a larger role in shaping the lives of individual citizens.

The cases of France, Sweden, and West Germany underscore the weak relationship between demographic trends and population policy. In these three countries at least, the relationship is the reverse of what would be anticipated if demographic trends were the determining factor in policy adoption. The study has shown that France, the country with the highest birth rates of the three and the largest growth potential in its age structure, has proceeded farthest in establishing a policy intended to reverse the trend. By contrast, West Germany, with a population already in decline, shows no sign of introducing a national pronatalist policy. Sweden, whose demographic status lies midway between the two, has attempted to remove financial obstacles to childbearing. A second point that bears reiteration is that none of the three countries is seriously contemplating a return to a positive rate of population growth.[1] In general the most that is hoped for, and considered desirable, is the achievement over the long term of zero population growth—a goal that envisages a rate of growth that would fluctuate somewhat around a mean level of zero. In Germany, as was noted in Chapter 6, population experts already discount the possibility of achieving stabilization at the present size of population. At best they envisage a slowing of the rate of decline prior to eventual stabilization at some lower but unknown level.

In the final chapter of his edited volume on population policy in twenty-four "developed" nations, Bernard Berelson concluded that the majority of these countries were already seeking to move in a mildly pronatalist direction.[2] Commenting on this assessment, Finkle and McIntosh observed that it seemed "difficult to substantiate on the basis of the formal policy pronouncements and governmental actions reported in the study." They suggested that the statement might nevertheless reflect the sentiment of a majority of political elites in developed countries.[3] The cases of France, Sweden, and West Germany which have been examined here permit us to elaborate on these remarks. It has been demonstrated that a good many of those in political elites and influential people in all three countries would feel more at ease if the fall in the birth rate could be halted. Yet in all these countries the evidence suggests that the 1980s are unlikely to see the adoption of strong, broadly based and coordinated policies intended to stimulate fertility.

In many ways the decades that passed between the pronatalist

---

[1]The goal adopted by the French Economic Planning Council, a fertility level "close to and preferably slightly above that required to ensure the replacement of generations," does not seem to differ significantly from zero.

[2]Berelson, *Population Policy in Developed Countries*, p. 773.

[3]Finkle and McIntosh, "Policy Responses to Population Stagnation," p. 275.

period of the 1930s and 1940s and the reemergence of concern over low fertility today mark a watershed in the attitudes of Western political elites toward population. Much less dominant is the earlier tendency of political elites to "view population questions from an 'Olympian' perspective which gives greater attention to the macro-effects of low fertility than to its micro-consequences."[4] In its place is a more pragmatic concern to safeguard the welfare of the individual and the family. In part the muted sense of nationalism is a consequence of the less threatening situation in which *individual* Western European nations find themselves in the 1970s compared with the earlier period. Whereas in the 1930s the countries of Western Europe were preparing for war among themselves, today it is the power and influence of the West as a whole—including the United States—that is challenged, and relative population growth rates within Europe have lost much of their significance. More fundamentally, as the calculus of national power has become more complex, taking into account the quality and morale of a people, their organizational ability, initiative, and enterprise, as well as the structure of their alliances, the role of population size is less direct and clear than in former times.[5]

In the 1980s there is uncertainty about the prospects for contin-ued economic growth in the context of a stable or declining population. Research on the complex relationships involved is not well advanced, but there is an awareness that population growth is only one factor in the equation. Until events prove otherwise, it is hoped that technological progress, improved hu-man productivity, and expanded world markets may offset the problems posed by smaller and aging work forces and reduced domestic demand. Moreover, many policy-makers today ques-tion whether the continued expansion of consumption at previ-ous rates is desirable in a world of finite resources. For all these reasons there is a tendency to regard the economic conse-

[4]Jason L. Finkle and Alison McIntosh, "Political Perceptions of Population Stabilization and Decline," *Policy Studies Journal* 6, 2 (Winter 1977), p. 157.

[5]Two attempts to identify the components of national power in this broader sense and to specify the relations among them are Cline, and Joseph J. Spengler, "Population and Potential Power," in *Studies in Economics and Economic History*, ed. Marcelle Kody (Durham, N.C.: Duke University Press, 1972), pp. 126–52.

quences of low fertility as matters for economic planning rather than indications for pronatalist policy.

Changes in the definition of national power and in the character of international tension have brought about a marked decrease in the importance attached to population size as the basis of national security. Instead there is heightened concern to preserve the cultural identity of the nation, a concern which has always been present but which was overshadowed in the 1930s by the more immediate anxiety over military power. Simultaneously, the possibility—if not yet the assurance—that means can be found to overcome the deleterious effect of declining population on economic growth has encouraged political elites to view the population-economy relationship from a more differentiated perspective. Although many of the policy-makers interviewed in France, Sweden, and West Germany clearly believed that the "health" of a nation is tied to its demographic vitality, there was a willingness to suspend judgment on this rather vague relationship and to focus on more specific consequences about which there is greater certainty. From this more microlevel perspective, the vital question in all three countries concerns the viability of the social security system.

In the minds of policy-makers and influential people in all three countries, the most immediate and pressing consideration today is the perceived effect of low fertility on the nations' ability to maintain social programs for the elderly and very elderly. In Sweden, Åberg and Nordin's study demonstrating the economic burden of the growing number of elderly seriously jolted elite complacency over the trend of domestic fertility. In both France and West Germany those who argue most forcefully for pronatalist policy do so on the grounds of the anticipated collapse of the social security system. While the likely effect of declining population on economic growth remains an open question, the disproportionate use by the elderly of increasingly costly medical care is well documented, as is the effect on pension funds of the ever-lengthening period of retirement. Thus the argument advanced by some experts that the financial burden of the elderly will be offset by reduced expenditures on the young do not appear to convince many. It is felt that so long as the number of retirees continues to grow more rapidly than the size of the active population, there will be a growing burden on the latter. Despite the problems that could follow from too rapid an increase in fertility, many policy-makers appear to feel that the effect of low fertility on social security systems justifies an attempt to stimulate the birth rate.

The cases of France, Sweden, and West Germany provide support, therefore, for the hypothesis that pronatalist sentiment in the liberal democracies is motivated in large measure by the need to prevent a deterioration in the economic well-being of individual citizens. It is worth noting that doubts about the ability of social security systems to sustain and extend existing programs under conditions of declining population growth spring from a new element in the relationship between population and the state. As late as the 1930s the effect of population growth on individual prosperity was largely indirect, mediated by improved job opportunities, higher wages, and generally rising standards of living. Although many of the pronatalist measures of the 1930s were also intended to alleviate the worst effects of the Depression, direct protection of living standards by the state was minimal and confined to special groups. Only since the development, largely after World War II, of elaborate, comprehensive, and universal systems of social security has the relationship between population growth and individual welfare been of such immediate concern to the state. As economic growth has declined in importance as a cause of pronatalist sentiment, the responsibility of the state for individual and family welfare looms larger as a justification for pronatalist measures.

Next to the anxiety displayed over the financing of social security, a desire to lessen dependence on immigration is the most salient concern underlying pronatalist sentiment in all three countries studied. Current efforts by the advanced industrialized nations to close their borders to foreign workers have been triggered by the prolonged economic recession and high unemployment, conditions that pose difficult political problems for governments. Beyond this the near universal rejection of labor immigration as a permanent solution to the problem of low population growth reflects a deeply rooted instinct in all three nations to preserve intact the cultural distinctiveness of the nation. In undefined ways it is believed that the cultural integrity of the nation forms the essential base on which is built its power and influence in the world. The determination of European countries to reduce their dependence on immigrant labor in the years to come stems from their expectation that future immigrants will be drawn predominantly from culturally as well as geographically remote parts of the world. Additionally, thinly populated rural areas are seen by many as an open invitation to immigrants whose impact on the receiving culture will be the greater as natural increase in the host population declines or becomes negative.

It is unlikely that immigration could ever be completely halted even if a total ban on immigration from outside the European Community—within which migration is free—were desired. But while current immigration policies often have a racist tinge, they may also serve another purpose. Restrictions on the inflow of aliens from culturally distinct lands may also be seen as efforts to slow down the rate of social, cultural, and political change, reducing it to a level that is tolerable.[6] In Sweden, at least, several scholars expressed the belief that the process of pluralization of an unusually homogeneous society will require time if serious and painful tensions and disruptions are to be avoided.

In sum, based on the cases of France, Sweden, and West Germany, Berelson's judgment about the mild pronatalism of developed nations seems an accurate summary of the situation. Among the persons interviewed for this study, pronatalist sentiment was particularly evident among government leaders and others with responsibility for directing the affairs of the country. The focus of concern has changed since the 1930s, not so much because national power and economic growth have assumed a lesser importance—although that may be the case—but because the evolution of technology and the growth of knowledge have cast a veil of uncertainty over the precise relationship of population growth to these national objectives. Instead, changes in the responsibility of the state for individual welfare and growing awareness that reliance on foreigners to solve one set of problems has brought with it problems of a different nature are

---

[6]As Polanyi notes, an important role of governments in the economic life of a nation consists in altering the rate of social change, speeding it up where appropriate or slowing it to prevent too great disruption. Polanyi's extended discussion treats especially the positive role played by the mercantilist policies of the Tudors and early Stuarts in retarding the process of enclosure, to the benefit of the common people. See Polanyi, pp. 35–39.

perceived as reasons for preferring a higher rate of natural increase. But while many political elites believe that higher fertility would be beneficial to the vitality of the nation, the welfare of its people, and its role in international affairs, the 1980s are unlikely to witness the introduction of comprehensive pronatalist policies in the liberal democracies of Western Europe. In order to understand this contradiction, it is necessary to appreciate the social context within which the decline of fertility has taken place.

The cause of low fertility has been the subject of recurrent discussion at least since the time of the Roman Empire. At various times the finger of blame has been pointed at the "love of luxury," "moral laxity," "selfish individualism," declining importance of the family, modern contraceptives, rising aspirations, increased costs of children, and many other factors. Although an understanding of the precise motivations to fertility would be enlightening, it is fallacious to assume that this knowledge would necessarily enable governments to act decisively to regulate the birth rate. Rather, it may be more helpful to look at low fertility today as a consequence of the convergence of a number of social revolutions, each of which exerts an antinatalist effect, and each of which undermines the inclination of a liberal democratic state to intervene. Most of these social trends had their origins in the early years of the century or before and were already starting to influence fertility during the 1930s. Since World War II, with gathering momentum, they have transformed society.

Important among these social revolutions has been the sharp increase in prosperity that has spread among all social classes since the war. Rising standards of living and the higher aspirations to which they have given rise, both for oneself and one's children, have exerted a strongly downward pressure on fertility. At all levels of society it no longer suffices merely to feed and clothe the children one brings into the world; social norms no less than personal inclination require that children receive an education to enable them to seize the social and economic opportunities that lie before them.[7] By itself the expense involved

---

[7]Since the early 1960s a considerable literature has grown up on the economics of fertility. Seminal studies include: Gary S. Becker, "An Economic

in equipping children for a fulfilling life would seem to place a declining emphasis on the size of the future family, even if other impediments to reproduction are overcome.

Even greater significance for fertility attaches to the urbanization of society, almost completed in developed countries, which has been accompanied by increasing nucleation of the family and an almost total separation of the functions of production and reproduction. In addition to the special problems of rearing children in urban societies—lack of space, higher costs—the burden of child care has been laid squarely on the nuclear family and especially the mother. This unrelieved burden on women is at odds with the concurrent movement for the political, social, and above all, economic emancipation of women. Claiming the right to self-fulfillment in areas outside the family, women today see no option but to demand the right of access to modern contraceptives and legal abortion, and to experiment with new patterns of family formation in order to free themselves from the burden of child care.

The movement for women's emancipation grows out of and has been accompanied by an egalitarian social and political ideology that has long distinguished Sweden and which has made significant inroads in the more traditional societies of France and West Germany since World War II. This movement toward equality embraces not only a reduction of the distinctions among social classes but also a push toward greater equality between men and women. Because of this new sexual ideology, governments in the liberal democracies no longer have available to them the "repressive" measures that were the hallmark of pronatalist policy in the 1930s and which are still available to

Analysis of Fertility," in Universities-National Bureau Committee for Economic Research (NBER), *Demographic and Economic Change in Developed Countries* (Princeton: Princeton University Press, 1960), pp. 209–31; Richard A. Easterlin, "Towards a Socio-Economic Theory of Fertility: A Survey of Recent Research on Economic Factors in American Fertility," in *Fertility and Family Planning: A World View*, ed. S. J. Behrman, Leslie Corsa, and Ronald Freedman (Ann Arbor: the University of Michigan Press, 1969), pp. 127–56. For an extensive bibliography on these issues, see Geoffrey Hawthorne, *The Sociology of Fertility* (London: Collier-MacMillan Ltd., 1970). For a recent comparative treatment of the Becker and Easterlin schools, see Warren G. Sanderson, "On Two Schools of the Economics of Fertility," *Population and Development Review* 2, 3–4 (September-December 1976), pp. 469–77.

governments in some Eastern European nations today. In Western Europe almost all governments now support family planning services, and in many, contraceptives are a charge on national health insurance. With the exception of a few predominantly Catholic countries,[8] all Western European governments have enacted legislation that permits abortion under a wide variety of social as well as medical indications; in many abortion is freely available on demand in the early weeks of pregnancy. Notwithstanding the reemergence of pronatalist sentiment among governments, it seems quite certain that in the liberal democracies the right of access to modern contraceptives is here to stay. Moreover, although some European governments are still in the process of determining the form of their abortion legislation, the trend is toward liberalization.[9] Secure in the knowledge that public opinion was behind it, the French government, for example, successfully steered its liberal abortion law through the National Assembly, despite the fact that most members of the parties that make up the majority coalition were opposed. It seems very unlikely that the opposition parties in West Germany could

[8]Spain, Portugal, and Ireland. Greece has very recently started to slightly liberalize its abortion legislation. The Netherlands has extremely restrictive legislation which is disregarded by the Justice Department as it is acknowledged to be outdated. In practice abortion is available virtually without restriction. Like Britain, the Netherlands in recent years has provided abortion services to women from many countries with restrictive laws.

[9]In 1979 Finland reduced the period of eligibility for abortion from 16 to 12 weeks, ostensibly to bring the law into line with those of other European countries. Abortion up to the sixteenth week of pregnancy is still permitted in the case of unmarried teenagers. See *Le Monde*, April 26, 1979, p. 6. Also in 1979 the Swedish parliament announced plans to review Sweden's liberal abortion legislation. There was concern over the rapid increase in the number of abortions, which is attributed in part to anxiety among Swedish women about the safety of the pill and the IUD. Announcing plans for the review, the minister of health said, "There can be no question of going back on the principles the legislation." *Le Monde*, December 1, 1979, p. 9. In the United Kingdom efforts to amend the law by reducing the duration of pregnancy within which abortion may be legally obtained, currently 28 weeks, have three times failed: in 1974, 1976, and 1979. See Maurice Kirk, ed., *Demographic and Social Change in Europe, 1975–2000* (Liverpool: University of Liverpool Press, 1981), p. 160.

force a restrictive amendment of the abortion law, although this is their stated intent.[10]

The changes in policy toward contraception and abortion are only the most obvious aspects of a broader change in what is regarded as the legitimate role of the state with regard to reproductive behavior. In the three countries in the study, the change appears to have been most profound in France, where the statism of former years has sharply declined. Respondent after respondent in France said that the greatest single obstacle to the development of a comprehensive pronatalist policy is that people do not want it. Since 1945 France has set up an elaborate and efficient machinery to monitor public opinion on matters of reproduction and, at least since the mid–1960s, has made serious efforts to respond to the preferences of the electorate, irrespective of party political differences. In West Germany, also, there has been a sharp retreat from statism, and the present government constantly invokes the provisions of the Basic Law to support its individualistic and antiinterventionist position on population growth. Only in Sweden was there no suggestion that an attempt to regulate fertility might exceed the limits of acceptable intervention in an area of private decision-making. It appears that the Swedish people are tolerant of mildly coercive moves by the state to shape the society in ways on which there is a broad consensus

Even if there were greater willingness to intervene in the private decision-making of couples, there remain practical obstacles to designing suitable and potentially effective measures to stimulate fertility. Feminist fears that pronatalist policies will send women back to the kitchen are surely unfounded, as modern economies rely greatly on the productive contribution of women. Even more, women's contributions are an essential element in the funding of social security. In all three countries, moreover, respondents observed that young women today are far too sophisticated to undertake the responsibility and burden of additional children for the sake of marginal financial incentives. Responsible officials in France called attention to the vast

---

[10]Land officials in Bavaria, which has an opposition (CSU) government, stated that there had never been any intention to attempt to restrict abortion as part of Bavaria's new pronatalist policy.

changes that have occurred in the socioeconomic status of the population since the 1930s. At that time there was widespread and genuine poverty that could be significantly relieved by comparatively small social transfers. There was also a large rural population with different family norms and aspirations from those of city people who could be expected to have large families if work could be found to keep them in the rural areas. Today serious poverty has all but disappeared. The cost of financial incentives large enough to make a real difference is far beyond what people would be willing to pay in additional taxation. Moreover, the rural population has decreased sharply, and those who remain on the land have adopted city norms. There is no longer a willingness, for example, to divide the family farm among several sons; additional children move to the city to find work. In France, Jacques Doublet observed that the ease with which the governments of Eastern European countries introduced vigorous pronatalist policies in the 1960s and 1970s can be explained in part by the fact that the stage of economic development reached by Eastern Europe more nearly approximates the level of Western Europe in the 1930s than the conditions that obtain in the West today. Thus there are still many things that can be done in Eastern Europe at a reasonable cost.

In sum, the muted sense of nationalism and the hope that a satisfactory level of economic growth will be obtainable even with a stable or declining rate of population growth have prevented the emergence of a sense of urgency over the need to stimulate the birth rate. Despite the warnings of demographers about the lead time needed to overcome the effects of demographic inertia, national leaders see little political advantage in campaigning for pronatalist policy at a time of high unemployment and fiscal constraint. The disinclination to act decisively is reinforced by uncertainty over the means that might be used to stimulate fertility. Deprived of, or lacking confidence in, the effectiveness of "traditional" pronatalist measures, governments in Western Europe are likely to move incrementally, as opportunity offers and economic conditions permit, to relieve the most obvious hardships experienced by families. A more enduring solution to low fertility in these rich, technologically sophisticated nations with their highly educated populations may lie in measures that will bring the organization of society into closer accord with the needs and aspiration of young couples. Some intimation of future possibilities can be seen in the efforts of the Swedish government—and to a lesser extent the government of France—to provide more leisure for young parents of both sexes in order to ease the strain between the productive and reproductive aspects of their lives. Even in Sweden, however, a lengthy educational effort will be needed to foster acceptance of these egalitarian policies by more conservative members of society, whether bourgeois or working-class.

In broad outline the responses of France, Sweden, and West Germany—and by extension of liberal democracies in North America, Australia, and elsewhere in Europe—are very similar. In all three countries earlier emphasis on the macroconsequences of low fertility has given way to a concern for economic effects at a more microlevel. Most significantly, the inclination and moral capacity of Western governments to intervene decisively in the area of reproductive decision-making has been much reduced, despite an uneasy feeling that a higher level of fertility is desirable. Notwithstanding the overall similarity among the three countries in the main lines of the response, there are variations among them that are likely to influence their actions in the coming years. In large measure these differences can be understood by reference to the explanatory variables identified in Chapter 2.

Historical experience

The most immediately striking characteristic of the attitudes and institutions of France and West Germany is the degree to which they are still shaped by both nations' historical experiences with population. French anxiety about the consequences of low fertility and French family policy, still the most fully developed in Western Europe, are clearly a continuing reaction to France's long history of low population growth and the military defeats of 1870 and 1940. In West Germany the inhibition exhibited by the present government, amounting to a psychological incapacity to deal with the population issue, is directly attributable to the Nazi legacy. As might be expected, there are signs in both countries that these traumatic events have much less power to shape the opinions of young persons who did not experience them at first hand. It is likely, therefore, that French pronatalism will decline further in future years and that German reluctance to deal with the issue will dissipate somewhat. Over and above the effect on attitudes toward low population growth, both countries carry with them more tangible signs of their demographic/ historical experience. INED, the superb research institution set up by the French in 1945, remains an important and positive force in the nation's policy-making capacity in the field of population. By contrast, the decentralization of West Germany's institutions of policy-making, a deliberate response to National Socialist authoritarianism, constitutes a serious obstacle to the formulation and implementation of a coherent federal population policy.

Political ideology

Within Western Europe political ideology is probable the best single predictor of attitudes toward fertility and pronatalist policy.[11] Since the middle of the nineteenth century, liberal and socialist opinion on population issues has differed sharply from that of political conservatives. While conservatives have tended to attach priority to the family and the nation as the primary objects of devotion, liberals and socialists have committed themselves to the furtherance of individual development and equality, including sexual equality. As this study has shown, these ideological orientations translate into vastly different perceptions of the relationship between population and society. His-

---

[11]This statement cannot be generalized to attitudes toward antinatalist policy outside of Europe. There is considerable evidence in Latin America, for example, of interaction between Marxism and Catholicism in attitudes toward antinatalist policy. Individuals who adhere strongly to either ideology tend to oppose antinatalist policy, though for different reasons. Some support for antinatalist measures tends to be forthcoming from moderates of both right and left. See, for example, J. Mayone Stycos, *Ideology, Faith and Family Planning in Latin America* (New York: McGraw-Hill, 1974); Axel Mundigo, "Factors Affecting the Population Attitudes of Latin American Elites," in Terry McCoy, ed., *The Dynamics of Population Policy in Latin America* (Cambridge, Mass.: Ballinger, 1974), pp. 37–57; and Peter McDonough and Amaury DeSouza, "Brazilian Elites and Population Policy," *Population and Development Review* 3, 4 (December 1977), pp. 377–401.

torically, as today, conservatives and nationalists have tended to view changes in population trends in terms of their consequences for the state and nation; following Marx, individuals who subscribe to socialist ideology regard population trends as dependent on conditions existing in the society. In designing pronatalist policy, parties and individuals of the right tend to express a preference for measures that promise to preserve intact the existing structure of the family, which is held to be the essential basis for the health and vitality of the nation and of Western civilization. Liberals and socialists, by contrast, characteristically opt for measures that will further the independence and equality of individuals, even if this means a disruption of traditional family relations.

In both France and Sweden members of the Communist Party most commonly ally themselves with the parties of the left when it comes to the vote.[12] Sharing the egalitarian and individualistic ideology of the socialists on women's issues, Western European communists tend to differ from socialists mainly in favoring greater financial assistance to the family. Nevertheless, communists in Western Europe clearly attach greater importance to the emancipation of women than to the size of the family. They tend to push for the provision of day care centers for children and vote against such measures as shorter working hours for mothers. There is thus a disjunction between the vigorous pronatalism of the communist governments of Eastern Europe, whose policies in recent years have registered some success in raising birth rates,[13] and the much less natalistic stance of communists in Western Europe.

An explanation for this difference can be found in the tension that exists between ideological principles and the hard facts of the real world. Like Western European socialism, Marxism contains a strong ideological commitment to the emancipation of women. Evidence of this commitment was the legalization of abortion in the Soviet Union as early as 1920.[14] As a result of

---

[12]The Communist Party in West Germany does not receive sufficient support to obtain a seat in the Bundestag.

[13]For a recent analysis of the impact of these policies, see Pressat, "Mesures nataliste."

[14]It should be pointed out that the rise of the birth control movement in Europe posed an ideological problem for many socialists who rejected the

this early liberalization, abortion became the principal means of controlling fertility throughout the Eastern European socialist world. Even today modern contraceptives are virtually unobtainable in many Eastern European countries, although they are not illegal. However, access to birth control services in socialist countries has tended always to take second place to the need of the state for labor. Abortion was banned in the Soviet Union in 1936, partly for medical reasons but also, it is thought, to ensure a rise in the birth rate. In the opinion of Frank Lorimer, who examined the issue in the 1950s, an important reason for the ban on abortion was the census of 1926, which showed the enormous loss of population that had occurred during the process of collectivization.[15] When the results of the census appeared, the nation's population research institutions were closed; and for at least twenty years, according to Lorimer, further census returns were kept secret. Even government officials responsible for planning were kept in ignorance of population trends. At the same time, a program of financial and symbolic incentives to fertility was introduced. Not until 1955 was abortion again legalized, an example that was immediately followed in most of the other socialist states. The rapid decline of fertility that ensued following the reintroduction of legal abortion prompted the adoption of comprehensive pronatalist policies in the socialist countries outside the Soviet Union.

Eastern European governments have made no attempt to hide the fact that their pronatalist policies are intended to ensure the continuing existence of an "adequately" growing work force.[16] In addition to the Marxian theoretical-ideological bias in

---

movement's bourgeois origins and Malthusian overtones. Not until Lenin separated the issue of birth control as an individual right from the question of population growth and the laws that govern it did socialism find a way to accept birth control for women. See, for example, William Petersen's discussion in *The Politics of Population* (Garden City: Doubleday, 1964), pp. 90–102. For an extended discussion of sexual equality, the family, and population in the Soviet Union, see Gail W. Lapidus, *Women in Soviet Society* (Berkeley: University of California Press, 1978).

[15]Frank Lorimer, "Population Policies and Politics in the Communist World," in *Population and World Politics*, Philip M. Hauser, ed. (Glencoe: The Free Press, 1958), pp. 214–36.

[16]See, for example, Berent, "Causes of Fertility Decline," p. 287; Heitlinger, p. 123. Heer cites one demographer from the Soviet Union who as late

favor of a growing population, the governments of Eastern
Europe face difficulties from the declining rate of growth of the
labor force that are not shared by their colleagues in the West.
Output per worker in Eastern Europe is lower than in the West,
the age of retirement is lower, and socialist countries cannot rely
on a large immigrant work force as Western nations have done
in the past. Furthermore, since nearly all women in socialist
societies are already in the work force, there are fewer untapped
reserves of labor. The case of East Germany is of special interest in this regard. Since the separation of East and West Germany, birth rates in both countries have remained at very much
the same level. There was, however, a drastic fall in East German fertility immediately after abortion became available on
demand in 1972. In an effort to recoup the loss, the government
introduced incentives to fertility, including, in 1977, the opportunity to take postmaternity leave of up to one year. Presumably
in response to these measures, there has been a significant rise
in the birth rate. Very recently, in a move to ameliorate the
labor shortage, the government has announced the introduction
of other measures, this time to encourage new mothers to go
back to work. Crèches are to be established that will take infants
from the age of ten weeks, and additional financial bonuses are
to be given. It is said that 81 percent of East German women are
in the labor force, a far higher proportion than in any Western
European country.[17]

Differences among the three countries of the study illustrate
the tension that also exists in Western Europe between ideology
and information. In France the availability of abundant, high-
quality demographic analysis has enabled the government to
keep abreast of changes in demographic trends and, at least,
their demographic implications. Evidence was presented in
Chapter 4 that showed how promptly the government reacted to
the downturn in fertility after 1964, even if political events prevented a policy response at that time. Of equal or greater importance, the regular soundings of public opinion relevant to fertil-

as 1968 advocated a pronatalist policy on grounds of national power. Speculat-
ing that this was prompted by a fear of China, Heer notes that he has been
unable to find any specific allusions to this issue. See "Recent Developments
in Soviet Population Policy," p. 259.

[17]*The Guardian*, August 7, 1979.

ity and reproduction have enabled the government to respond rapidly and with flexibility to the preferences of the people—most notably over the abortion issue but also in other areas.

By contrast, much of the delay in responding to the decline of fertility in Sweden and West Germany can be attributed to the more ideological positions of their governments on the population question. In both countries an ideologically based commitment to equality and the welfare of the individual has been reinforced by a lack of demographic analysis and less systematic effort to sample public opinion. In Sweden the lack of relevant information is itself partly a consequence of the ideological position of the Social Democratic government on domestic vis-à-vis international population growth and its neglect of demographic research and training. At present efforts are being made to overcome this handicap. In West Germany the inflexibility of the Federal government's response to low population growth is in large measure attributable to the nation's poorly developed research base in population—a consequence of the government's urgent desire not to appear interventionist.

The advantage conferred by the availability of information can also be illustrated by reference to the countries of Eastern Europe. For two reasons it seems no accident that it was the socialist states outside the Soviet Union that responded most rapidly and decisively to the fertility decline that followed the legalization of abortion in 1955. For one thing, the ideological commitment to orthodox Marxism is less absolute in these countries. For another, several of the Eastern European countries, notably Hungary, have well-developed population research institutions that have been used to good effect to monitor fertility trends and to assist in the design of flexible legislation that is responsive to change.[18] As a result, political leaders appear to have readily accepted the arguments of demographers that demographic trends are conditioned by factors other than the relations of production—whether socialist or capitalist—and that they are, therefore, susceptible to regulation by demographic policies.[19] By contrast, a stronger adherence to orthodox inter-

[18]For a discussion of these policies and their flexibility, see McIntyre, "Pronatalist Programs in Eastern Europe."

[19]For examples of non-Soviet, socialist demographic thinking on the relationship between demographic trends and the Marxist "law of population." see

pretations of Marxian population theory in the Soviet Union, and the secrecy that for many years surrounded demographic issues, may largely explain the slower acceptance by political leaders that demographic trends are in large measure "autonomous" and therefore regulable.[20]

Information

On the basis of the earlier discussion of the social revolutions that have accompanied and "caused" the decline of fertility, it may be hypothesized that basic research information on the determinants of fertility may not be so essential to governments as is often assumed by those responsible for formulating policy. As social conditions change, not only do different environmental factors come to play a role in shaping the reproductive decisions of individuals, they also produce shifts in the objectives and priorities of governments. Thus in times of rapid social change, it seems likely that research findings may lag behind the motivations of both individuals and governments. It can be argued, furthermore, that basic research may best be viewed as a cooperative and cumulative endeavor engaged in by the intellectual community on a worldwide basis. My research suggests that the needs of democratic governments in the population field are much better served by the availability of reliable and up-to-date information on demographic trends, their implications for the economy and society, and public opinion about possible policy interventions. While France has excellent information on both demographic trends and public opinion about them, all advanced countries need to support much more research on the economic and social implications of declining population.

---

the statement by Srb, and György Acsádi's discussion, "Recent Problems in Population Policies in the European Region of Socialist Countries," in *Proceedings of the IUSSP Population Conference, London, 1969*, vol. 2 (Liège: IUSSP, 1969), pp. 1381–93.

[20]The paper by Weber and Goodman and the statement by Ryabushkin both suggest that a more pragmatic view of population dynamics is now becoming officially more acceptable in the Soviet Union. See also the discussion of this issue in Besemeres, pp. 95–103.

Another important aspect of the population information available to governments is the nature of the relationship between research institutions and the policy-making institutions of government. In Chapter 5, for example, it was seen that Sweden did not entirely lack population research of relevance to policy formulation; however, the information was scattered among a number of independent university research departments and did not systematically reach the policy-making system. It is noteworthy that once some significant research findings did attract the notice of political elites, there was an immediate reaction that set in motion a train of investigations and inquiries. By contrast, in France the very close ties between INED and the coordinating agency for population policy, wherever it happens to be located, provides an effective mechanism for the rapid transfer of research information to those responsible for policy formulation.

At first glance the cases of France and Sweden suggest that government-based population research centers may be more effective than are independent agencies in providing necessary inputs to policy formulation. It seems obvious that the transmission of information will be easier among government departments than between governmental and nongovernmental agencies. The case of West Germany casts doubt on this assumption, however. The Federal Institute for Population Research is a government agency located within the ministry responsible for population; yet since its creation in 1974, it has remained small and has not played a significant role in population policy formulation. In part this lack of effectiveness can be attributed to the organizational distance between the agency and the centers of governmental power; in part it may be a function of the government's *a priori* distaste for a pronatalist policy. It is not possible on the basis of three cases to fully assess the relative effectiveness of governmental versus nongovernmental research institutions in alerting political elites to demographic trends that may pose problems for the society. Nevertheless, the data from both Eastern and Western Europe suggest that where the inclination to develop a policy exists, the availability of high-quality governmental research is likely to facilitate the process of policy formulation.

Centralized decision-making and
interministerial coordination

My last point touches on the difficult question of coordinating policy initiatives in different parts of government. It seems highly probable that the decisive response of Eastern European governments to declining fertility was facilitated by their use of centralized planning which, of necessity, takes account of demographic trends. None of the three countries in this study makes use of centralized planning to the extent found in Eastern Europe. Yet it is significant that recent moves toward the development of a pronatalist policy in France were heralded by the adoption by the Economic Planning Council of something in the nature of a population growth target. Likewise, it is noteworthy that government officials in West Germany felt that the decentralized structure of government in that country, and the division of responsibility between the Federal and Land governments, would prevent the development of a pronatalist policy at the federal level.

The coordination of broadly based policy always presents problems for governments, even those in Eastern Europe. While all governments can create formal structures to encourage cooperation and some centralization of decision-making, the multiple and pressing responsibilities of government leaders frequently preclude sustained and serious attention to a single issue. In addition, there is a natural tendency among government leaders to preserve and extend the scope of their autonomy rather than relinquish claim to areas of competence. Of the three countries in this study, therefore, Sweden shows the most promise of a capacity to coordinate policy initiatives to encourage fertility. The small size of the government bureaucracy, the extended practice of informal interaction among political leaders and senior civil servants, and the functions of government commissions all provide opportunities for cooperation. In the last analysis, however, the ability of a government to coordinate its policies depends on the conviction of its members that the issue is serious and that intervention is essential to the well-being of the nation. As this study has attempted to demonstrate, this sense of urgency over population decline is still far from acute in the liberal democracies of Western Europe.

APPENDIX A

A NOTE ON DEMOGRAPHIC TERMS AND MEASURES

The purpose of the present note is to specify the meaning of the terms "low fertility," "low population growth," and "replacement level fertility" which are used throughout this study to characterize the demographic situation confronting advanced industrialized nations today. Only the last of these terms has a precise demographic meaning, the other two being used loosely to denote either a level of fertility that approximates the level required to assure replacement of the population or a rate of natural increase just a little above zero. "Replacement level fertility," on the other hand, denotes a level of fertility at which the rate of population growth—disregarding migration—is or will gradually become zero.[1]

The notion of replacement is central to an understanding of the demographic predicament of industrialized nations at the present time. Replacement is a complex concept most easily approached through the idea of natural increase or the balance between births and deaths: if the balance is positive, the population will increase, barring out-migration; and if it is negative, the population will decline. The measurement of fertility is complicated by the fact that the absolute number of births and deaths in a society is influenced not only by current rates of fertility per woman but also by the age composition of the population, which is itself determined by the levels of fertility and mortality current in former years. If, as a result of higher fertility in earlier years,

[1]For a lucid discussion of replacement and the New Reproduction Rate (NRR), see Roland Pressat, *Demographic Analysis*, trans. Judah Matras (Chicago-New York: Aldine-Atherton Inc., 1972), pp. 335–56.

there is a relatively large number of women in the reproductive period of their lives, the actual number of births in a given year may be large enough to exceed the number of deaths even if the underlying current fertility per woman is not sufficient to ensure replacement of the population in the long run. Under these circumstances the population will continue to grow, fertility remaining constant, until such time as the large cohorts of women have moved out of the reproductive years. The length of time for which growth continues will depend on the level of earlier fertility and the speed of the fertility decline. Some years ago, for example, it was calculated that if replacement level fertility were to be achieved in all the industrialized nations somewhere between 1970 and 1975 and to remain at that level, the amount of growth inherent in the age structure would vary from 5 and 6 percent for East and West Germany to 36 and 41 percent for the United States and Canada.[2] It should be borne in mind when reading statistics on population growth that the zero or negative growth of an indigenous population may be masked by a high level of immigration which, as in West Germany in the early 1970s, may enable a population to grow after natural increase has ceased.

The most useful measure of replacement, the Net Reproductive Rate (NRR), was developed specifically to overcome the confounding effect of age structure on the measurement of natural increase.[3] In essence the NRR takes a cohort of 1,000 women from the moment of their birth, reduces them by the mortality experienced by the cohort from birth until they have passed out of the reproductive years at age 50, and counts the number of live female children born to them.[4] The NRR is constructed in such a way that a value of 1.0 denotes exact replacement of the population. More specifically, a value of 1.0 signifies that each of the 1,000 women in the cohort was re-

[2]Michael S. Teitelbaum, "U.S., Population Growth in International Perspective," in Charles F. Westoff et al., *Toward the End of Growth* (Englewood Cliffs, N.J.: Prentice-Hall Inc., 1973), pp. 76–78.

[3]The NRR became known largely through its use by Robert R. Kuczynski in his study *Fertility and Reproduction* (New York: Falcon Press, 1932). Kuczynski notes that the measure was developed by Richard Boeckh, director of the Berlin Statistical Office in 1884. See, ibid., p. 15.

[4]Age 45 is sometimes used to denote the end of the reproductive period.

placed by one daughter on the average. Correspondingly, an NRR of 0.94 signifies fertility 6 percent below the level required for long-term replacement of the population, while an NRR of 1.25 denotes fertility 25 percent in excess of replacement.

Although it is possible to base the calculation on a real cohort, in practice the NRR is most commonly calculated from a hypothetical cohort to which is applied the age-specific fertility and mortality current in the population for the year under consideration. The two methods of calculation—that is, using real or hypothetical cohorts—give slightly different results depending on the pattern of mortality rates over a reproductive lifetime. In a period of stable low mortality such as characterizes industrialized societies today, the differences are small and of little significance. However, the NRR has another serious limitation which should be noted: in a contracepting population in which the number, timing, and spacing of births may change dramatically over a short period in response to fashion or transient changes in social or economic conditions, the NRR based on the experience of a particular year can be misleading when projected into the future. Many of the prognostications of doom and decline that were made during the 1920s and 1930s appeared because there was little accumulated experience of either contracepting populations or the NRR, and the assumption was made that the subreplacement fertility implied by the new measure would persist.

Two other measures of fertility, the Total Fertility Rate (TFR) and the Gross Reproduction Rate (GRR), bear a number of resemblances to the NRR but also differ from it in important ways. The GRR is similar to the NRR in that it is based on female births only. It differs from the NRR in that it does not take into account mortality and, therefore, does not embody the notion of replacement. Conceptually, the TFR differs from the GRR only in the fact that the former measure includes both male and female births; it therefore gives the average *total* fertility per woman.[5] Because of their conceptual relatedness, the GRR and TFR can be estimated from each other by means of the prevailing sex ratio at birth.

The particular value of the TFR which denotes replacement

---

[5]For a discussion of the TFR, see Pressat, *Demographic Analysis*, pp. 188–90.

fertility for a society will vary in accordance with the mortality experienced by the society at the time for which the index is being constructed. At the present time replacement of the population in industrialized societies calls for a TFR of approximately 2.11 children per woman on the average. It should be noted that this is very close to the minimal value the TFR can take if replacement is assumed; should mortality fall to zero between birth and age 50, the index would fall only to 2.05. Moreover, since mortality decline in developed countries is now very slow, replacement of the population, barring a revolutionary breakthrough in the prevention of infant mortality, will be determined almost entirely by trends in fertility.

Like the NRR, calculation of the TFR can be based on either a real or hypothetical cohort of 1,000 women from birth to age 50. The use of a real cohort is only feasible after the women have passed through the reproductive years and have completed their childbearing. In this case the measure, sometimes known as the "index of lifetime fertility" or, more loosely, as "completed family size," is the best available measure of the fertility actually experienced by a cohort. When constructed by the application of age-specific fertility rates to a hypothetical cohort, the measure, sometimes referred to as the "period fertility index," is subject to the same limitations that affect the NRR and should be interpreted and projected with caution.

APPENDIX B

A CONCEPTUAL FRAMEWORK

Political scientists have developed a number of concepts and models of politics that can be used to organize and guide the study of public policy. Each of these models directs attention to a different aspect of public policy, providing a particular perspective on the process of policy formulation and a characteristic explanation of policy. Among the models that scholars have found most useful for analyzing policy processes, public policy has been variously conceived as: the output of a political system which is responding to inputs from its environment;[1] the "equilibrium" reached in the struggle among interest groups for influence over official policy-makers;[2] and as the preferences and values of a governing elite whose social and occupational positions, wealth, education, interest, and involvement allow them to exert a disproportionate amount of political power and influence.[3] A fourth approach attempts essentially to analyze the relationship between the process of policy-making or the content of policy and the structures and institutions of government.[4] All

[1]David Easton, "An Approach to the Analysis of Political Systems," *World Politics* 9 (1957), pp. 383–400; idem, *A Framework for Political Analysis* (Englewood Cliffs, N.J.: Prentice-Hall Inc., 1965).

[2]Earl Latham, "The Group Basis of Politics," *American Political Science Review* 46, 2 (June 1952), pp. 376–97; David B. Truman, *The Governmental Process* (New York: Alfred A. Knopf, 1951).

[3]For a discussion and bibliography of classical theorists of elites see T. Bottomore, *Elites and Society* (London: C. A. Watts and Co. Ltd., 1964); for a bibliography of elite studies in general, see Robert D. Putnam, *The Comparative Study of Political Elites* (Englewood Cliffs, N.J.: Prentice-Hall Inc., 1976).

[4]Carl J. Friedrich, *Man and His Government* (New York: McGraw Hill Book Co. Inc., 1963).

of these and other models have proved capable of generating insights and illuminating parts of the policy process. Since no single one can furnish a full explanation of any specific piece of policy-making, it is important to exercise some care in selecting the most appropriate approach and in laying out its elements for the convenience and understanding of the reader.

This book adopts an elitist approach which focuses attention on the perception and opinions of political elites and influential people responsible for or closely involved in population issues. Beyond the fact that the elite "model" provides the most direct test of the study's three most fundamental hypotheses, there are two additional reasons for stressing the views of public officials and influential elites. First, there is considerable evidence that political elites are more alert than are the mass of ordinary citizens to the development of conditions that may come to present problems for the society. Much of the communication concerning problems that need attention, moreover, flows downward from elites to mass rather than upward from mass to elite.[5] V. O. Key, for example, has explained:

> The political elite . . . mediate between the world of remote and complex events and the mass of the public. A great function of political leadership is the clarification of public problems and the presentation of courses of action.[6]

In particular, "elite opinion is apt to run ahead of mass opinion in periods of rapid change and on topics that are new to the national agenda."[7] It seems reasonable to assume, therefore, that political elites are more likely than are private individuals to appreciate the widely ramifying societal consequences of a new and complex issue like low population growth and will be more likely to attempt to deal with it. Even on a common sense level, it is not unreasonable to assume that in a country which has a

[5]See, for example, Karl W. Deutsch, *The Analysis of International Relations* (Englewood Cliffs, N.J.: Prentice Hall Inc., 1968) pp. 101–10; Philip E. Converse, "The Nature of Belief Systems in Mass Publics," in *Ideology and Discontent*, ed. David E. Apter (New York: The Free Press, 1964), pp. 206–61.

[6]V. O. Key, *Public Opinion and American Democracy* (New York: Alfred A. Knopf, 1961).

[7]Putnam, p. 140.

low birth rate as a consequence of the deliberate decisions of most couples to have small families, demands for pronatalist policy are unlikely to come from the public. It is much more probable that pronatalist sentiment will first appear within government itself or in elite circles close to government.[8]

Second, even when policy is adopted in response to public demand, decisions binding on the whole society are made only by a relatively small circle of public officials who have responsibility for specific issues or issue areas. Focusing research on the attitudes and opinions of these "proximate decision-makers" and those who advise and influence them therefore constitutes a convenient and economical way to identify the critical determinants of public policy.[9] Even though the contributions of political parties, interest groups, substantive specialists, and the mass public may significantly shape certain aspects of the policy process, their effect on policy choices is always mediated by their influence on the opinions and actions of those who are authorized to make decisions on behalf of government.

Determinants of elite values and perceptions

We have argued that the primary reason for the weak relationship between demographic variables and population policy is that objective conditions, by themselves, do not shape the decisions of governmental leaders; rather, it is elite perceptions of empirical realities and the significance attached to them that determine the policy responses of governments. This statement does not explain the relationship but simply marks the point of

[8]For a discussion of the types of policy that are most likely to be initiated by elite action, see Robert Cobb, Jennie Keith-Ross, and Marc Howard Ross, "Agenda Building as a Comparative Political Process," *American Political Science Review* 70, 1 (March 1976), pp. 132–34.

[9]Richard C. Snyder, "A Decision-Making Approach to the Study of Political Phenomena," in *Approaches to the Study of Politics*, ed. Roland Young (Evanston, Ill.: Northwestern University Press, 1958), pp. 15–16; see also, Richard C. Snyder, Henry Bruck, and Burton Sapin, *Decision-Making as an Approach to the Study of International Politics* (Foreign Policy Analysis Series, no. 3, 1954).

departure for my analysis. The immediate task, therefore, is to identify the forces that are most influential in shaping elite perceptions of demographic trends.

It is a commonplace that behavior is powerfully influenced by the attitudes and values of the actor; yet there is abundant evidence that in many field situations attitudes are poor predictors of behavior.[10] One reason for the gap that often appears between elite opinions and policy outputs is that governmental decision-making is normally a joint function of multiple actors with different perceptions of the problem and different bases of power, whose relative weights are difficult to assess.[11] A more profound reason for the discrepancy is that the relationship between attitudes and behavior is not simple but emerges from a dynamic interaction between the complex psychological predispositions brought to the situation by the actor and the objective situation in which he finds himself. In common with many attitude theorists, Fred Greenstein in his work on personality and politics writes that "it is the situation, *as perceived by the actor*, an attitudinal datum, that is of central importance for predicting and explaining behavior."[12] Greenstein continues with the suggestion that it may be instructive "to think of attitude and situation as being in a kind of push-pull relationship: the stronger the attitudinal press for a course of action, the less the need for a situational stimulus, and vice versa."[13] While perceptions thus represent a fusion of predispositions and empirical situational

---

[10]For representative discussions of the discrepancy between attitudes and behavior, see, for example, A. M. Wicker, "Attitudes versus Actions: The Relationship of Verbal and Overt Behavioral Responses to Attitude Objects," *Journal of Social Issues* 25, 4 (1969), pp. 41–78; Martin Fishbein and James J. Jaccard, "Theoretical and Methodological Considerations in the Prediction of Family Planning Intentions and Behaviors," *Representative Research in Social Psychology* 4, 1 (1973), pp. 37–51; Herbert C. Kelman, "Attitudes are Alive and Well and Gainfully Employed in the Sphere of Action," *American Psychologist* 29, 5 (May 1974), pp. 310–24.

[11]For a useful discussion of methods for assessing the relative value of leverage points, see Kenneth J. Gergen, "Assessing the Leverage Points in the Process of Policy Formation," in *The Study of Policy Formation*, ed. Raymond A. Bauer and K. J. Gergen (New York: The Free Press, 1968), pp. 181–203.

[12]Fred I. Greenstein, *Personality and Politics* (Chicago: Markham Publishing Company, 1969), p. 28.

[13]Ibid., p. 29.

realities, it is both necessary and possible to separate them analytically and, without entering the deep waters of personality and political behavior, identify those features which are likely to be most significant for explaining population policy.

Situational determinants

Among the complex situational variables that constrain the actions of policy-makers, there are three which may be thought to have exceptional significance for the process of policy-making. First, it may be hypothesized that the amount and quality of the *information* reaching responsible decision-makers will largely determine the time at which the issue reaches the political agenda, the substance of the discussion, and the content of the policy proposals that emerge. In addition to the basic census and vital-statistical information necessary for projecting population trends, which can be assumed to be generally available in good quantity and quality to governments in industrialized countries, three types of information would seem to be particularly important. They are:

a) reliable assessments of the consequences of trends in fertility and population growth for different sectors of the economy and society as a basis for deciding about the type of policy response called for;
b) sophisticated demographic and socioeconomic-demographic analyses of fertility as a basis for rational selection of appropriate measures to raise fertility;
c) reliable indicators of the reception likely to be accorded specific measures by the people who will be most affected by them.

The need for dependable information on which to base policy decisions, moreover, draws attention to the number, quality, and location of population research institutions and the relationship between policy-makers and research personnel.

Two propositions follow from these considerations of the relationship between information and policy decisions.

I. There will be a tendency for governments which routinely use demographic data in the formulation of national economic plans to attach greater importance to the attainment of a positive rate of population growth than will governments which do not engage in centralized economic planning.

II. Where there is a deficiency of reliable information on the causes and consequences of demographic trends, there will be a tendency for governments to act on the basis of attitudinal predispositions rather than on the objective demographic facts of the situation.

A second situational variable of significance for population policy formulation may be conceived as the degree of *coordination* within and between the departments and agencies of government which have responsibility for population issues. It is helpful for certain purposes to regard a government as a formal organization engaged in a search for solutions to complex problems. From this perspective a government may be viewed not as a unitary structure but as a collectivity of loosely articulated ministries and departments among which responsibility for discrete parts of the problem is divided. At the top of the structure sits the government proper, much like the board of directors of a company. Viewed in this way, each ministry or department constitutes a separate organization acting independently in pursuit of its own goals, invested with its own responsibilities, bases of power, and sources and types of information, and constrained by its own set of previous commitments, budgetary restrictions, and statutory obligations.[14] The "organization model" of policy formulation thus directs attention to the particular constellation of ministries involved in population issues and to the institu-

---

[14]The writings of Herbert A. Simon and his colleagues have been especially influential in this field. See, for example, Simon, "A Behavioral Model of Rational Choice," *Quarterly Journal of Economics* 69 (February 1955), pp. 99–118; idem, *Models of Man* (New York: John Wiley and Sons Inc., 1957); James G. March and Herbert A. Simon, *Organizations* (New York: John Wiley and Sons, 1958); Richard M. Cyert and James G. March, *A Behavioral Theory of the Firm* (Englewood Cliffs, N.J.: Prentice-Hall, Inc., 1963). For an empirical application of the organization model compared with other models, see Graham T. Allison, *Essence of Decision: Explaining the Cuban Missile Crisis* (Boston: Little, Brown and Co., 1971).

tional and informal mechanisms for coordinating policy both within and among ministries. it also underscores the need to examine the division of responsibility among national, regional, and local levels of government.

The organization model suggests the following proposition.

III. When fertility falls to replacement level and/or the rate of population growth approaches zero, both the speed at which a government will initiate corrective action and the degree of policy coordination it will achieve will be positively related to the degree of centralization of government.

The third situational variable influencing policy-maker's definitions of the situation is essentially political—the limits on governmental maneuverability imposed by widely shared societal values relevant to population issues and existing policies that express them. Foremost among these *constraints* is the movement for women's independence which has spread throughout the Western world with gathering momentum, especially since the end of World War II. As a result of this movement, Western governments have become deeply committed to policies which, taken together, undermine the desire for children and make it easier to avoid unplanned and unwanted births. It seems unlikely that governments will take the risk of alienating women by restricting their access to means of family planning, including legal, safe abortion, or by attempting to limit women's educational and occupational opportunities. Indeed, women's participation in the labor force will become increasingly necessary to maintain labor force growth once the smaller birth cohorts reach the age of employment. Moreover, the contributions of working women are already a vital element in the financing of social security programs.[15] Bearing in mind these and similar constraints, it is hypothesized that governments will endeavor to find ways to link public discussion of low fertility with other causes being pursued by women, and that they will attempt to

[15]For an explicit statement of this position, see the remarks of Monique Pelletier, French minister delegate for women's conditions in the Giscard d'Estaing government, "Donner la possibilité de choisir," *Le Monde*, March 14, 1979, p. 2.

present their policy choices as providing a wider range of options for women.

Attitudinal predispositions

A reading of the policy literature in population and in other issue areas suggests that the attitudinal predispositions brought by political elites to the consideration of population issues will depend most significantly on three determining influences in their environments: (a) occupational role perceptions; (b) political ideology; and (c) the shared cognitive, normative, and affective understandings of the society relevant to demographic questions, the role of the state, and the rules of political conduct in the society.

At the level most immediate to governmental decision-making, we can expect that opinions and attitudes of policy-makers will be influenced by interests and concerns specific to their work roles. A number of studies have found that elites in similar occupational positions in different countries tend to be more similar along certain dimensions than individuals in different positions in the same society.[16] These similarities and differences appear to be explicable in terms of the situations in which elites find themselves. Facing similar problems and responsibilities, possessed of similar types of information and similar constraints on their actions, it is not surprising that elites in similar positions tend to think and act in in similar ways—and differently from elites in different positions. A full exploration of this hypothesis is beyond the scope of the present research. Nevertheless, the influence of role perceptions on attitudes toward low population growth may be viewed as an aspect of the organizational structure of government that was discussed above. Furthermore, the varied perceptions of policy-makers in different positions underline the importance for policy formulation of mechanisms for coordinating diverse opinions.

---

[16]A number of these studies are cited in Allen H. Barton, "Determinants of Leadership Attitudes in a Socialist Society," in Barton, Bogdan Denitch, and Charles Kadushin, *Opinion-Making Elites in Yugoslavia* (New York: Praeger, 1973), pp. 229–30, 242. See also, Putnam, pp. 96–98.

The positions of policy-makers on the left-right continuum of *political ideology* constitutes a second potential influence on elite attitudes to population issues. There is evidence from the history of pronatalism in Western Europe that intellectuals and states-men of the political right have tended to view population issues from a nationalistic and militaristic perspective, while elites of the political left have paid more attention to the consequences of demographic trends for the well-being of individuals.[17] These considerations give rise to the following proposition:

IV. *Within the liberal democracies* there will be a tendency for individuals and parties of the political right to perceive low population growth in terms of its macroeffects on the economy and national power, whereas indviduals and parties of the political left will tend to perceive it in terms of its microconsequences at the level of the individual and the community.[18]

Finally, the most fundamental of the attitudinal determinants of elite perceptions of low population growth are likely to be those that spring from the common understandings of the society relative to population growth, the role of the state, and the rules of the political game. Thus it is hypothesized that the attitudinal predispositions of policy-makers will be shaped in large measure by the same concerns that have animated the actions of rulers vis-à-vis population throughout history: that is, by a care for the relationships between population and national power, national wealth, and international influence. In addition, it is hypothe-sized that policy-makers will be profoundly influenced by the demographic experiences of their countries in the recent past.

Sources of Data

This book was designed to explore the perceptions of policy-makers relevant to declining fertility and negative population

[17]Koenraad W. Swart; Kälvemark, *More Children of Better Quality?*, pp. 50–55; Hatje; Glass, *Policies and Movements*, p. 279, n. 4.

[18]There is an obvious inconsistency between the attitudes of political parties of the left in the liberal democracies of the West and the policies of leftist governments in the socialist states in Eastern Europe. This issue is taken up in the concluding chapter.

growth and to assess the significance today of perceived relations between population and national power, economic prosperity, and the role of the state. The data for the study were drawn from a number of sources. For the historical period (Chapter 3), full reliance has been placed on secondary studies written contemporaneously with the events or more recently. For the contemporary period (Chapters 4–6), the primary data source was a series of semistructured interviews with the government officials, politicians, research personnel, and other influential people most closely involved in the formulation of population policy in the countries of the sample. Some additional interviews were obtained with scholars in other Western European countries who are working on aspects of population policy in Europe and with officials responsible for population policy issues in six international organizations: the UN Economic Commission for Europe (Geneva); the Council of Europe (Strasbourg); the Organization for Economic cooperation and Development (Paris); the European Economic Community (Brussels); and the UN Population Division (New York). Finally, the interview materials are supplemented by data drawn from published and unpublished documents and research reports collected from government departments and international organizations, scholarly journals, and the mass media.

BIBLIOGRAPHY

Åberg, Carl Johan, and Allan Nordin. *Befolkning och Ekonomi*. Stockholm: Trygg Hansa, 1977.

Abgeordnetenhaus von Berlin. l Enquete-Komission, 7. Wahlperiode, *Schlussbericht*. Drucksache 7/11/71, Berlin, March 15, 1978.

Acsädi, György. "Recent Problems in Population Policies in the European Region of Socialist Countries." In *Proceedings of the IUSSP Population Conference, London, 1969*, vol. 2. Liège: IUSSP, 1969, pp. 1381–93.

Akkermann, Dr., and Karl-Heinz Mehlan. "Law and Fertility in the German Democratic Republic." In *Law and Fertility in Europe*. Ed. Maurice Kirk, Massimo Livi-Bacci, and Egon Szabady. Dolhain, Belgium: Ordina Editions, 1976, pp. 274–97.

Allison, Graham T. *Essence of Decision: Explaining the Cuban Missile Crisis*. Boston: Little, Brown, 1971.

An Arab Philosophy of History. Selections from the Prologomena of Ibn Khaldun of Tunis (1332–1406). Trans. and arr. Charles Issawi. London: John Murray, 1950.

Anton, Thomas J. "Policy Making and Political Culture in Sweden." *Scandinavian Political Studies*. Ed. Olof Ruin, vol. 4, 1969, pp. 88–102.

Anton, Thomas J. *Administered Politics: Elite Political Culture in Sweden*. Hingham, Mass.: Martinus Nijhoff, 1980.

Barton, Allen H. "Determinants of Leadership Attitudes in a Socialist Society." In Allen H. Barton, Bogdan Denitch, and Charles Kadushin. *Opinion-Making Elites in Yugoslavia*. New York: Praeger, 1973, pp. 220–62.

Basic Law of the Federal Republic of Germany. Adopted at Bonn by the Parliamentary Council, September 1948–May 1949. Agreed Anglo-American translation. (No publication details available).

Baude, Annika. "Public Policy and Changing Family Patterns in Sweden, 1930–1977." Trans. Jeanne Rosen. Stockholm: National Board of Health and Welfare, n.d. (mimeo).

Bavarian State Ministry of Labor and Social Affairs. "Bisherige und Künftige Bevölkerungsentwicklung und ihre Auswirkungen im Sozialbereich." Munich: State Ministry of Labor and Social Affairs, Planningsgruppe 407/56/77, 1977.

———. "Situationsanalyse und Projektionen der Bevölkerungsentwicklung." First Action Report of the Interministerial Working Group on Population Trends and Family Policy. (Munich: n.d., mimeo).

Bebel, August. *Woman and Socialism*, 50th Ed. Trans. Meta L. Stern (Hebe). New York: Socialist Literature, 1910 (first published in Germany, 1894).

Becker, Gary S. "An Economic Analysis of Fertility." Universities-National Bureau Committee for Economic Research (NBER). *Demographic and Economic Change in Developed Countries*. Princeton: Princeton University Press, 1960, pp. 209–231.

Berelson, Bernard. *Population Policy in Developed Countries*. New York: McGraw Hill, 1974.

———. "Romania's 1966 Anti-Abortion Decree: The Demographic Experience of the First Decade." *Population Studies* 33, 2 (July 1979), pp. 209–22.

Berent, Jerzy. "Fertility Decline in Eastern Europe and the Soviet Union." *Population Studies* 24, 2 (July 1970), Parts 2 and 3, pp. 247–92.

———. "Fertility Trends and Policies in Eastern Europe in the 1970's." In *Social, Economic, and Health Aspects of Low Fertility*. Ed. Arthur A. Campbell. Washington, D.C.: U.S. Government Printing Office, 1979.

Bernhardt, Eva. *Trends and Variations in Swedish Fertility: A Cohort Study*. URVAL no. 5. Stockholm: National Central Statistical Bureau, 1971.

Besemeres, John F. *Socialist Population Politics*. White Plains, N.Y.: M. E. Sharpe, 1980.

Bidou, Dominique. "Le débat est politique." *Le Monde*, December 29, 1978, p. 2.

Blayo, Chantal. "Les interruptions volontaires de grossesse en France en 1976." *Population* 34, 2 (March-April, 1979), pp. 307–42.

Bleuel, Hans P. *Strength Through Joy: Sex and Society in Nazi Germany*. Trans. by Maxwell Brownjohn. London: Seker and Warberg, 1973.

de Bliokh, Ivan Stanislavovich. "Population Pressures as a Cause of War." Trans. Michael Boylsov. *Population and Development Review* 3, 1–2 (March-June, 1977), pp. 129–36. Excerpted from *The Future War from the Point of View of Technology, Economy and Politics*. St. Petersburg, 1898.

Bottomore, T. B. *Elites and Society*. London: C. A. Watts, 1964.

Bourgeois-Pichat, Jean. "Evolution de la population française depuis le XVIIIe siècle." *Population* 6, 4 (1951), pp. 635–62.

———. "France." In *Population Policy in Developed Countries*. Ed. Bernard Berelson. New York: McGraw Hill, 1974, pp. 545–91.

———. "Baisse de la fécondité et decendance finale." *Population* 31, 6 (November-December 1976), pp.1045–97.

———. "La transition démographique: vieillissement de la population." In *Population Science in the Service of Mankind*. Papers presented at the Conference on Science in the Service of Life, convened by the Institute of Life and IUSSP, Vienna, 1979. Liège, Belgium: IUSSP, 1979, pp. 211–39.

———. "Recent Demographic Change in Europe: An Assessment." *Population and Development Review* 7, 1 (March 1981), pp. 19–42.

Brand, Jack. "Reforming Local Government: Sweden and England Compared." In *The Dynamics of Public Policy: A Comparative Analysis*. Ed. Richard Rose. Beverly Hills: Sage Publications, 1976, pp. 35–56.

Brandelius, Pia. "Taxes: One of the Main Issues in the 1979 Election." *Election Year '79*. New York: Swedish Information Center, July 1979.

Brisset, Claire. "L'avortement, tabou de la campagne électoral." *Le Monde*, March 8, 1978, p. 15.

———. "Le débat sur l'avortement." *Le Monde*, October 4, 1979, pp. 1, 26, and October 9, 1979, pp. 1, 16.

———. "La loi française." *Le Monde*, April 26, 1979, p. 14.

Bumpass, Larry, and Charles F. Westoff. *The Later Years*. Princeton: Princeton University Press, 1970.

Calot, Gérard. "La baisse de la fécondité depuis quinze ans." *Colloque national sur la démographie française*. Paris: Ministry of Labor and Population, June, 1980, pp. 29–39.

————, and Jacqueline Hecht. "The Control of Fertility Trends." In *Population Decline in Europe*. Ed. Council of Europe. New York: St. Martin's Press, 1978, pp. 178–96.

Campbell, Arthur A. (Ed.). *Social, Economic and Health Aspects of Low Fertility*. Washington, D.C.: U.S. Government Printing Office, 1979.

Carr-Saunders, Alexander. *World Population: Past Growth and Present Trends*. Oxford: The Clarendon Press, 1936.

Chesnais, Jean-Claude. "La baisse de la natalité et ses conséquences sur l'enseignements." *Problèmes Economiques*, no. 1.715, March 18, 1981, pp. 20–28. Paris: La Documentation Française.

————. "Le modèle économique de l'Allemagne Fédérale est-il compatible avec son modèle démographique?" *Revue d'Ecomomie Politique* 91, 2 (1981), pp. 163–77.

Clark, Colin. *Population Growth and Land Use*. London: Macmillan and Co., 1967.

————, and Margaret Haswell. *The Economics of Subsistence Agriculture*, 3rd ed. London: St. Martin's Press, 1967.

Cline, Ray S. *World Power Assessment: A Calculus of Strategic Drift*. Boulder, Colo.: Westview Press, 1975.

Coale, Ansley J. "Should the United States Start a Campaign for Fewer Births?" *Population Index* 34, 4 (October-December 1968), pp. 467–76.

Cobb, Robert, Jennie Keith-Ross, and Marc Howard Ross. "Agenda Building as a Comparative Political Process." *American Political Science Review* 70, 1 (March 1976), pp. 126–38.

Converse, Philip E. "The Nature of Belief Systems in Mass Publics." In *Ideology and Discontent*. Ed. David E. Apter. New York: The Free Press, 1964, pp. 206–61.

Cramer, James C. "Fertility and Female Employment: Problems of Causal Direction." *American Sociological Review* 45 (April, 1980), pp. 167–90.

Cyert, Richard M., and James G. March. *A Behavioral Theory of the Firm*. Englewood Cliffs, N.J.: Prentice-Hall, 1963.

Dabernat, René. "Le 'Questionnaire' de M. Giscard d'Estaing: la référence allemande." *Le Monde*, October 18, 1978, pp. 1, 42.

Dahl, Robert A., and Charles E. Lindblom. *Politics, Economics, and Welfare*. New York: Harper Torchbooks, 1953.

Dahlström, Edmund (Ed.). *The Changing Roles of Men and Women*. Trans. Gunilla and Steven Anderman. London: Gerald Duckworth, 1967, and Boston: Beacon Press, 1971.

David, Henry. *Family Planning and Abortion in the Socialist Countries of Central and Eastern Europe*. Washington, D.C.: International Research Institute, American Institutes for Research, 1970.

Davis, Kingsley. "The Nature and Purpose of Population Policy." In *Califor-*

nia's Twenty Million. Eds. K. Davis and Frederick Styles. Berkeley: University of California Press, 1971, pp. 3–29.

Debré, Michel. "Donner des Français à la France." *Revue des Deux Mondes,* December 1976, pp. 514–24.

———. "La menace démographique et politique." *Le Monde,* April 21, 1978, p. 9.

———. "Ce jour que j'attendais . . . " *Le Monde,* August 12, 1978, pp. 1, 6.

———. "Pour un Grenelle des familles." *Le Monde,* December 14, 1978, p. 1.

———, and Alfred Sauvy. *Des Français pour la France.* Paris: Gallimard, 1946.

Desabie, Jacques. "Projections démographiques à moyen terme (2000) et à longue terme (2020, 2050) pour la France." *Colloque national sur la démographie française.* Paris: Ministry of Labor and Participation, June 1980, pp. 83–95.

Deutsch, Karl W. *The Analysis of International Relations.* Englewood Cliffs, N.J.: Prentice-Hall, 1968.

Di Maio, Alfred J. "The Soviet Union and Population." *Comparative Political Studies* 13, 1 (April 1980), pp. 97–136.

Doublet, Jacques. *L'Aide aux familles.* Geneva: International Labor Organization, 1975.

———, and Hubert de Villedary. *Law and Population Growth in France.* Law and Population Monograph Series, no. 12. Medford, Mass.: The Fletcher School of Law and Diplomacy, Tufts University, 1973.

Driver, Edwin. *Essays on Population Policy.* Lexington, Mass.: Lexington Books, D. C. Heath, 1972.

Dumont, Arsène. *Dépopulation et civilization: étude démographique.* Paris: Lecrosnier et Babe, 1890.

Dumont, Gérard-François, with the collaboration of Pierre Chaunu, Jean Legrand, and Alfred Sauvy. *La France rideé.* Paris: Le Livre de Poche, "Pluriel," 1979.

Dumont, Jean-Pierre. "La réduction du temp de travail." Parts 1–3. *Le Monde,* May 31–June 2, 1979.

———. "Social Security: Balancing the Ins and Outs." *Manchester Guardian Weekly,* July 5, 1979, p. 14 (trans. and reprinted from *Le Monde,* July 5, 1979).

———. "Innovation et précipitation." *Le Monde,* May 29, 1981, p. 7.

Dupont, Jean-Marie. "Faut-il encourager la reprise de la natalité?" *Le Monde,* May 2, 1979, p. 28.

Dyer, Colin. *Population and Society in Twentieth Century France.* New York: Holmes and Meier Publishers, 1978.

Easterlin, Richard A. "Towards a Socio-Economic Theory of Fertility: A Survey of Recent Research on Economic Factors in American Fertility." In *Fertility and Family Planning: A World View.* Ed. S. J. Behrman, Leslie Corsa, and Ronald Freedman. Ann Arbor: University of Michigan Press, 1969, pp. 127–56.

Easton, David. "An Approach to the Analysis of Political Systems." *World Politics* 9 (1957), pp. 383–400.

————. *A Framework for Political Analysis.* Englewood Cliffs, N.J.: Prentice Hall, 1965.

Elder, Neil. *Government in Sweden.* Oxford-New York: Pergamon Press, 1970.

Ericsson, Bo A. "The Unemployment Situation in Sweden: Some Main Issues Looking Ahead to the 1980's." *Election Year '79.* no. 2. New York: Swedish Information Service, June 1978.

Espenshade, Thomas J. "Zero Population Growth and the Economies of Developed Nations." *Population and Development Review* 4, 4 (December 1978), pp. 645–80.

————, and William J. Serow. *The Economic Consequences of Slowing Population Growth.* New York: Academic Press, 1978.

Eversley, David E. C. *Social Theories of Fertility and the Malthusian Debate.* Oxford: The Clarendon Press, 1959.

————. "Welfare." In *Population Decline in Europe.* Ed. Council of Europe. London: Edward Arnold, 1978, pp. 115–42.

Federal Republic of Germany, Federal Statistical Office. *Statistisches Jahrbuch, 1980.* Stuttgart and Mainz: W. Kolhammer, 1980.

————. "Langfristige Bevölkerungsentwicklung." Reply of the Federal Government. Deutscher Bundestag, 8. Wahlperiode. Drucksache 8/680, of June 24, 1977.

————. "Langfristige Sicherung des Generationenvertrages in der Alterssicherung im Zusammenhang mit der Geburtenentwicklung." Reply of the Federal Government. Deutscher Bundestag, 8. Wahlperiode. Drucksache 8/1982 of June 10, 1978.

————, Ministry of the Economy. *Wirtschaftspolitische Implikationen eines Bevölkerungsrückgangs: Gutachten des wissenshaftlichen beim Bundesministerium für Wirtschaft.* Bonn, 1980.

————, Ministry of Family, Youth, and Health. *Erster Familienbericht: Bericht über die Lage des Familien in der Bundesrepublik Deutschland.* Bonn: Bundesministerium für Jugend, Familie und Gesundheit, 1968.

————. *Zweiter Familienbericht: Familie und Sozialisation-Leistungen und Leistungsgrenzen der Familie hinsichtlich des Erziehungs- und Bildungsprozesses der jungen Generation.* Bonn-Bad Godesberg: Bundesministerium für Jugend, Familie und Gesundheit, 1975.

————, Ministry of the Interior. *Bericht über Bevölkerungsentwicklung in der Bundesrepublik Deutschland.* Bonn: Deutscher Bundestag, 8 Wahlperiode. Drucksache 8/4437. August 1980.

————, Sachverständigen komission der Bundesregierung. "Die Lage der Familien in der Bundesrepublik Deutschland." Dritter Familienbericht. Deutscher Bericht, Drucksache 8/3120, August 20, 1979.

————. *Verhandlungen des Deutschen Bundestages, 7. Wahlperiode, 1972.* Stenographische Berichte, vol. 93. Bonn, 1975.

Finer, Samuel E. "State- and Nation-Building in Europe: The Role of the Military." In *The Formation of National States in Western Europe.* Ed. Charles Tilly. Princeton: Princeton University Press, 1975, pp. 84–163.

Finkle, Jason L., and Alison McIntosh. "Political Perceptions of Population

Stabilization and Decline." *Policy Studies Journal* 6, 2 (Winter 1977), pp. 155–67. Reprinted in *Policy Studies Review Annual*, 1977. Ed. Stewart Nagel. Beverly Hills: Sage Publications, 1978, pp. 574–86.

———. "Policy Responses to Population Stagnation in Developed Societies." In *Social, Economic, and Health Aspects of Low Fertility*. Ed. Arthur A. Campbell. Washington, D.C.: U.S. Government Printing Office, 1979, pp. 275–97.

Fishbein, Martin, and James J. Jaccard. "Theoretical and Methodological Considerations in the Prediction of Family Planning Intentions and Behaviors." *Representative Research in Social Psychology* 4, 1 (1973), pp. 37–51.

France, Ministry of Labor and Participation, Secretariat of State for Immigrant Workers. *La nouvelle politique de l'immigration*. n.d. (circa 1978).

———. *Septième rapport sur la situation démographique de la France*. Paris, 1978.

———. *Neuvième rapport sur la situation démographique de la France*. Paris, 1980.

———. *Colloque national sur la démographie française*. Paris, June 1980.

———. *Rapport de synthèse de travaux du Haut Comité de la Population*. Paris, June 1980.

Freedman, Ronald, Pascal K. Whelpton, and Arthur A. Campbell. *Family Planning, Sterility and Population Growth*. New York: McGraw Hill, 1959.

Frejka, Tomas. "Fertility Trends and Policies: Czechoslovakia in the 1970's." *Population and Development Review* 6, 1 (March 1980), pp. 65–93.

Frercks, Rudolf. *German Population Policy*. Berlin: Terramare Publications, no. 5, 1938.

Friedrich, Carl J. *Man and His Government*. New York: McGraw Hill, 1963.

Gendell, Murray. "Sweden Faces Zero Population Growth." *Population Bulletin* 35, 2. Washington, D.C.: Population Reference Bureau, June 1980.

Gergen, Kenneth J. "Assessing the Leverage Points in the Process of Policy Formation." In *The Study of Policy Formation*. Ed. Raymond A. Bauer and K. J. Gergen. New York: The Free Press, 1968, pp. 181–203.

Girard, Alain, and Louis Roussel. "Fecondité et conjoncture: une enquête d'opinion sur la politique démographique." *Population* 34, 3 (May-June, 1979), pp. 567–88.

Giscard d'Estaing, Valéry. *Une politique pour la famille*. Supplement to Actualités-Service, no. 306. Paris: Service d'Information et de Service, n.d.

Glass, David V. "Population Policy." In *Democratic Sweden*. Ed. Margaret Cole and Charles Smith. New York: The Greystone Press, 1939, pp. 277–93.

———. *Population: Policies and Movements in Europe*. Oxford: The Clarendon Press, 1940.

Godwin, R. Kenneth (Ed.). *Comparative Policy Analysis*. Lexington, Mass.: Lexington Books, D. C. Heath, 1975.

Grand-Duchy of Luxembourg, Ministry of National Economy. *La démographie du Luxembourg: passé, présent, et avenir.* Report prepared by Gérard Calot. Luxembourg: Service Central de la Statistique et des Etudes Economiques (STATEC), 1978.

Greenberg, D. S. "Birth Control: Swedish Help to Underdeveloped Nations." *Science* 137 (September 1962), pp. 1038–39.

Greenstein, Fred J. *Personality and Politics.* Chicago: Markham Publishing, 1969.

Hajnal, John. "The Analysis of Birth Statistics in the Light of the Recent International Recovery of the Birth-Rate." *Population Studies* 1,2 (September 1947), pp. 137–64.

———. "European Marriage Patterns in Perspective." In *Population in History.* Ed. David V. Glass and David E. C. Eversley. London: Edward Arnold, 1965, pp. 101–43.

Hale, Oran J. "Adolf Hitler and the Post-War German Birth Rate: An Unpublished Memorandum." *Journal of Central European Affairs* 17, 2 (July 195), pp. 166–73.

Hansen, Alvin H. "Economic Progress and Declining Population Growth." *The American Economic Review* 29 (March 1939), pp. 1–15.

Harmsen, Hans. "Notes on Abortion and Birth Control in Germany." *Population Studies* 3, 4 (March 1950), pp. 402–05.

Hatje, Ann-Katrin. *Befolkningsfrågan och Välfärdin: Debatten om Familje politik och Nativitesökning under 1930–och 1940–talen.* Stockholm, 1974. English summary, pp. 237–45.

Hauser, Phillip M. "Introduction." In *Population and World Politics.* Ed. P. Hauser. Glencoe, Ill.: The Free Press, 1958, pp. 9–23.

Hawthorne, Geoffrey. *The Sociology of Fertility.* London: Collier-McMillan, 1970.

Hecht, Jacqueline. "La politique familiale française depuis 1939." In *La France et sa population aujourd'hui.* Les Cahiers Français, no. 184. Paris: La Documentation Française, 1978, pp. 50–53.

Heer, David M. "Recent Developments in Soviet Population Policy." *Studies in Family Planning* 3, 11 (November 1972), pp. 257–64.

———. "Three Issues in Soviet Population Policy." *Population and Development Review* 3, 3 (September 1977), pp. 229–52.

Heidenheimer, Arnold J., and Donald P. Kommers. *The Governments of Germany.* 4th ed. New York: Thomas Y. Crowell, 1975.

Heitlinger, Alena. "Pronatalist Population Policy in Czechoslovakia." *Population Studies* 30, 1 (March 1976), pp. 123–35.

Helmut, Otto. *Volk in Gefahr.* Munich: J. S. Lehmanns Verlag, 1933.

Henry, Louis. *Anciennes familles génevoises.* Institute National d'Etudes Démographiques, Travaux et Documents. Cahier no. 26. Paris: Presses Universitaires de France, 1956.

———. "The Population of France in the 18th Century." Trans. Peter Jimack. In *Population in History.* Ed. David V. Glass and David C. Eversley. London: Edward Arnold, 1965, pp. 434–56.

———, and Yves Blayo. "La population de la France." *Population* (Special Issue: Démographie Historique) November 1975, pp. 71–122.

Hofsten, Erland. "Non-Marital Cohabitation: How to Explain its Rapid In-crease, Particularly in Scandinavia." In *Economic and Demographic Change: Issues for the 1980's*. vol. 3. Proceedings of the IUSSP Confer-ence, Helsinki, 1978. Liège: IUSSP, 1979, pp. 303–11.

———, and Hans Lundström. *Swedish Population History, 1750–1970*. Stock-holm: National Central Statistical Bureau, 1976.

Holmberg, Ingvar. "The Population Debate in Sweden in Recent Years." *Current Sweden*. No. 169. Stockholm: The Swedish Institute, August 1977.

Huntford, Roland. *The New Totalitarians*. New York: Stein and Day, 1972.

Hutchinson, Edward P. *The Population Debate*. Boston: Houghton Mifflin, 1967.

"Immigrants in Sweden." *Facts Sheets on Sweden*. Stockholm: The Swedish Institute, April 1978.

Institut National d'Etudes Démographiques (INED). *Natalité et politique démographique*. Travaux et Documents, no. 76. Paris: Presses Universi-taires de France, 1976.

International Birth Control Conference, Fifth, London, 1922. *Report*. Ed. Raymond Pierpont. London: William Heinemann, 1922.

Jonsson, Lena. "Law and Fertility in Sweden." In *Law and Fertility in Europe*. Ed. Maurice Kirk, Massimo Livi-Bacci, and Egon Szabady. Dolhain, Bel-gium: Ordina Editions, 1976, pp. 544–65.

Kaiser, Karl. "Schmidt's Foreign Policy." *New York Times*, January 21, 1979, p. 21.

Kälvemark, Ann-Sofie. "Swedish Emigration Policy in an International Per-spective, 1840–1925." In *From Sweden to America*. Ed. Harold Runblom and Hans Norman. Minneapolis, Minn.: Minnesota University Press, and Uppsala: Acta Universitatis Upsaliensis, 1976.

———. *More Children of Better Quality?* Studia Historica Upsaliensia, no. 115. Uppsala: Acta Universitatis Upsaliensis, 1980.

Kamerman, Sheila B., and Alfred J. Kahn (Eds.). *Family Policy: Government and Families in Fourteen Countries*. New York: Columbia University Press, 1978.

Kelman, Herbert C. "Attitudes are Alive and Well and Gainfully Employed in the Sphere of Action." *American Psychologist* 29, 5 (May 1974), pp. 310–24.

Key, V. O. *Public Opinion and American Democracy*. New York: Alfred A. Knopf, 1961.

Keynes, John Maynard. "Some Economic Consequences of a Declining Popu-lation." *Eugenics Review* 29 (1937), pp. 13–17.

Kirk, Maurice (Ed.). *Demographic and Social Change in Europe, 1975–2000*. Liverpool: Liverpool University Press in association with the Council of Europe, 1981.

———, Massimo Livi-Bacci, and Egon Szabady (Eds.). *Law and Fertility in Europe*. Dolhain, Belgium: Ordina Editions, 1976.

Knarr, John R. "Population Politics and the Soviet Polity." Unpublished Ph.D. dissertation, University of California, Los Angeles, 1976.

Knodel, John E. *The Decline of Fertility in Germany, 1871–1939.* Princeton: Princeton University Press, 1973.

Kozlowska, Ewa, and Jan Wojtyla. "Law and Fertility in Poland." In *Law and Fertility in Europe.* Vol. 2. Ed. Kirk et al. pp. 495–519.

Kuczynski, Robert René. *Fertility and Reproduction.* New York: Falcon Press, 1932.

———. *The Measurement of Population Growth.* London: Sidgwick and Jackson, 1935.

Lapidus, Gail Warshofsky. *Women in Soviet Society.* Berkeley: University of California Press, 1978.

Last, Hugh. "The Social Policy of Augustus." Cambridge Ancient History, vol. 10. *The Augustan Empire, 44 B.C.-A.D. 70.* Cambridge: The University Press, 1934. pp. 425–64.

Latham, Earl. "The Group Basis of Politics." *American Political Science Review* 45, 2 (June 1952), pp. 376–97.

Law File. September 1979. London: International Planned Parenthood Federation.

Le Bras, Hervé, and Georges Tapinos. "Les perspectives démographiques à longue terme et leurs consequences." *Population* 34, Special Number (December 1979), pp. 1391–1451.

Lecaillon, Jean-Didier. *L'économie de la sous-population.* Paris: Presses Universitaires de France, 1977.

Le Conseil Permanent de l'Episcopat Français. *Faire vivre: L'Eglise catholique et l'avortement.* Paris: Editions du Centurion, 1979.

"Legislation on Family Planning." *Fact Sheets on Sweden.* Stockholm: The Swedish Institute, March 1980.

"Le haut comité de la population." Unsigned and undated document of the Division of Population and Migration, Ministry of Labor and Participation, circa 1975.

Leichter, Howard M. *A Comparative Approach to Policy Analysis.* Cambridge: Cambridge University Press, 1979.

Lenin, Vladimir I. "Agrarian Question and the 'Critics of Marx'." *Selected Works*, vol. 12, pp. 51–63. New York: International Publishers, 1938.

Le Play, Fréderic. *La réforme sociale en France détruite de l'observation comparée des peuples européens.* Paris: E. Dentu, 1867.

Levy, Claude, and Louis Henry. "Ducs et pairs sous l'ancien régime: caractéristiques démographiques d'une caste." *Population* 15, 4 (October-December 1960), pp. 807–30.

Levy, Michel Louis. "Les étrangers en France." *Population et Sociétés* 137 (July-August 1980).

———. "Préoccupations natalistes en Europe de l'Est." *Population et Sociétés* 143 (January 1981).

———. "Divorces et divorcés." *Population et Sociétés* 144 (February 1981).

Liljeström, Rita. "Children-Parents-Jobs: 'Rearranging' the Swedish Society." *Social Change in Sweden.* Introductory Issue. New York: Swedish Information Service, May 1977.

———. "Are Children Better Off in the Post-Industrial Society?" *Social*

Change in Sweden, no. 2. New York: Swedish Information Service, November 1977.

————. "Integration of Family Policy and Labor Market Policy." Paper presented at the Conference on Equal Pay and Equal Opportunity Policy for Women: Europe, Canada, and the United States, Wellesley College Center for Research on Women, Wellesley, Mass., 1978 (mimeo).

————. "Integration of Family Policy and Labor Market Policy." *Social Change in Sweden*, no. 9. New York: Swedish Information Service, December 1978.

————. "Sweden." In *Family Policy: Government and Families in Fourteen Countries*. Ed. Sheila B. Kamerman and Alfred J. Kahn. New York: Columbia University Press, 1978, pp. 19–48.

————, Gunilla Furst Melstrom, and Gillan Liljeström Svensson. *Roles in Transition*. Stockholm, 1978.

Lipson, Leslie. *The Great Issues of Politics*. New York: Prentice-Hall, 1954.

Livi-Bacci, Massimo. "Population Policies in Western Europe." *Population Studies* 28, 2 (July 1974), pp. 191–204.

Lorimer, Frank. "Population Policies and Politics in the Communist World." In *Population and World Politics*. Ed. Philip M. Hauser. Glencoe: The Free Press, 1958. pp. 214–36.

Louros, N., J. Danezis, and D. Trichopoulos. "Greece." In *Population Policy in Developed Countries*. Ed. Bernard Berelson. pp. 151–92.

McDonough, Peter, and Amaury DeSouza. "Brazilian Elites and Population Policy." *Population and Development Review* 3, 4 (December 1977), pp. 377–410.

McIntyre, Robert J. "The Effects of Legalized Abortion Laws in Eastern Europe." In *Research in the Politics of Population*. Ed. Richard L. Clinton and R. Kenneth Godwin. Lexington, Mass.: D. C. Heath, 1972. pp. 183–216.

————. "Pronatalist Programs in Eastern Europe." *Soviet Studies* 27, 3 (July 1975), pp. 366–80.

Macura, Milos. "Population Policies in the Socialist Countries of Europe." *Population Studies* 28, 3 (September 1974), pp. 369–79.

Malthus, Thomas Robert. *An Essay on the Principle of Population*. Ed. Philip Appleman. New York: W. W. Norton, 1976. First published in 1789.

March, James G., and Herbert A. Simon. *Organizations*. New York: John Wiley, 1958.

Marx, Karl. *Capital*. Vol. 1. Trans. from the Third German Ed. Samuel Moore and Edward Aveling. Chicago: Charles H. Kerr, 1915.

Mayntz, Renate, and Fritz W. Scharpf. *Policy-Making in the German Federal Bureaucracy*. Amsterdam-London-New York: Elsevier, 1975.

Meijer, Hans. "Bureaucracy and Policy Formulation in Sweden." *Scandinavian Political Studies*. Ed. Olof Ruin. vol. 4, 1969. pp. 103–16.

Melsted, Lillemor. "Swedish Family Policy." *Election Year '79*, no. 6. New York: Swedish Information Service, July 1979.

Meusel, Alfred. "National Socialism and the Family." *Sociological Review* 28 (April, October 1936). pp. 166–80, 389–411.

More, Adelyne. *Fecundity Versus Civilization*. London: George Allen and Unwin, n.d. The catalogue of the British Museum Reading Room gives the date 1916 for this book.

Morgenthau, Hans J. *Politics Among Nations*. 5th Ed. New York: Alfred A. Knopf, 1973.

Moskoff, William. "Pronatalist Policies in Romania." *Economic Development and Cultural Change* 8, 3 (April 1980), pp. 602–3.

Mosse, George. *Nazi Culture: Intellectual, Cultural and Social Life in the Third Reich*. New York: Grosset and Dunlap, 1966.

Mundigo, Axel. "Factors Affecting the Population Attitudes of Latin American Elites." In *The Dynamics of Population Policy in Latin America*. Ed. Terry L. McCoy. Cambridge, Mass.: Ballinger, 1974. pp. 37–57.

Murray, John. "Population Policies in Europe." Paper presented at the Conference of the Population Study Group of the Institute of British Geographers. Durham, England. September 1978. Mimeo.

Myrdal, Alva. *Nation and Family*. New York: Harper and Brothers, 1941. Reprinted in 1968 by M.I.T. Press, Cambridge, Mass.

————, and Viola Klein. *Women's Two Roles*. London. Routledge and Kegan Paul, 1956.

Myrdal, Gunnar. *Population: A Problem for Democracy*. Cambridge, Mass.: Harvard University Press, 1940. Reprinted in 1962.

Neidhardt, Friedhelm. "The Federal Republic of Germany." In *Family Policy: Government and Families in Fourteen Countries*. Ed. Sheila B. Kamerman and Alfred J. Kahn. New York: Columbia Univeristy Press, 1978, pp. 217–38.

Neumann, Robert G. *The Government of the German Federal Republic*. New York-Evanston-London: Harper & Row, 1966.

Noonan, John T., Jr. *Contraception*. Cambridge, Mass.: Harvard University Press, 1965.

Organski, A. F. K., Bruce Bueno des Mesquita, and Allen Lamborn. "The Effective Population in International Politics." U. S. Commission on Population Growth and the American Future. Research Reports, vol. 4. *Governance and Population*. Washington, D. C.: U. S. Government Printing Office, 1972, pp. 235–50.

Organski, Katherine, and A. F. K. Organski. *Population and World Power*. New York: Alfred A. Knopf, 1961.

Overbeek, Johannes. *History of Population Theories*. Rotterdam: Rotterdam University Press, 1974.

Paillat, Paul. "Economic and Social Assistance to Families." In *Law and Fertility in Europe*, vol. 1. Ed. Maurice Kirk, Massimo Vivi-Bacci, and Egon Szabady. Dolhain, Belguim: Ordina Editions, 1976, pp. 66–79.

————. "Le vieillissement de la France rurale. Intensité, évolution, diffusion et typologie." *Population* 31, 6 (November-December 1976), pp. 1147–88.

Pelletier, Monique. "Donner la possibilité de choisir." *Le Monde*, March 14, 1979, p. 2.

————. "Des lieux de bonheur et de sociabilité." *Le Figaro*, April 26, 1979, p. 2.

Petersen, William. *The Politics of Population*. Garden City: Doubleday, 1964.
———. *Population*. 2nd Ed. New York: Macmillan, 1969.
Plischke, Elmer. With the assistance of H. J. Hille. *The West German Federal Government*. Office of the U. S. High Commissioner for Germany, Historical Division, 1952.
Polanyi, Karl. *The Great Transformation*. New York: Rinehart, 1944.
Population Decline in Europe. Ed. The Council of Europe. New York: St. Martin's Press, 1978.
Population Index 47, 2 (Summer 1981). Princeton, N. J.: Office of Population Research, Princeton University and Population Association of America.
van Praag, Philip and Louis Lohlé-Tart. "The Netherlands." In *Population Policy in Developed Countries*. Ed. Bernard Berelson. New York: McGraw Hill, 1974, pp. 294–318.
"President Mitterrand on Population Policy in France." Statement prepared for the National Alliance Against Depopulation. Published in *Population et Avenir*. Trans. and rep. in *Population and Development Review* 7, 3 (September 1981), pp. 568–69.
Pressat, Roland. *Demographic Analysis*. Trans. Judah Matras. Chicago-New York: Aldine Atherton, 1972.
———. "Mesures natalistes et relèvement de la fécondité en Europe de l'Est." *Population* 34, 3 (May-June 1979), pp. 533–48.
Putnam, Robert D. *The Comparative Study of Political Elites*. Englewood Cliffs, N. J.: Prentice-Hall, 1976.
Questiaux, Nicole, and Jacques Fournier. "France." In *Family Policy: Government and Families in Fourteen Countries*. Ed. Sheila B. Kamerman and Alfred J. Kahn. New York: Columbia University Press, 1978, pp. 117–82.
Der Regeirender Bürgermeister von Berlin. *Bericht über Leitlinien die Stadtenwicklung*. Berlin: Senatskanzlei/Plannungsleitstelle, n.d. (circa 1978).
Ridley, Frederick, and Jean Blondel. *Public Administration in France*. London: Routledge and Kegan Paul, 1964.
Rosenberg, Alfred. *Der Mythus des 20. Jahrhunderts: Eine Wertung der Seelischgeistigen*. Munich: Hoheneichen-Verlag, 1930.
Roussel, Louis. "La cohabitation juvénile en France." *Population* 33, 1 (January 1978), pp. 15–42.
———. "Changements démographiques et nouveaux modèles familiaux." In France, Ministry of Labor and Participation, *Colloque national sur la démographie française*, Paris, June 1980, pp. 61–70.
Rückert, Gerd-Rüdiger. "The Employment of Women as a Cause of a Declining Number of Births." *Materialien zur Bevölkerungswissenschaft*, no. 5, 1978. Wiesbaden: Federal Institute for Population Research, 1978, pp. 197–222.
Runblom, Harald, and Hans Norman (Eds.). *From Sweden to America*. Minneapolis: Minneapolis University Press, and Uppsala: Acta Universitatis Upsaliensis, 1976.
Rupp, Leila J. *Mobilizing Women for War*. Princeton: Princeton University Press, 1978.
Ryabushkin, Timon. "Social Policy and Demography in the Soviet Union."

Population and Development Review 4, 4 (December 1978), pp. 715–20. Reprinted from *Social Sciences Today*. Moscow, 1978.

Ryder, Norman B., and Charles F. Westoff. *Reproduction in the United States, 1965*. Princeton: Princeton University Press, 1971.

Sabine, George H. *A History of Political Theory*. New York: Henry Holt, 1937.

Sanderson, Warren G. "On Two Schools of the Economics of Fertility." *Population and Development Review* 2, 3–4 (September-December 1976), pp. 469–77.

de Sandre, Paolo. "Critical Study of Population Policies in Europe." In *Population Decline in Europe*. Ed. The Council of Europe. New York: St. Martin's Press, 1978, pp. 145–70.

Sartre, Jean Paul. *Roads to Freedom*. Vol. 1, *The Age of Reason*; Vol. 2, *The Reprieve*; Vol. 3, *Iron in the Soul*. Trans. Gerard Hopkins. London: Hamish Hamilton, 1950.

Sauvy, Alfred. *L'Europe et sa population*. Paris: Les Editions Internationales, 1953.

———. *La montée des jeunes*. Paris: Calmann-Levy, 1959.

———. *Le Plan Sauvy*. Paris: Calmann-Levy, 1960.

———. *A General Theory of Population*. Trans. Christopher Campos. New York: Basic Books, 1969.

———. *La prévention des naissances: "Birth Control."* France: Presses Universitaires de France, 1972.

———. *Zero Growth*. Trans. A. McGuire. Oxford: Blackwell, 1975.

———. "La nécessité d'une nation jeune." *Le Figaro*, April 27, 1979, p. 2.

———. "Les conséquences du vieillissement de la population." In *La France Ridée*. Ed. Gérard-François Dumont et al. Paris: Le Livre de Poche, 1979, pp. 61–118.

Schubnell, Hermann. "West Germany." In *Population Policy in Developed Countries*. Ed. Bernard Berelson. New York: McGraw Hill, 1974, pp. 679–703.

———, and Sabine Rupp. "Federal German Republic." In *Law and Fertility in Europe*. Ed. Maurice Kirk, Massimo Livi-Bacci, and Egon Szabady. Dolhain, Belguim: Ordina Editions, 1976, pp. 298–336.

Schwarz, Karl. "La baisse de la natalité en Allemagne fédérale." *Population* 33, 4–5 (July-October 1978), pp. 999–1016.

———. "Regional Differences in Natality and Consquences of the Decline of the Birth Rate for Problems of Regional Planning." *Materialien zur Bevölkerungswissenschaft*, no. 5, 1978. Wiesbaden: Federal Institute for Population Research, 1978, pp. 223–33.

Scott, Hilda. *Does Socialism Liberate Women?* Boston: Beacon Press, 1974.

Siampos, George. "Law and Fertility in Greece." In *Law and Fertility in Europe*. Ed. Maurice Kirk, Massimo Livi-Bacci, and Egon Szabady. Dolhain, Belgium: Ordina Editions, 1976, pp. 337–61.

Simon, Herbert A. "A Behavioral Model of Rational Choice." *Quarterly Journal of Economics* 69 (February 1955), pp. 99–118.

———. *Models of Man*. New York: John Wiley, 1957.

Snyder, Richard D. "A Decision-Making Approach to the Study of Political Phenomena." In *Approaches to the Study of Politics.* Ed. Roland Young. Evanston, Ill.: Northwestern University Press, 1958, pp. 3–38.

————, Henry Bruck, and Burton Sapin. *Decision-Making as an Approach to the Study of International Politics.* Foreign Policy Analysis Series, no. 3, 1954.

SOPEMI, 1980. Continuous Reporting System on International Migration. Paris: Organization for Economic Cooperation and Development, 1980.

Sorokin, Pitirim A. *Social Philosophies of an Age of Crisis.* Boston: Beacon Press, 1950.

Spengler, Joseph J. *Frances Faces Depopulation.* Durham, N. C.: Duke University Press, 1938.

————. "Mercantilist and Physiocratic Growth Theory." In *Theories of Economic Growth.* Ed. Bert F. Hoselitz. New York: The Free Press, 1960, pp. 3–64, 299–334.

————. "Population and Potential Power." In *Studies in Economics and Economic History.* Ed. Marcelle Kody. Durham, N. C.: Duke University Press, 1972, pp. 126–52.

————, and Otis Dudley Duncan. *Population Theory and Policy.* Glencoe: The Free Press, 1956.

Spengler, Oswald. *Decline of the West.* Trans. C. F. Atkinson. New York: Alfred A. Knopf, 1926–28.

Srb, Vladimir. "On the Issue of Population Laws of Socialism and Communism." *International Demographic Symposium, Zakopane, 1964.* Warsaw: Panstwowe Wydawnictwo Naukowe, 1966, pp. 51–56.

Stoffel, Eugène. *Rapports Militaire Ecrits de Berlin de 1866–1870.* Paris, 1871.

Stoleru, Lionel. "Entre le bouc et l'autruche." *Le Monde,* June 15, 1979, p. 38.

Strangeland, Charles Emil. *Pre-Malthusian Doctrines of Population: A Study in the History of Economic Theory.* Studies in History, Economics and Public Law, vol. 21, no. 3. New York: Columbia University Press, 1904.

Stycos, J. Mayone. *Ideology, Faith and Family Planning in Latin America.* New York: McGraw-Hill, 1974.

Suleiman, Ezra N. *Politics, Power, and Bureaucracy in France.* Princeton: Princeton University Press, 1974.

————. *Elites in French Society: The Politics of Survival.* Princeton: Princeton University Press, 1978.

Sullerot, Evelyne. *La démographie de la France: bilan et perspectives.* Paris: Journaux Officiels and La Documentation Française, 1978.

Sundquist, James L. "A Comparison of Policy-Making Capacity in the United States and Five European Countries: The Case of Population Distribution." *Policy Studies Journal* 6, 2 (Winter 1977), pp. 194–200.

Swart, Koenraad W. *The Sense of Decadence in Nineteenth-Century France.* The Hague: Martinus Nijhoff, 1964.

Sweden, Department of Social Affairs. *Flerbarnsfamiljerna—kartläggning och analys.* February 1981. Stockholm, 1981.

————, National Central Statistical Bureau. *Information i Prognosfrågor,* 1973: 3.

————, Royal Ministry for Foreign Affairs. *The Biography of a People*. Stockholm, 1974.

————. *Snabbprotokoll från Riksdagsdebatterna*. 1977/78, no. 149, Thursday, May 18, 1978.

————. *Sveriges Officiella Utredningar* (SOU). 1977/78 No. 32. Socialutskottets betänkande. *Befölkningsutvecklingen*, 1978.

————. 1978/78. *Langtidsutredning*. 1978.

"The Swedish Government in Crisis, Spring 1981." *Political Life in Sweden*, no. 10, July 1981. New York: Swedish Information Service.

"Swedish Legislation on Birth Control: Contraception, Sterilization and Abortion." *Fact Sheets on Sweden*. Stockholm: The Swedish Institute. July 1977.

Symonds, Richard, and Michael Carder. *The United Nations and the Population Question*. New York: McGraw-Hill, 1973.

Szabady, Egon. "Interdependence Between Fertility Changes and Socio-Economic Development in East European Countries." *Population Review* 16, 1–2 (January-December 1972), pp. 9–17.

Teitelbaum, Michael S. "Fertility Effects of the Abolition of Legal Abortion in Romania" *Population Studies* 26, 3 (November 1972), pp. 405–17.

————. "U. S. Population Growth in International Perspective." In *Toward the End of Growth*. Ed. Charles F. Westoff et al. Englewood Cliffs, N. J.: Prentice-Hall, Inc., 1973, pp. 69–83.

Toman, Walter, Siglinde Hölzel, and Volker Koreny. "Factoren der Bevölkerungsentwicklung—Ursachen und Beweggründe für den Kinderwunsch." Munich: Bavarian State Ministry of Labor and Social Affairs, 1977.

Toynbee, Arnold J. *A Study of History*. London: Oxford University Press, 1934–39.

Trebici, Vladimir. "Law and Fertility in Romania." In *Law and Fertility in Europe*, vol. 2. Ed. Maurice Kirk, Massimo Livi-Bacci, and Egon Szabady. Dolhain, Belgium: Ordina Editions, 1976, pp. 520–43.

————. "Law and the Social Status of Women." In *Law and Fertility in Europe*, vol. 1. Ed. Maurice Kirk, Massimo Livi-Bacci, and Egon Szabady. Dolhain, Belgium: Ordina Editions, 1976, pp. 80–106.

Trochu, Louis. *L'Armée française en 1867*. Paris: 1867.

Trost, Jan. "A Renewed Social Institution: Non-Marital Cohabitation." *Acta Sociologica* 21, 4 (1973), pp. 303–15.

Truman, David B. *The Governmental Process*. New York: Alfred A. Knopf, 1951.

United Kingdom, Central Policy Review Staff. *Report of the Population Panel*. London: Her Majesty's Stationery Office, 1973.

————, Office of Population Censuses and Surveys. *Demographic Review: A Report on Population in Great Britain*. London: Her Majesty's Stationery Office. Series DR. no. 1, 1978.

————, Royal Commission on Population. *Report*. London: Her Majesty's Stationery Office, June 1949. Cmd. 7695.

United Nations. *Demographic Yearbook*. New York: United Nations, annual.

————, Department of International Economic and Social Affairs. *Population Policy Briefs: Current Stituation in Developed Countries, 1980*. New York: United Nations, January 1981. Serial No. ESA/P/WP.72.

————, Department of International Economic and Social Affairs. *Selected Demographic Indicators by Country, 1950–2000*. New York: United Nations, 1980.

————, Department of International Economic and Social Affairs. *World Population Trends and Policies: 1979 Monitoring Report*, vol. 2. New York: United Nations, 1980.

————, Department of International Economic and Social Affairs. *World Population Trends and Prospects by Country, 1950–2000*. New York: United Nations, 1979. Serial No. ST/ESA/Ser.R/33.

————. *Determinants and Consequences of Population Trends*. New York: United Nations, 1973.

————, Economic Commission for Europe (ECE). *Economic Survey in Europe in 1974*, Part 2. New York: United Nations, 1975.

————, Economic and Social Council. *World Population Trends and Policies: 1977 Monitoring Report*, vol. 2. New York: United Nations, 1979.

————, International Conference on Human Rights, Teheran. April-May 1968. (UN Doc. A/CONF.32/41.)

United States, Commission on Population Growth and the American Future. *Population and the American Future*. Washington, D. C.: Government Printing Office, 1972. (This report was also published by Signet Books, New York, 1972.)

————, House of Representatives. 95th. Congress. Second Session. *Final Report of the Select Committee on Population*. Domestic Consequences of Population Change, pp. 43–57 (1978).

————, Library of Congress, Law Library. "The Abortion Decision of February 25, 1975 of the Federal Constitutional Court, Federal Republic of Germany." Trans. and introduced by Edmund C. Jann. (European Law Division, 75–5 LL, November 1975.)

————, National Resources Committee. *The Problems of a Changing Population*. Washington, D. C.: U. S. Government Printing Office, 1938.

Vasaria, Pravin. "Sex Ratio at Birth in Territories with Relatively Complete Registration." *Eugenics Quarterly* 14 (1967), pp. 132–42.

Veil, Simone. "A propos de politique familiale." Extracted from a press conference given by Veil on December 31, 1975. "La France et sa population aujourd'hui." Supplement no. 4. *Les Cahiers Français*. No. 184. Paris: La Documentation Française, 1978.

————. "Human Rights, Ideologies, and Population Policies." Trans. David B. Doty. *Population and Development Review* 4, 2 (June 1978), pp. 313–21.

Vinde, Pierre, and Gunnar Petrie. *Swedish Government Administration*. 2nd Ed. Trans. Patric Hort. Stockholm: Bökforlaget Prisma-The Swedish Institute, 1978.

Vinocur, John. "Sweden's Economic Success Sours." *New York Times*, March 24, 1978, pp. A1, D3.

van de Walle, Etienne. "Alone in Europe: The French Fertility Decline Until 1850." In *Historical Studies of Changing Fertility*. Ed. Charles Tilly. Princeton: Princeton University Press, 1978, pp. 257–88.

Wander, Hilde. "The Working Population." In *Population Decline in Europe*. Ed. Council of Europe. New York: St. Martin's Press, 1978, pp. 53–71.

―――. "Zero Population Growth Now: The Lessons in Europe." In *The Economic Consequences of Slowing Population Growth*. Ed. Thomas J. Espenshade and William J. Serow. New York: Academic Press, 1978, pp. 41–69.

Weber, Cynthia, and Ann Goodman. "The Demographic Policy Debate in the USSR." *Population and Development Review* 7, 2 (June 1981), pp. 279–95.

Westoff, Charles F. "Marriage and Fertility in the Developed Countries." *Scientific American* 239, 6 (December 1978), pp. 51–57.

―――, Robert G. Potter, Jr., Philip C. Sagi, and Eliot G. Mishler. *Family Growth in Metropolitan America*. Princeton: Princeton University Press, 1961.

―――, Robert G. Potter, Jr., and Philip C. Sagi. *The Third Child*. Princeton: Princeton University Press, 1963.

―――, and Norman B. Ryder. *The Contraceptive Revolution*. Princeton: Princeton University Press, 1977.

Wheeler, Christopher. *White Collar Power*. Urbana, Ill.: University of Illinois Press, 1975.

Whelpton, Pascal K. "Why the Large Rise in the German Birth Rate?" *American Journal of Sociology* 41, 3 (November 1935), pp. 299–313.

―――, and Clyde V. Kiser (Eds.). *Social and Psychological Factors Affecting Fertility*, 5 Vols. New York: Milbank Memorial Fund, 1946–58.

―――, Arthur A. Campbell, and J. E. Patterson. *Fertility and Family Planning in the United States*. Princeton: Princeton University Press, 1966.

Wicker, A. M. "Attitudes versus Actions: The Relationship of Verbal and Overt Behavioral Responses to Attitude Objects." *Journal of Social Issues* 25, 4 (1968), pp. 41–78.

Wilkinson, L. P. "Classical Approaches to Population and Family Planning." *Population and Development Review* 4, 3 (September 1978), pp. 439–55.

"Women in Swedish Society." *Facts Sheets on Sweden*. Stockholm: The Swedish Institute, May 1979.

Woodrow, Alain. "Crime et Châtiment." *Le Monde*, April 24, 1979, p. 14.

Wright, Quincy. *A Study of War*. Chicago: Chicago University Press, 1942.

―――. *The Study of International Relations*. New York: Appleton-Century-Crofts, 1955.

Ziolkowski, Janusz A. "Poland." In *Population Policy in Developed Countries*. Ed. Bernard Berelson. New York: McGraw-Hill, 1974, pp. 445–88.

Index

About the Author

After a career in international health, Alison McIntosh, a New Zealand citizen, became interested in population in the mid–1970s. In this field, her recent work has included studies of population policy and international migration. Dr. McIntosh is currently engaged in teaching and research as a member of the Center for Population Planning at the University of Michigan.